Punishing Immigrants

Policy, Politics, and Injustice

Edited by Charis E. Kubrin, Marjorie S. Zatz, and Ramiro Martínez, Jr.

NEW YORK UNIVERSITY PRESS
New York and London

NEW YORK UNIVERSITY PRESS
New York and London
www.nyupress.org

References to Internet websites (URLs) were accurate at the time of writing.
Neither the author nor New York University Press is responsible for URLs
that may have expired or changed since the manuscript was prepared.

LIBRARY OF CONGRESS CATALOGING-IN-PUBLICATION DATA

Punishing immigrants : policy, politics, and injustice / edited by Charis E. Kubrin, Marjorie
S. Zatz, and Ramiro Martinez, Jr.
p. cm.
Includes bibliographical references and index.
ISBN 978-0-8147-4902-9 (cloth : alk. paper)
ISBN 978-0-8147-4903-6 (pbk. : alk. paper)
ISBN 978-0-8147-4904-3 (ebook)
ISBN 978-0-8147-4949-4 (ebook)
1. United States—Emigration and immigration—Government policy. 2. United States—
Emigration and immigration—Political aspects. I. Kubrin, Charis Elizabeth. II. Zatz,
Marjorie Sue, 1955- III. Martinez, Ramiro.
JV6483.P86 2012
325.73--dc23
2012016650

New York University Press books are printed on acid-free paper,
and their binding materials are chosen for strength and durability.
We strive to use environmentally responsible suppliers and materials
to the greatest extent possible in publishing our books.

Manufactured in the United States of America
c 10 9 8 7 6 5 4 3 2 1
p 10 9 8 7 6 5 4 3 2 1

CONTENTS

ACKNOWLEDGMENTS

From inception to completion this project would have been impossible without funding from the National Science Foundation (NSF). We are indebted to NSF program officers Patricia White in Sociology, and Scott Barclay, Susan Haire, and Wendy Martinek in Law and Social Sciences, for making possible an award that supported a Workshop on Social Science Research on Immigration: The Role of Transnational Migration, Communities, and Policy, on September 10–11, 2009, at Arizona State University. We are also grateful to workshop participants Alice Cepeda, Elizabeth Chacko, Leo Chavez, Susan Coutin, Evelyn Cruz, Scott Decker, Godfried Engbersen, Corina Graif, Belinda Herrera, Laura Hickman, Charles Keely, Paul Lewis, Tiffany Lightbourn, Cecilia Menjívar, Ruth D. Peterson, Doris Marie Provine, Holly E. Reed, Katja Rusinovic, Robert J. Sampson, Avelardo Valdez, Marianne van Bochove, Monica Varsanyi, María Vélez, James Walsh, Michael Welch, Patricia White, and Sheldon Zhang. Special thanks to ASU faculty, students, and community workshop participants for contributing in immeasurable ways to facilitating the project and for helping lay the foundation for this book.

We owe a special debt to Ruth D. Peterson and Lauren J. Krivo, who, with NSF funding, helped create a community of scholars now known as the Racial Democracy, Crime and Justice Network (RDCJ-N) that has met for the past eight summers at The Ohio State University. The RDCJ-N has provided us with an intellectual home for thinking about research on race, ethnicity, immigration, crime, and criminal justice, and the members have contributed in numerous ways to the overall effort that eventually culminated in this volume. They have provided assistance and comments at workshops and in other academic settings, helping make this book a better finished product.

We also benefited from institutional support from Arizona State University who, along with NSF, helped support the workshop. Throughout, we were fortunate to have worked with a number of ASU staff, especially Nancy Newcomer, Maureen Roen, and Melissa Weimer from Justice and Social Inquiry, and graduate research associates David Berg, Katherine Abbott, and Lisa Jaeger. As always, our editor at New York University Press, Ilene Kalish, and her assistants, particularly Aiden Amos, provided thoughtful comments along the way. Much of the material in this book is based upon work supported by the National Science Foundation under Grant No. 0913033. Any opinions, findings, conclusions, or recommendations expressed in this material are those of the authors and do not necessarily reflect the views of the National Science Foundation.

In closing, rather than continue to thank the many individuals who require special mention for helping us bring this project to completion, we take another path. We have been engaged in the writing and editing of this book during a period of national angst and concern over the growth of immigration across the nation. Unfortunately, this anxiety is likely to continue. We believe that social science research can inform policy debates and broader societal understandings of immigration. Accordingly, we dedicate this volume in the spirit of creating a more just immigration policy and comprehensive immigration reform. In the end, our hope is that this goal is within reach.

1

Introduction

CHARIS E. KUBRIN, MARJORIE S. ZATZ, AND RAMIRO MARTÍNEZ, JR.

Most scholarly research on immigration and crime has focused on a subset of questions: Are immigrants more crime-prone? Do areas where immigrants reside experience higher crime rates? What are the larger connections between immigration and crime in the United States and abroad? For the most part, these questions have been satisfactorily addressed. Contrary to public opinion, it is now well-established in the scholarly literature that, in fact, immigrants commit less crime, particularly less violent crime, than the native-born and that their presence in communities is not associated with higher crime rates. Consequently, scholars are eager to move beyond the question: "Does a connection exist?"

This edited volume does just that by broadening the focus to encompass issues relevant to law and society, immigration and refugee policy, and victimization, as well as crime. There has been relatively little research on victimization among immigrants, and even fewer studies analyze legal issues of concern to immigrants and the communities in which they reside. Clearly, though, the three are interdependent and researchers must begin to consider how each intersects with the others to shape immigrants' experiences and realities.

Within the larger context of immigration and crime, law, and victimization, the edited volume focuses on two critical areas: First, chapters uncover and identify the unanticipated and hidden consequences of immigration policies and practices here and abroad at a time when immigration to the United States is near an all-time high. In the United States, these collateral consequences include harms to individuals (e.g., victimization by unscrupulous employers, human traffickers, etc.) and to communities (a result of reduced crime reporting, reduced efficacy of public health and school systems, etc., when immigrants are fearful of interacting with public institutions and authorities). In other contexts, these state-created vulnerabilities may include, for example, forced relocations and displacement, rape and other assaults, and ethnic cleansing. We expand the analysis to also consider the ramifications of deportation for individuals who grew up in the United States but who are forcibly removed and must adapt to new laws and social norms in a nation of origin which is not "home" to them.

Second, chapters in this volume illuminate the nuanced and layered realities of immigrants' lives and describe the varying complexities surrounding immigration and crime, law, and victimization. These nuanced realities and complexities include, most especially, the racialized and gendered overlays. For example, many state-created vulnerabilities have patterned outcomes, with some immigrants particularly vulnerable to victimization as well as deportation (e.g., women may be at greater risk of intimate partner violence and less able to protect themselves when their immigration status is tied to that of their husband; immigrants from some countries can claim refugee status more readily than others; linguistic and cultural differences make some groups more readily identifiable as immigrants than others; day laborers may experience special vulnerabilities, and so on). Moreover, immigrant status may intersect with schooling, labor market, and other institutional structures to differentially affect employment opportunities and these patterns may, in turn, vary across nations and regions.

We situate these themes—the hidden consequences of immigration policies and practices and the nuanced and layered realities of immigrants' lives—within the larger context of immigration and social control, particularly new modes of control in a post-9/11 era.

In essence, this edited volume focuses on the hidden consequences, nuanced realities, and complexities that emerge when we delve beyond the immigration-crime nexus to consider multiple forms of victimization, the impacts of socio-legal policies and practices on communities, and the responses of individual immigrants and immigrant communities to their victimization. Throughout, the chapters interweave U.S. and global patterns, concerns, and reactions to the movement of people and labor across borders. Equally important, they do so from explicitly interdisciplinary perspectives, with contributions from scholars, politicians, and practitioners trained in anthropology, criminology, geography, law, political science, social work, and sociology. By drawing on multiple locations and cross-cutting themes, the collection expands our understanding of the multifaceted, complex linkages among immigration policy, crime, law, and victimization, and points legal and social science research on immigration in these new directions.

Change and Continuity in Immigrant Flows

Worldwide, close to 190 million people, representing 3 percent of the world's population, lived outside their country of origin in 2005. The United States and Western Europe have seen the greatest increases of immigrant and refugee flows, with marked increases also evident in Canada, Australia, and Russia, among other sites. In contrast, emigration has been greatest from Mexico, Central America, China, India, and parts of Africa, Eastern Europe, and Central Asia (New York Times 2007). While much of the migration flow reflects the movement of labor, as individuals and families seek better employment opportunities, the movement of political refugees is also an important and growing component. In 2007, 338,000 new asylum applications were made in European and non-European industrialized nations. Half of the asylum-seekers were from Asia, and another 21 percent from Africa. The United States, France, and the United Kingdom received the greatest share of asylum requests, with significant numbers also appealing to Sweden, Canada, Germany, Australia, and New Zealand (UNHCR 2008).

Considering just the United States, the Pew Hispanic Center estimates that roughly 12 percent of the U.S. population in 2010, or 40 million persons, were born outside of its borders (Passel and Cohn 2011). Of these, most are naturalized citizens or legal permanent residents, students and temporary workers on temporary visas, and refugees, with about 28 percent estimated to be undocumented (2011: 10). About half of the undocumented residents (58 percent) are from Mexico and another 23 percent are from other Latin American countries, with one-fifth (18 percent) coming to the United States from other parts of the world (Passel and Cohn 2011).

These statistics remind us that the stream of immigrants currently reshaping the United States, unlike at the turn of the last century, is no longer primarily of European origin. The racial/ethnic/immigrant composition of many communities and cities has grown increasingly diverse, and while most newcomers are from Latin America, others are born in Asian and European countries. Still, the U.S.-Mexican border has supplanted Ellis Island as the most prominent entry point into the nation, and many politicians and pundits are concerned about the potential of chaos and disruption in border communities (Rodríguez, Saenz, and Menjívar 2008). This concern is linked, in part, to the burgeoning Latino (Hispanic) population in the United States and projections that these numbers will continue to grow (ibid.). While Latinos and Asians are still concentrated in the west and southwest, immigrants also have settled in other regions of the country and are working in diverse sectors of the economy. Newcomers are now moving into cities with older immigrant populations that have long served as traditional settlement points in the northeast and midwest regions. Others have moved into rural areas where few immigrants historically resided, contributing to residents' concerns about their growth, hardening residents' attitudes toward the newcomers, and generating angst over the perceived political, economic, and criminal threat of Latino and other immigrants.

Immigrant growth, legality aside, has implications for the nation. Stereotypes regarding newcomers dominate public discourse in the United States and paint immigrants as dangerous threats to the nation (Chavez 2008; Nevins 2002; Ngai 2005). Immigration policy now reflects, in part, local concerns about economic competition, racialized political threat, and fear of crime, even in the absence of systematic evidence revealing a connection between immigration and crime (Johnson 2007; Martínez and Valenzuela 2006; Newton 2008). Moreover, policy mandates for controlling the American border and "illegals," who are primarily of Mexican origin, are encouraged by politicians and commentators for the sake of enhancing "national security" and preventing crime. Such mandates include demanding proof of citizenship, deploying the National Guard, building a fence on the border between Mexico and the United States, encouraging the growth of self-styled "militias," and labeling "undocumented" immigrants as criminal aliens (Doty 2009). Taking this one step further based on arguments that the federal government is not doing enough to curb immigration, states and local governments across the country are enacting laws and approving ballot referendums designed to "get tough" on immigration. Most notably, in April 2010, the governor of Arizona signed into law Senate Bill 1070, which makes it a crime to be undocumented and threatens law enforcement officials perceived to be lax in enforcing immigration law with lawsuits.

New Modes of Social Control

These numerous and varied immigration policies, we argue, constitute new and expanding modes of social control in the United States. The first set of chapters in this volume outlines new modes of control by discussing recent laws and policies designed to control immigrants and immigration more generally. What emerges from this collection of policies and practices, as described in the chapters, is a nationwide re-visioning of immigration enforcement driven by federal law and policy, as well as by politics at the local level. These enhanced control strategies, as we come to find out, are not unique to the United States but can be found elsewhere, including in Europe and Australia.

In the first chapter of this section, Panic, Risk, Control: Conceptualizing Threats in a Post-9/11 Society, Michael Welch argues that part of the recent concern over immigrants is linked to fear of terrorism, which rose after the attack on the World Trade Center in 1993 and, later, on 9/11. States like Florida, Texas, and California denied basic education, health, and social services to immigrants—actions that were eventually seen as the first step in controlling newcomers. Further steps have included giving federal agencies "unprecedented authority" to target immigrants and deport newcomers under the guise that they constituted threats to national security. The chapter by Welch contributes to our understanding of the overlap of criminal and administrative laws post-9/11 and documents how subsequent attempts to control immigration have contributed to the growth of an industry benefiting from the overlapping wars on crime, "illegal" immigration and, of course, terrorism. Drawing from literature on moral panics and risk societies, Welch demonstrates how our thinking about immigration and terrorism has escalated from panic to a more permanent state of feeling at risk, thus making concern about growth of immigration and the need for enhanced control more understandable in the larger context of the potent social and political forces shaping control strategies. Welch compares trends in the United States with trends in Australia, providing a comparative approach for understanding linkages among panic, risk, and control of immigrant populations.

Within the United States, concern about the growth in immigration has also led to legislation flourishing at the city, county, and state levels, measures which are viewed by many as anti-Latino or anti-immigrant. Yet research on the possible mechanisms that give rise to such sentiment across collectivities is underdeveloped. Moreover, little is known about the ways in which social processes contribute to this sentiment or anti-immigrant reactions. In their chapter, Growing Tensions between Civic Membership and Enforcement in the Devolution of Immigration Control, Doris Marie Provine, Monica Varsanyi, Paul Lewis, and Scott Decker address these issues, focusing specifically on Latinos. They first remind us that while much of the Latino growth has been in traditional settlement areas in the southwestern United States, there is substantial movement to places that are new destinations or where few Latinos resided in previous decades (Rodríguez et al. 2008). The emergence of anti-immigrant laws or ordinances has proliferated in these new destination points. They have been aimed at preventing "illegals" from securing housing, punishing business owners for employing the undocumented, and allowing local police to search for "illegals" or ask about legality status, the latter historically left for the federal domain (Varsanyi 2010). Many communities now encourage local police to engage in federal immigration activities and enforce immigration laws through the investigation, apprehension, and detention of undocumented immigrants, part of what is known as the 287(g) program, a clause in the Illegal Immigration Reform and Immigrant Responsibility Act of 1996 (Khashul 2009). This agreement also allows local police officers to use federal databases to check the immigration status of individuals and to process them for deportation hearings when necessary.

Most police departments and local governments have not rushed to assume federal responsibility, but some are actively enforcing immigrant-status violations (see Decker et al. 2009) including policing internal immigration enforcement through the so-called Secure Communities initiatives, as discussed by Provine and her colleagues in their chapter. Other draconian anti-immigrant initiatives are apparent in new destination points such as Hazleton, Pennsylvania. According to the 2000 Census, Hazleton had about 23,000 residents, 5 percent of whom were Latino. In 2006, local officials passed the Illegal Immigration Relief Act, a measure that would have resulted in racial profiling, discrimination, and denial of benefits to legal immigrants. This ordinance imposed fines of up to $1,000 to landlords who rented to "illegal" immigrants, denied business permits to corporations who employed undocumented immigrants, and made English the official language of the village (Rodríguez et al. 2008). The consequences of anti-immigrant/Latino initiatives are that all immigrants and Latinos are singled out by politicians, the media, and authorities and, thus, presumed illegal (ibid.).

If this is going to happen anywhere, perhaps it is most likely to occur in states such as Arizona, which have enacted some of the harshest anti-immigration laws on the books. Consider Senate Bill 1070, mentioned earlier, which makes it a crime to be undocumented and threatens legal action against law enforcement officials perceived to be lax in enforcing immigration law. Critics of SB 1070 argue it is the broadest and strictest anti-immigration measure in decades. They further claim it encourages racial profiling. Where did this law come from and how did it emerge so quickly? As Arizona state senator Kyrsten Sinema demonstrates in her chapter, No Surprises: The Evolution of Anti-Immigration Legislation in Arizona, such legislation does not materialize overnight. Rather, momentum builds until the political climate normalizes what previously had seemed unreasonable. Sinema takes readers on a legislative journey by tracing the development of anti-immigrant legislation in Arizona, highlighting the steady, organized movement from the initial introduction of such legislation to the passage of SB 1070 and beyond. Her analysis demonstrates that Arizona's legislative journey was, in fact, carefully crafted and executed by a coalition of state elected officials and national activists, with the intent to utilize Arizona as a model for other states. Importantly, Sinema's chapter evaluates the impact of Arizona's laws on other states and looks ahead to the movement's next steps in Arizona and beyond.

Consequences for Individuals and Communities

One of the lessons prior research has demonstrated repeatedly is that laws and policies are political, and often symbolic, responses to larger social problems. As such, they frequently result in both anticipated and unanticipated consequences (see, for example, Beckett and Herbert 2008; Chambliss and Zatz 1993; Clear 2007; Fine 2006; Ganapati and Frank 2008; Simon 2007). Immigration law is no exception; indeed, symbolic politics with unintended "collateral" consequences may be the norm when it comes to immigration legislation.

Immigration policy is inherently contradictory as it tries to balance a variety of strains within and among nations. For instance, political and economic relations have created lopsided labor markets and economic opportunities in the global North and South. Looking just within the United States, immigration policies and practices have sought to respond to a number of conflicting needs. These include, for example, religious and ethical demands regarding the place of immigrants in our society and understandings of what constitutes citizenship, the desire for cheap labor on the part of some business sectors (e.g., agribusiness, the hospitality industry, and the meatpacking industry) and individuals (e.g., for nannies, house cleaners, and gardeners), and racialized and gendered educational and employment structures.

At the same time, as noted earlier, immigration policies are often reflective of unfounded fears and moral panics (Cohen 1972; Goode and Ben-Yehuda 1994; Welch 2003). As immigration policies attempt to address these often contradictory realities and fears, they can create new sets of problems for individuals and communities (Calavita 1984, 1996; Chavez 2008; Gardner 2005; Johnson 2004, 2007; Newton 2008).

Some of these consequences can be anticipated. For example, individuals who immigrate without proper authorization may be deported and employers who hire undocumented workers may be sanctioned. Individuals make choices in light of these risks. A second set of consequences, while readily apparent, is less likely to be anticipated. These include, for example, the devastating effects of parents' deportation on children and other family members, some of whom may be citizens. And, because attorneys practicing in criminal or family law may not have a complete understanding of immigration law, they may unknowingly recommend actions that have devastating ramifications for their client's immigration status.

Yet a third group of consequences are what we call hidden, state-created vulnerabilities. These include harms to individuals (e.g., increased victimization by unscrupulous employers, fear of reporting violence in the home, risks from human traffickers, etc.) and to communities (e.g., reduced willingness of victims and witnesses to report crime, reduced efficacy of the public health sector and school systems because immigrants fear interacting with government employees). In other contexts, these state-created vulnerabilities may include forced relocations and displacement of refugees, rape and other assaults against displaced persons, or finding oneself in unfamiliar and unsafe settings following deportation or relocation.

The chapters included in this section of the volume exemplify some of these anticipated and unanticipated collateral consequences. As a set, they help us understand the myriad ways in which our policies and practices create new dilemmas even as they seek, often unsuccessfully, to resolve other problems confronting societies today. Evelyn Cruz's chapter, Unearthing and Confronting the Social Skeletons of Immigration Status in our Criminal Justice System, examines the breach of trust that can arise when criminal defense attorneys are unaware of the immigration consequences of the advice they offer to clients. Without such knowledge, attorneys may unwittingly recommend legal actions that result in deportation and permanent bars against re-entering the country. Examining just such a situation in the case of the Postville workers, Cruz takes us beyond the consequences for individuals to help us confront the ramifications for our legal order when clients cannot trust that their attorneys will give them competent legal advice.

Workplace and community raids may result in the arrest and deportation of persons who have lived in the host country for many years. Also, lawful permanent residents convicted of "aggravated felonies" are subject to mandatory deportation. The 1996 Antiterrorism and Effective Death Penalty Act (AEDPA) and the Illegal Immigration Reform and Immigrant Responsibility Act (IIRIRA), in combination, expanded the category of aggravated felonies to include a range of minor and nonviolent offenses and made deportation mandatory even for persons who had already served their criminal sentence or when the offense did not fit the criteria for mandatory deportation at the time of conviction. The 1996 immigration laws also eliminated immigration hearings for legal permanent residents facing deportation based on aggravated felony convictions (International Human Rights Law Clinic 2010: 3). If these individuals come into contact with the criminal justice system or immigration officials for any reason, they risk immediate deportation. This broader net includes many immigrants who have lived in the United States for years and have raised families here.

The chapter by Kathleen Dingeman-Cerda and Susan Coutin, The Ruptures of Return: Deportation's Confounding Effects, examines the ramifications of deportation for such individuals. By focusing on the experiences of persons who lived in the United States for many years and now find themselves in what is a truly foreign country for them—their country of origin—Dingeman-Cerda and Coutin explore the ramifications of mandatory deportation policies. Based on interviews with deportees in El Salvador, they report that the experiences of deportees and their families are varied and complex. Some deportees adjust successfully to life in their country of origin. Others suffer from depression and alienation, which may be exacerbated by the negative reactions of fellow citizens, discrimination, and harassment because they are perceived to be foreign, and from loss of custody and sometimes even communication with their children. Some of these deportees remain in El Salvador; others defy their deportation orders through unauthorized reentry or by recreating U.S. communities on small scales in El Salvador. Dingeman-Cerda and Coutin develop the concept of "secondary victimization" to help us understand the confounding effects of deportation for disrupted communities and family members remaining in the United States.

Finally, the chapter by Wenona Rymond-Richmond and John Hagan, Race, Land, and Forced Migration in Darfur, examines the hidden consequences of the Darfur genocide. They shift attention from the genocidal intent to its aftermath in order to understand the challenges and complexities associated with surviving genocide and becoming a refugee. In their analysis based on survey and interview data, Rymond-Richmond and Hagan document refugees' experiences with victimization post-genocide, describing their victimization experiences during the journey to the camps, while at the camps, and even upon returning to their homeland. Although victimization is a reality for all refugees, Rymond-Richmond and Hagan underscore the racialized and gendered nature of victimization in this case, describing how, for example, rape is used as a control mechanism against women, most of whom are Black African, and how the children of these rape victims are considered Arabic rather than Black African. Such racialized and gendered overlays occur, they point out, in a political context where the government of Sudan continues to be predominantly Arabic, leaving Black Africans underrepresented in political positions of power.

These consequences and state-created vulnerabilities have patterned outcomes, with some immigrants particularly vulnerable. Accordingly, in the remainder of this volume, we turn our attention to the ways in which these consequences and vulnerabilities are structured along gender, racial, and class lines and to the stresses and strains which they create for individuals and communities.

Layered Realities

As just noted, there are significant hidden consequences and collateral costs associated with immigration policies and practices, including but not limited to those discussed. As the chapters herein reveal, these consequences and costs are substantial and wide-ranging, affecting millions of immigrants and non-immigrants alike, as well as families and entire communities. Of critical importance is the fact that these consequences are not randomly distributed across populations or communities; rather, they have patterned outcomes, with some immigrants and communities particularly vulnerable. Which types of immigrants and communities are most affected? Why?

We argue it is impossible to answer these questions without examining the layered realities of immigrants' lives and the varying complexities surrounding immigration and crime, law, and victimization. In terms of immigrants, this requires attention to how identity may condition the relationships among immigration, crime, law, and victimization. So, for example, attention to racialized and gendered overlays, as just noted, is essential. The hidden consequences of immigration policies and practices affect men and women differently, and the same can be said based on one's race or ethnicity as evidenced, for example, by fears that Arizona's new legislation will exacerbate racial profiling. In terms of communities, this requires attention both to historical trends and to contextual analyses of the effects of policies and practices, which are undoubtedly variant across time and place.

Regardless of focus, the key point is that the consequences of policies and practices associated with immigration are not simple; nor are they uniform. Accordingly, research must explore and document nuances, complexities, and layered realities for immigrants and communities. Only then can we begin to understand how the costs and consequences associated with these policies and practices are patterned and structured.

Unfortunately, very few studies accomplish this. As mentioned at the outset of this chapter, most scholarly research has focused on a subset of questions limited to immigrants' participation in criminal activity. Rarely are fundamental differences in race, class, gender, or social context given serious consideration. To address this gap in the literature, the final section of this volume explores these patterned relations to better understand the nuances of immigration policies and practices and their effects on immigrants and communities. While the costs and consequences are likely structured in many different ways, the remaining chapters consider four of the most important: race/ethnicity, socioeconomic status, gender, and community or regional context.

The chapter by María Vélez and Christopher Lyons, Situating the Immigration and Neighborhood Crime Relationship across Multiple Cities, considers how metropolitan context moderates the relationship between immigration and crime. Although most research documents that immigration and crime are not significantly associated across neighborhoods and cities, Vélez and Lyons argue this relationship is likely conditioned by the degree to which cities historically have been, and currently are, receptive to immigrants. They therefore compare the relationship between immigration and crime in traditional gateway cities long accustomed to immigration, and non-gateway cities, which historically have incorporated far fewer immigrants. Their findings show that the protective effect of immigration is heightened in gateway cities, suggesting that immigrants fare better in contexts that are receptive to them.

The chapter by Paola Bertolini and Michele Lalla, Immigrant Inclusion and Prospects through Schooling in Italy: An Analysis of Emerging Regional Patterns, also considers the importance of context, more specifically, regional context. Their analysis takes us to the European Union, which is grappling with enormous immigration pressures. Bertolini and Lalla examine school participation rates among immigrants in the Northern and Southern regions of Italy. Northern Italy is one of the most developed regions in the European Union, while Southern Italy is among the less developed areas. Comparing native Italians, first-generation immigrants, and second-generation immigrants, they document distinct differences in school participation rates, type of school attended (pre-university or vocational), and labor market opportunities of the groups—differences that can be traced back to individual, familial, and community characteristics including, among other factors, the social and economic structures of the region where the family lives. Their chapter demonstrates the importance of educational opportunities, and of policies supporting such opportunities, for successful integration of immigrant youth into the larger society.

In some cases, the nuanced realities of immigrants encompass multiple layers that simultaneously affect the relationships among immigration and crime, law, and victimization, as evidenced in the chapter by Alice Cepeda, Nalini Negi, Kathryn Nowotny, James Arango, Charles Kaplan, and Avelardo Valdez, Social Stressors, Special Vulnerabilities and Violence Victimization among Latino Immigrant Day Laborers in Post-Katrina New Orleans. In this chapter, the authors explore the myriad challenges immigrant day laborers face on a daily basis, and document how their unique set of vulnerabilities makes them particularly susceptible to victimization. According to Cepeda and her colleagues, these vulnerabilities are shaped by gender, race/ethnicity, socioeconomic status, and even community context, all of which interact to make Latino immigrants working as day laborers in post-Katrina New Orleans especially susceptible. Through interviews with day laborers across four New Orleans research sites, Cepeda and her colleagues collected rich data that detail the various vulnerabilities and social stressors experienced by these immigrants. They describe how such processes and stressors contribute to increased victimization among this population. Of particular interest is their analysis of how this unique constellation of vulnerabilities goes beyond those faced by immigrants in more traditional settlement destinations. Cepeda and her colleagues also document how these vulnerabilities are confounded by the highly racialized social context of New Orleans, a city characterized by high crime rates, thriving drug markets, and drug use, especially post-Katrina.

The final chapter of this volume, the Conclusion, draws on lessons learned from the readings and applies them to assist in informing emerging policy and research agendas. Here, we summarize the major findings crosscutting the research presented in individual chapters, identify key research themes for future studies, and initiate a conversation on how social science research can better inform immigration policy. By drawing on studies from multiple disciplines and from various sites within the United States as well as Africa, Europe, Central America, and Australia, we are better able to understand the confounding effects of immigration policies on individuals and communities, and the varied responses of immigrants. Our exploration of the lived realities of immigrants, deportees, and relocated persons helps us to see the ways in which those experiences are systematically nuanced and layered. The next step, we suggest, is to translate this social science research into more informed policies and practices for addressing the relationships among immigration, crime, law, and victimization. Accordingly, we conclude with suggestions both for future research and for those individuals designing and enforcing immigration policy.

REFERENCES

Beckett, Katherine and Steve Herbert. 2008. "The Punitive City Revisited: The Transformation of Urban Social Control." In *After the War on Crime: Race, Democracy, and a New Reconstruction*, ed. Mary Louise Frampton, Ian Haney Lopez, and Jonathan Simon, 106–22. New York: New York University Press.

Calavita, Kitty. 1984. *U.S. Immigration Law and the Control of Labor: 1820–1924*. Orlando: Academic Press.

———. 1996. "The New Politics of Immigration: 'Balanced Budget Conservatism' and Prop 187." *Social Problems* 43:284–305.

Chambliss, William J. and Marjorie S. Zatz (eds.). 1993. *Making Law: The State, The Law, and Structural Contradictions*. Bloomington: Indiana University Press.

Chavez, Leo R. 2008. *The Latino Threat: Constructing Immigrants, Citizens, and the Nation*. Stanford: Stanford University Press.

Clear, Todd R. 2007. *Imprisoning Communities: How Mass Incarceration Makes Disadvantaged Neighborhoods Worse*. New York: Oxford University Press.

Cohen, Stanley. 1972. *Folk Devils and Moral Panics: The Creation of the Mods and Rockers*. London: McGibbon and Kee.

Decker, Scott H., Paul G. Lewis, Doris M. Provine, and Monica W. Varsanyi. 2009. On the Frontier of Local Law Enforcement: Local Police and Federal Immigration Law. In *Sociology of Crime, Law, and Deviance*, ed. W. F. McDonald, 261–78. Bingley, UK: Emerald/JAI Press.

Doty, Roxanne Lynn. 2009. *The Law Into Their Own Hands: Immigration and the Politics of Exceptionalism*. Tucson: University of Arizona Press.

Fine, Gary. 2006. "The Chaining of Social Problems: Solutions and Unintended Consequences in the Age of Betrayal." *Social Problems* 53:3–17.

Ganapati, Sukumar and Howard Frank. 2008. "Good Intentions, Unintended Consequences—Impact of Adker Consent Decree on Miami-Dade County's Subsidized Housing." *Urban Affairs Review* 44:57–84.

Gardner, Martha, 2005. *The Qualities of a Citizen: Women, Immigration, and Citizenship, 1870–1965*. Princeton, NJ: Princeton University Press.

Goode, Erich and Nachman Ben-Yehuda. 1994. *Moral Panics: The Social Construction of Deviance*. Cambridge: Blackwell.

International Human Rights Law Clinic, University of California, Berkeley, Chief Justice Earl Warren Institute on Race, Ethnicity and Diversity, University of California, Berkeley, and Immigration Law Clinic, University of California, Davis. 2010. *In the Child's Best*

Interest? The Consequences of Losing a Lawful Immigrant Parent to Deportation. March. Retrieved June 24, 2011 from http://www.law.ucdavis.edu/news/images/childsbestinterest.pdf.

Johnson, Kevin R. 2004. *The "Huddled Masses" Myth: Immigration and Civil Rights.* Philadelphia: Temple University Press.

———. 2007. *Opening the Floodgates: Why America Needs to Rethink Its Borders and Immigration Laws.* New York: New York University Press.

Khashul, Anita. 2009. *The Role of Local Police: Striking a Balance Between Immigration Enforcement and Civil Liberties.* Washington, DC Police Foundation. Retrieved May 9, 2010 from http://policefoundation.org/indexStriking.html.

Martínez, Ramiro, Jr. and Abel Valenzuela, Jr. (eds.). 2006. *Immigration and Crime: Race, Ethnicity and Violence.* New York: New York University Press.

Nevins, Joseph. 2002. *Operation Gatekeeper: The Rise of the "Illegal Alien" and the Remaking of the U.S.-Mexico Boundary.* New York: Routledge.

New York Times. 2007. Snapshot: Global Migration. June 22. Retrieved June 24, 2011 from http://www.nytimes.com/ref/world/20070622_CAPEVERDE_GRAPHIC.html.

Newton, Lina. 2008. *Illegal, Alien, or Immigrant: The Politics of Immigration Reform.* New York: New York University Press.

Ngai, Mae M. 2005. *Impossible Subjects: Illegal Aliens and the Making of Modern America.* Princeton, NJ: Princeton University Press.

Passel, Jeffery S. and D'Vera Cohn. 2011. *Unauthorized Immigrant Population: National and State Trends, 2010.* Washington, DC: Pew Hispanic Center.

Rodríguez, Havidan, Rogelio Saenz, and Cecilia Menjívar. 2008. Preface. In *Latinas/os in the United States: Changing the Face of America,* xv–xxiii. New York: Springer.

Simon, Jonathan. 2007. *Governing Through Crime: How the War on Crime Transformed American Democracy and Created a Culture of Fear.* New York: Oxford University Press.

United Nations High Commissioner for Refugees (UNHCR). 2008. *Asylum Levels and Trends in Industrialized Countries, 2007.* Retrieved June 24, 2011 from http://www.unhcr.org/statistics/STATISTICS/47daae862.pdf.

Varsanyi, Monica W. (ed.). 2010. *Taking Local Control: Immigration Policy Activism in U.S. Cities and States.* Stanford: Stanford University Press.

Welch, Michael. 2003. "Ironies of Social Control and the Criminalization of Immigrants." *Crime, Law and Social Change* 39:319–37.

PART I

New Modes of Control

2

Panic, Risk, Control

Conceptualizing Threats in a Post-9/11 Society

MICHAEL WELCH

Since the early 1990s, we have witnessed another round of events that contribute to a historical pattern of punishing immigrants. In the wake of the 1993 bombing of the World Trade Center and again following the attack on September 11, 2001, Congress passed tough new laws that essentially scapegoat racial, ethnic, and religious minorities (Welch 2002, 2006a, 2009). Those policies, driven by conservative and populist politics, are not confined to the United States, as similar responses to 9/11 also have taken effect in Europe and Australia (Bosworth and Guild 2008; Grewcock 2009; Melossi 2003; Pickering 2005; Welch and Schuster 2005a, 2005b). While progressive scholars should continue their efforts to confront and correct these forms of injustice, it is important not to overlook the emergence of new modes of social control. By recognizing precisely how threats are conceptualized, we are better able to understand the ways in which certain groups of people are perceived and managed by government. Among the concepts that deserve special attention are panic, risk, and control. Correspondingly, this chapter delves into the phenomenon of threat and considers the economic forces shaping strategies to contain certain "dangers" in a post-9/11 era. Indeed, the new modes of social control are coupled with related industries that benefit from the overlapping wars on crime, illegal immigration, and terror. It is fair to say that those wars have become so consuming that no end is in sight. In the words of a former CIA officer quoted in the documentary titled *Why We Fight*: "When war becomes profitable, we will see more of it" (Jarecki 2006).

While engaging in a theoretical analysis, this chapter frequently breaks from the abstract to focus on the collateral consequences of unreasonably harsh policies. Further demonstrating that panic, risk, and control resonate beyond the United States, awareness is turned to other countries, in particular, Australia, where similar anxieties over "outsiders" have recently surfaced. In Australia, a comparative survey found that its citizens out-worry Americans on the issue of illegal immigration. The study reports that 69 percent of Australian respondents agree that their country "is taking too many immigrants," as compared to 62 percent of Americans. Overall, "76 percent of Australians believe that increasing numbers of asylum seekers and illegal immigrants are an important problem for the country" (United States Studies Centre 2010, 1; also Iyengar and Jackman 2010). Much like their U.S. counterpart, the Australian government has instituted tough measures for those entering its territory illegally, including mandatory detention. In doing so, both nations have created financial opportunities for private corrections companies. While attending to these developments in both the United States and Australia, the chapter emphasizes the importance of deciphering how threat is conceptualized along lines of crime, immigration, and terror. Discussion concludes with some suggestions for challenging the new modes of social control and the markets they produce.

Panic over Immigrants

In the early 1990s, anti-immigrant attitudes spread throughout key states such as Florida, Texas, and most notably California, where voters overwhelmingly supported California's Proposition 187: a measure intended to deny basic services to anyone suspected of not being a citizen or legal resident, including education, health, and social services. Eventually, the problem of illegal immigration—embodied in the threat of terrorism—emerged as a national issue in 1993 when an explosion ripped through the World Trade Center in New York City. Two years later, when the Murrah Federal Building in Oklahoma City was bombed, the immediate reaction of law enforcement officials and many citizens was to assume that it, too, was the act of foreign terrorists (Cole 1999; Tebo 2000). Although investigations led to U.S.-born Timothy McVeigh, and not foreign terrorists, as the person responsible for the bombing, public hostility toward immigrants heightened. In swift order, politicians weighed into the controversy. In 1996, Congress passed the *Anti-Terrorism and Effective Death Penalty Act*. Combining concerns over terrorism with other crimes committed by illegal aliens, the anti-terrorism law greatly complemented the *Illegal Immigration Reform and Immigrant Responsibility Act* of 1996. Under those Acts, increased funding for the fight against illegal immigration made the Immigration and Naturalization Service (INS) the largest federal law enforcement agency. More significantly, both statutes granted the agency unprecedented authority to seek out and deport immigrants deemed a threat to national security (see Welch 1996, 2000b; Zatz and Smith 2008).

Moral panic theory has made significant inroads into immigration research, especially in light of exaggerated and turbulent reactions to "outsiders" (Welch 2002, 2003b). Drawing inspiration from Marshall McLuhan's *Understanding Media* (1964), the term "moral panic" was initially used by Jock Young (1971) in his examination of the police and how they negotiate reality and translate fantasy, but his colleague Stanley Cohen elaborated more fully on the concept in *Folk Devils and Moral Panics*. In its infancy, the moral panic paradigm incorporated an emerging sociology of deviance and cultural studies, reflecting the changing social mood of the late 1960s. According to Cohen, a moral panic has occurred when: "a condition, episode, person or group of persons emerges to become defined as a threat to societal values and interest; its nature is presented in a stylized and stereotypical fashion by the mass media and politicians" (1972: 9). Together, media and members of the political establishment move to publicize putative dangers; in turn, such claims were used to justify enhanced police powers and greater investment in the traditional criminal justice apparatus (see Beckett and Sasson 2000; Herman and Chomsky 2002).

Scholars have pinpointed the ways moral panics lead to legislation imposing new restrictions on existing freedoms, liberties, and due process (Goode and Ben-Yehuda 1994; Hall et al. 1978; Welch 2000a). The 1996 immigration and anti-terrorism laws did just that, especially considering that for many years the immigration review process was becoming progressively more fair. In fact, INS hearing judges had been attending to individual circumstances while the courts reviewed the officers' decisions, acting as final arbiters of whether particular cases met constitutional muster. The new statutes, by contrast, gutted due process, issuing the INS unparalleled powers and limiting judicial review of deportation and detention decisions made by immigration judges. Those laws authorized the INS to use secret evidence to detain and deport suspected terrorists and expanded the scope of crimes considered aggravated felonies that are grounds for deportation. Compounding matters, that provision was made retroactive, meaning any person convicted of a crime now reclassified as an aggravated felony could be deported, regardless of how old the conviction (ACLU 2000).

Legislation on immigration in 1996 was imbued with an undifferentiated fear of crime and terror as well as of minorities and outsiders. Legal expert Margaret Graham Tebo concurs: "some speculate it's because the INS knows that despite rhetoric to the contrary, Congress wants the agency to tighten the nation's borders, particularly to minority immigrants" (2000: EV9). Similarly, Gregory T. Nojeim, an ACLU Legislative Counsel, opined: "Everyone in Congress knew that the '96 anti-terrorism law was in large part an immigration law" (ibid.). The clampdown on illegal—and criminal—immigrants remains riddled with contradictions, exhausting vast resources in efforts to apprehend persons who have committed minor, not serious, offenses (ACLU 2000). Other observers agree that the impact of the Illegal Immigration Reform and Immigration Responsibility Act has been not primarily on illegal immigrants, but on lawful permanent residents of the United States who at some time in the past ran afoul of the criminal law (Greenhouse 2001).

In Australia, scholars have not ignored the interaction between the government and the media, particularly since together they portray illegal immigration (e.g., "bogus" asylum-seekers) as a threat to the state and national security. Examining news discourses on asylum-seekers during the administration of Prime Minister John Howard (1997–1999), Pickering (2001) adopted a Gramscian perspective on "ideological work" and the production of "common sense." Three thematic categories of representation were discovered: the invading deviant, the racialized deviant, and the diseased deviant. While also attending to nationalistic identities, Pickering argues that the media constitute an important site for hegemonic activity aimed at achieving public consent for tighter control over refugees. Overall, such policies and practices as mandatory detention are presumed to secure the nation and its borders (see Pickering 2005; Refugee Council of Australia 2000).

Klocker and Dunn (2003) also studied how asylum-seekers in Australia were depicted by the state and the media. Their content analysis of media releases (2001–2002) revealed the decidedly negative manner in which members of the federal government spoke about asylum-seekers, relying on such characterizations as "threat," "other," "illegality," and "burden." Newspaper articles during the same time show that the media largely adopted the negativity and specific references of the government, thereby demonstrating media's dependence upon government statements and spokespersons. Klocker and Dunn contend their "findings generally support the 'propaganda model' that holds a pessimistic view of the news media's critical abilities" (2003: 71). Still, their study also indicates the media departed somewhat slightly from the government's unchanging stance following some key events and revelations, particularly the disinformation campaign generated by the Howard government over the "Children Overboard" controversy.

On October 7, 2001, amid worldwide anxiety over 9/11, Australian Prime Minister John Howard, Immigration Minister Phillip Ruddock, and Defence Minister Peter Reith accused Iraqi asylum-seekers intercepted north of Australian territory of "throwing their children overboard" into the ocean in an attempt to pressure the crew of an Australian naval ship to pick them up and take them to Australia. The event caused a major stir in Australia, prompting its citizens to feel threatened by an influx of boat people from Asia and the Middle East. Eventually, skeptics began investigating the veracity of the report and learned that the Howard government had duped the media as well as the public:

> There were, in fact, images of adults and children fleeing their sinking vessel, in an attempt to save their own lives. The initial story, however— as constructed by the Howard government—appeared to demonise the asylum seekers, depicting them as evil and inhuman. The government interpreted the event as a threat to the inherent "goodness" of Australian citizenship and considered the Australian nation as in need of protection from an "evil," thereby establishing the moral high ground. This had the effect of supporting the government's immigration and border control policies. (Slattery 2003: 93–94)

In a similar evaluation of the "Children Overboard" event, Saxton (2003) delves further into the meaning of Howard's reaction to the incident: "I certainly don't want people like that here" (Mares 2001: 135). Saxton's discourse analysis reveals how asylum-seekers have been represented as illegal, nongenuine, and threatening. Much like the aforementioned studies, she finds that nationalist rhetoric (e.g., protect Australia's territory) was used to legitimize the government's actions and public opinion concerning asylum-seekers (see Weber 2002; Welch 2010a, 2010b).

Further refining the sociology of moral panic, Cohen (2002) distinguishes between noisy and quiet constructions. As the term suggests, noisy constructions manifest in moral panic accompanied by high levels of public, political, and media attention. By contrast, quiet constructions emerge as a more contained entity in which the "claims makers are professionals, experts, or bureaucrats working in an organization with little or no public or media exposure" (2002: xxiii). At first glance, the idea of a quiet panic appears oxymoronic: how can a moral panic be quiet? Unfortunately, Cohen offers little guidance on how to answer this question other than the aforementioned quotation. Still, it is important to pursue that facet of moral panic theory in an attempt to break new ground. Toward that end, comparative research has set out to decipher reactions to asylum-seekers (Welch 2004; Welch and Schuster 2005a, 2005b). Much like in Australia, moral panic over so-called bogus asylum-seekers in Britain represents a noisy construction whereby claims-making is loud and public. Whereas there is considerable panic over undocumented immigrants in the United States, especially those entering illegally through the border with Mexico, the controversy over asylum-seekers is relatively quiet. Despite the absence of public anxiety over asylum-seekers, government officials have quietly instituted policies and practices that adversely affect those seeking refuge, particularly post-9/11 (e.g., Operation Liberty Shield, Blanket Detention Order of 2003).

Risk in a Post-9/11 Society

The third edition of *Folk Devils and Moral Panics* allowed Cohen to look back on how moral panic as a concept has been used—and misused—by academics as well as journalists. By doing so, he considers further the explanatory power of moral panic with respect to risk:

> Some of the social space once occupied by moral panics has been filled by more inchoate social anxieties, insecurities and fears. These are fed by specific risks: the growth of new "techno-anxieties" (nuclear, chemical, biological, toxic and ecological risk), disease hazards, food panics, safety scares about traveling on trains or planes, and fears of international terrorism. (2002: xxv)

These developments offer conceptual bridges between the moral panic paradigm and the risk society, again refining a critical understanding of shifting sites of social anxiety. The construction of risk refers not only to basic information about harmful conditions and events but also the manner of evaluating, classifying, and reacting to them (Beck 1992; O'Malley 2010, 2008). Those activities inevitably involve claims made by experts and authorities, raising questions over whether there is a moral enterprise in the making (Welch 2002; Zatz 1987).

While there is overlap between the moral panic theory and the risk society literatures, there is a key distinction: namely, the notion of volatility. To determine whether a moral panic has actually occurred, there must be evidence of volatility whereby panic over a putative problem eventually wanes and dissipates from public concern (Goode and Ben Yehuda 1994; Welch 2008). Assessing the aftermath of 9/11, some scholars point to incidents of moral panic that have since subsided (Bonn 2010; Rothe and Muzzatti 2004). Those developments notwithstanding, it seems useful to also theorize along lines of the risk society. From that standpoint, what is important is not so much momentary bursts of hostility aimed at various scapegoats (e.g., immigrants, asylum-seekers, minorities) but the long-term shifts in the political, economic, and legal architecture of post-9/11 society alongside its new modes of social control. Those changes have certainly made their way into a reinvigorated sense of sovereignty, state, and territory, particularly given how threat is conceptualized (Pickering and Weber 2006; Welch 2007, 2008).

In Australia, among the key features of the controversy over asylum-seekers is Howard's decision to use offshore detention centers. During his term, the government instituted what it called the Pacific Solution, a controversial strategy to deal with boatloads of asylum-seekers. Under the policy, so-called boat people would be transported by the Australian navy to neighboring states (e.g., Nauru) rather than to the mainland. It was presumed by the Howard government that detention offshore would deter boat people from seeking asylum in Australia. In addition, Australian officials claimed that offshore detention would curb threats from terrorists and people-smugglers in the region, thereby protecting Australian borders and national security. Although legal scholars argue that preventing asylum-seekers from filing claims in Australia violates international law, the Pacific Solution gained considerable momentum, especially before the "Children Overboard" story had been discredited (Grewcock 2009; Pickering 2005).

In 2007, the Rudd Labor government officially abandoned the Pacific Solution and relaxed some aspects of the detention policy, but "the fundamental dynamics of border policing policy have not changed" (Grewcock 2009: 11). In 2009, Prime Minister Rudd met with his Indonesian counterpart to urge his government to detain asylum-seekers in Indonesia as part of a regional strategy to keep those seeking asylum from reaching Australia. Since 2010, the newly elected Gillard government has kept open plans to use offshore detention and asylum processing. Those immigration policies point to a significant shift in practice whereby border policing occurs externally. In essence, the territory of a particular state extends its borders as a means to prevent asylum-seekers from reaching the mainland; otherwise, that government would be obligated to file asylum claims. The strategy to *externalize* the border for purposes of immigration policing is not unique to Australia. In Europe, the Italian government has transported unauthorized migrants to Libya, a state that is not a signatory to the 1951 convention on refugees (Trucco 2005).

Although the European parliament condemned Italy's tactic, Britain prompted the European Commission to consider regional management sites and offshore detention centers to control the flow of unauthorized migration and asylum-seeking. Some potential offshore sites include Somalia, Turkey, and Ukraine, all of which have a record of mistreating refugees (Dietrich 2005). For decades, the U.S. government has policed the Caribbean in ways that appear to externalize the border, sweeping up boats of migrants and asylum-seekers, particularly those fleeing Haiti. Coupling that mode of social control, American officials have instituted new immigration policing strategies that appear to *internalize* the border. Although the bulk of U.S. immigration patrols target the southern border with Mexico, the government has quietly expanded transportation checks along the north. As Bernstein (2010) notes:

> The little-publicized transportation checks are the result of the Border Patrol's growth since 9/11, fueled by Congressional antiterrorism spending and an expanding definition of border jurisdiction. In the Rochester area, where the border is miles away in the middle of Lake Ontario, the patrol arrested 2,788 passengers from October 2005 through last September [2009]. (p. 3)

According to Rafael Lemaitre, a spokesperson for U.S. Customs and Border Protection, the checks are "a vital component to our overall border security efforts" to prevent terrorism and illegal entry. He went on to explain the patrol had jurisdiction to enforce immigration laws within 100 miles of the border, and that "one mission was preventing smugglers and human traffickers from exploiting inland transit hubs" (Bernstein 2010: 3). Critics of the northern border patrol argue that the concept of the border is becoming more fluid and consequently erodes constitutional limits on search and seizure. And, unlike the recent state law in Arizona referenced in this volume's introductory chapter and discussed in greater detail in chapter 4, the shift in enforcement is happening without public debate. Cary M. Jensen, director of international services for the University of Rochester, said: "It's turned into a police state on the northern border. It's essentially become an internal document check" (Bernstein 2010: 4). The internalization of the border marks a new development in the modes of control aimed at assessing risk and detecting threats in post-9/11 America. Those manifestations are not confined to policing U.S. territory but have clearly spilled over to the global war on terror.

Counter-Law: Laws against Law

The reconfiguration of American power in the wake of 9/11 has not gone unnoticed, especially in the realm of an executive office that has overreached its constitutional limits. Indeed, the expansion of presidential power has become a defining feature of the global war on terror as it suspends federal as well as international law (i.e., unlawful enemy combatants, torture, and the invasion of Iraq) (Welch 2009). These developments have prompted scholars to consider the links between recent legal transformations and a neoliberal political culture preoccupied with uncertainty. According to Ericson (2007), as uncertainty intensifies, a precautionary logic leads to extreme—and frantic—security measures intended to ward off imagined sources of harm (see Agamben 2005; Butler 2004; Taylor 2004). In the realm of national security, terrorism is the politics of uncertainty since as a form of political violence it plays on randomness to push entire populations into mind-sets of fear and anxiety. Terrorism also exposes an inherent feature of modern societies— their potential ungovernability whereby those with little power can undo formidable institutions.

In response to such threats, state actors move toward intensified security measures by putting into motion key legal maneuvers. Foucault recognized that asymmetries of power are widened by suspensions of law, a phenomenon that he called counter-law, or laws against law (1977: 30). Drawing on Foucauldian thought, Ericson characterizes counter-law as the enactment of new laws (and civil and administrative devices) so as "to erode or eliminate traditional principles, standards, and procedures of criminal law that get in the way of preempting imagined sources of harm" (2007: 24). To be clear, Ericson's use of the term "counter-law" should not be separated from his theoretical insights into risk. Counter-law is not simply a power shift that passes new legislation to replace existing ones. It is a socio-legal transformation within the state as it strives to harness risk. While many crimes, including terrorism, fall into the purview of criminal law, counter-law serves to justify reassigning those offenses (and even mere threats or suspicions of such harm) into the sphere of civil and administrative proceedings where there is less uncertainty in trying to manage a particular threat:

The legal transformation through counter-law is not only a response to scientific uncertainty about risk, but also the law itself as a source of uncertainty. For example, when it sustains high standards of due process, evidence, proof and culpability, criminal law creates a great deal of uncertainty in the capacity of the criminal justice system to prevent, discover, build a case against, and successfully prosecute criminal behavior. In the precautionary urge for greater certainty in crime control, these standards of criminal law are weakened [and] the lower standards of civil and administrative law are substituted. (Ericson 2007: 25–26; see Ericson and Haggerty 1997)

Counter-law is a tactic used by the executive to gain the upper hand in the politics of authority. This is particularly significant in the wake of catastrophic events, such as September 11, which reveal key weaknesses in the government's capacity to protect national security. Consequently, counter-law becomes a dominant political strategy representing the boldest statement of authoritative certainty by the state, even when its authority and certainty may be at its weakest (Ericson 2007; Welch 2009).

While proponents of counter-law claim to have achieved an advantage in managing society as it faces risks embedded in late modernity, such new modes of social control undermine democratic institutions and provide a dangerous foundation for human rights abuses. In its war on terror, the U.S. government has adopted several counter-law tactics that restrict the rights of its own citizens (e.g., U.S. Patriot Act). Additionally, there are other maneuvers that target persons outside of America's borders. The unlawful enemy combatant designation, the opening of Guantanamo Bay, and revised definitions of torture are all counter-terrorism measures that operate beyond law as conventionally conceived. Turning critical attention to these matters, Ericson discusses the importance of counter-law as it emerges in a state of exception, an idea developed by Agamben (2005). The state of exception stems from a catastrophic event that the state depicts as an emergency, thereby justifying a suspension of normal legal principles and procedures. As a national (or even international) emergency expands, so do uncertainty and threat; as one might expect, a state of exception has profound socio-legal effects. For Agamben (2005: 26): "The legal order must be broken to save the social order." Ericson and Agamben share the view that counter-law and the state of exception are not momentary suspensions of the legal order but have become the new "normal," serving as the dominant paradigm of government (see American Civil Liberties Union 2010; Welch 2011).

Immigration Law as Counter-Law

Especially since 9/11, Justice Department officials in concert with immigration authorities have developed another new mode of control, the misuse of immigration law. This form of counter-law stands out for its capacity to bypass constitutional guarantees afforded under criminal law (Welch 2006c). These tactics have caught the attention of lawmakers who view them as undermining basic checks and balances in governance. Senator Patrick Leahy, chairman of the Senate Judiciary Committee, stated in a letter to then Attorney General John Ashcroft: "I am deeply troubled at what appears to be an executive effort to exercise new powers without judicial scrutiny or statutory authorization" (Reuters 2001: EV2). Lawyers and legal scholars are equally worried about the wider implications to criminal procedure and due process:

> Under immigration law, the Justice Department is both accuser and judge, with its Immigration and Naturalization Service serving as police and prosecutor and its Executive Office for Immigration Review running special courts that decide whether resident aliens should be detained or deported. INS agents need no warrant to arrest noncitizens, and immigration courts don't provide lawyers for indigent suspects. (Bravin et al. 2001: 1)

Professor David Martin elaborates on the government's use of executive power: "There may not be evidence right now to hold someone on a criminal charge." But with immigration charges, it is often "very easy to demonstrate a violation" of immigration law, allowing officials to deport or detain suspects (Bravin et al. 2001: 1).

Although since the 1980s the government has turned to immigration law to contain and expel criminal aliens, its use in the war on terror is considered more troublesome. Several groups released reports documenting serious violations of civil liberties and human rights (American Civil Liberties Union 2001; Amnesty International 2003; Lawyers Committee for Human Rights 2003). Chief among the complaints of civil liberties and immigration attorneys is that the government, in waging a war on terror, inappropriately applies immigration law to circumvent its obligations under the criminal justice system. Moreover, the Department of Justice has established new immigration policies and procedures that undermine previously existing safeguards against arbitrary detention by immigration authorities. These violations are cataloged into three key areas: arbitrary detention, mistreatment of detainees, and abusive interrogations (Human Rights Watch 2002).

Moreover, each problem was exacerbated by the government's reliance on secrecy whereby the Justice Department refused to release information concerning the persons being detained.

In the realm of arbitrary detention, civil liberties and human rights groups remind us that physical liberty is a fundamental human right affirmed in international law and in the U.S. Constitution, contained in the due process clauses of the Fifth and Fourteenth Amendments. Correspondingly, arbitrary detention violates that right: "An individual who is arbitrarily detained is rendered defenseless by the coercive power of the state. While arbitrary detention is a hallmark of repressive regimes, democratic governments are not immune to the temptations of violating the right to liberty" (Human Rights Watch 2002: 46; Amnesty International 2003). Regrettably, many detainees swept up during the early phase of the post-9/11 investigation were subjected to arbitrary detention and held for lengthy periods of time. Such violations were not merely inadvertent due to the confusion surrounding the events of September 11. Instead, arbitrary detention became a systematic tool in the Justice Department's campaign against terror under which new procedural rules had been created. Those rules provided greater power to the government and undermined previously existing protections for detainees. The new rules enabled the government to use immigration detention as a form of preventative detention for criminal procedures even though it lacked evidence that detainees were flight risks or presented a danger to the community (Lawyers Committee for Human Rights 2003).

In line with the U.S. Constitution as well as international human rights law, all persons, citizen or non-citizen, have the right to be represented by legal counsel after being deprived of liberty for alleged criminal or immigration law violations. Human Rights Watch (2002) discovered that "special interest" detainees (those the government suspected of being involved in terrorism-related activity) were questioned in custody as part of a criminal investigation, even though they were subsequently charged with immigration violations. Many of those detainees were interrogated by FBI and INS agents concerning criminal matters as well as their immigration status. To reiterate, immigration attorneys complain that the government relies on administrative proceedings under the immigration law as a proxy to detain and interrogate terrorism suspects without affording them the rights and protections that the U.S. criminal system provides. Among those safeguards are the requirements of public notice, complete judicial review, and the right to have a lawyer present during custodial interrogations, including free legal counsel if necessary (Cole 2003; Cole and Dempsey 2002).

Convergence as a New Mode of Social Control

Legal scholars have examined the misuse of immigration law in the war on terror. Teresa A. Miller, for instance, contributes to a conceptual explanation of the phenomenon by looking beyond the practical advantages for implementing immigration law rather than criminal law: "One reason immigration and criminal law continue to converge after September 11 is immigration law's development as a more efficient mechanism for social control of noncitizens than the criminal justice system" (2005: 95). Such convergence, however, has attracted relatively little scrutiny from the legal community, in part because the two areas of law are doctrinally distinct. Compared to criminal law, immigration law is tremendously administrative and lacks considerable judicial overview and constitutional lawmaking. Criminal law and immigration law also operate within separate legal systems, each of which has a different set of short-term objectives and long-term goals (see Kanstroom 1999, 2000; Stichter 2002). Nevertheless, the convergence of immigration and criminal laws is gaining attention from scholars of different disciplines, all of whom conclude that the merger of these fields of law is decidedly coercive and punitive. Feeley and Simon (1992) point to shifts in the penological paradigm that increasingly emphasizes mechanisms aimed at controlling high-risk aggregates through risk management, relying on greater surveillance and detention. Kanstroom's (2004) approach to the convergence of crime control and deportation law demonstrates how post-9/11 immigration reforms have further embraced the doctrine of criminal retribution. Moreover, the mere threat of removal contributes to an already tense atmosphere for noncitizens residing in the United States.

The convergence of immigration and criminal law is escalated further by economic incentives whereby a growing jail complex thrives on immigration detainees who serve as raw materials for private profit. The detention industry also benefits government-operated facilities that siphon funds from local, state, and federal budgets (Welch 2002, 2000b). Altogether the convergence between the immigration and criminal justice systems illustrates the "severity revolution" (Simon 2001), a phenomenon described by some as a "criminalization" of immigration law (Adams 2002; Medina 1997; Morris 1997). Regardless of how the phenomenon is characterized, there is consensus on a blurring of the boundaries between immigration and crime control: "After September 11, immigration law functions as a powerful adjunct to the criminal justice system in its pursuit not only of terrorists, but of a host of objectives, including the apprehension, incarceration, and expulsion of undocumented workers and noncitizens with criminal convictions, some of whom are long-term residents with remote criminal convictions" (Miller 2005: 123).

By "criminalizing" immigration law as well as revamping criminal law to resemble immigration law so as to appear more administrative and less judicially reviewable, a new hybrid crime/immigration system of social control has been established (Miller 2003). In theorizing on these transformations, it is useful once again to consider the concept of counter-law, especially since it lends itself to the sociological literature focusing on the notion of risk in late modernity (Beck, Giddens, and Lash 1994; Ericson 2007; O'Malley 2010). The obvious downside to counter-law is its undermining effects on democratic institutions. In the war on terror, policies involving torture, the unlawful enemy combatant designation, and the misuse of immigration law proceed without the rule of law as traditionally understood. These developments have strong implications for the new modes of social control and the markets they produce.

Markets of Social Control

Thinking in terms of markets allows us to theorize about the role of economics in establishing and perpetuating certain forms of social control as well as the industries they create (Christie 1993; Welch 2003b). Of particular relevance to this discussion is the emergence of the detention-industrial complex. This type of industry operates with a market that pursues private profit not only at the expense of taxpayers but also those who are held in immigration detention. Since the 1980s, when deregulation regained prominence, the field of corrections has become big business for politicians, business leaders, and criminal justice officials, setting the groundwork for another industry of domination. The detention-industrial complex resembles its military-industrial counterpart insofar as it is formed around an iron triangle of criminal justice where subgovernment control is established. Operating well below the radar of public visibility, key players in the corrections subgovernment strongly influence the course of policy and spending. The triangle includes (a) private corporations eager to profit from incarceration, (b) government agencies anxious to secure their continued existence (e.g., Bureau of Justice Assistance, National Institute of Justice), and (c) professional organizations (e.g., the American Bar Association, the American Correctional Association) (Lilly and Deflem 1996). The iron triangle of criminal justice draws on power from each of these sectors in a formidable alliance and, according to critics, is a daunting source of influence over government (Welch 2000b; Welch and Turner 2008).

The Immigration and Customs Enforcement (ICE; formerly INS) detains thousands of undocumented immigrants and asylum-seekers who are either waiting to have a hearing or are scheduled to be deported. Because of its limited jail capacity, however, the immigration authorities rent cells from other correctional facilities, including county jails and private correctional facilities. In so doing, the agency has become an influential participant in the corrections industry (Welch 2002). Despite complaints from human rights groups, the business of detaining undocumented immigrants and asylum-seekers has produced a vast network of more than 900 jails nationwide, all eager to cash in on lucrative government contracts that usually pay twice the cost of housing inmates charged with criminal offenses (Casimir 2001). Local jail administrators have taken comfort in the fact that Congress remains deeply committed to its fight against illegal immigrants. In 2000, the budget for the INS totaled $4.27 billion, an 8 percent increase over the previous year; by 2001, federal lawmakers increased the budget once again, to $4.8 billion, an 11 percent increase. More significantly, the detention budget jumped from $800 million in 2000 to $900 million in 2001 (INS 2001). Immigration officials use more than a third of the detention budget to rent cells, mostly in remote rural counties where the costs are low and there are beds to spare (Welch and Turner 2008).

Immigration detainees are the fastest-growing segment of the nation's correctional population. In 1997, 8,200 detainees were held by the INS, and by 2001, that figure leaped to more than 20,000 (INS 2001). The agency's policy shift toward detention and away from parole has not occurred in a vacuum. For the past two decades, immigration officials have been responding to key ideological and market forces driving the uncritical acceptance that greater law enforcement activities coupled with fewer social services not only is rational and legitimate but lucrative as well. On the business side of detention (and incarceration), there is considerable speculation that privatization will continue to flourish, thus fulfilling its enormous potential by generating significant capital and handsome dividends. The economic formula is simple. Investors in private corrections are anticipating more detainees (and prisoners) to be incarcerated for longer periods of time. Consequently, CEOs and other financial players expect to profit opulently from the prison enterprise. By 2005, industry analysts projected the private share of the prison market to double (Welch and Turner 2008). Evidence of current and future financial gain in private corrections is another blunt reminder of the market forces driving the new modes of social control. While many corporations and their investors benefit financially from the privatization of corrections, there are tragic consequences, including the unjust detention of undocumented immigrants and asylum-seekers who, in effect, become raw materials for the detention business (Welch 2007, 2002, 2000b).

Since the events of September 11, 2001, there has been increased economic interest in detention. Months following the attacks, the U.S. government rounded up more than 1,000 foreigners. In response to signals that additional jail space is needed, stocks of private companies that build and operate prisons for governments zoomed as high as 300 percent. James Mac-Donald, prisons-security analyst at First Analysts Securities, notes: "Unfortunately, these are becoming good investments" (Tharp 2001). Owing to the detention prospects contained in the war on terror, six publicly traded prison companies expect good financial news from the Federal Bureau of Prisons as it plans to expand its holding capacity for immigration detainees. The BOP opened the bidding process for two prisons to hold criminal aliens in Georgia, and in early 2002 the government solicited bids for three more prisons in the Southwest deserts that can hold more than 1,500 detainees. Among those companies poised to cash in on the new crop of detainees is Wackenhut Corporation. Still, other companies, such as Corrections Corporation of America (CCA), are expected to be in the race for prison revenue. CCA was on the brink of bankruptcy in the summer of 2001, but a new management team and new business in the aftermath of the September 11 terror attacks changed its prospects. Financial analysts noted that many security companies received huge and immediate profits in the aftermath of the terror attack (Welch and Turner 2008).

These *privatized* modes of social control have global reach, especially in regions grappling with the influx of unwanted migrants, refugees, and asylum-seekers. In Britain, for instance, key developments have led to significant growth in the detainee population which in turn has created opportunities for private detention firms. Prior to 1988, asylum-seekers averaged approximately 5,000 per year and were rarely deported or detained. Occasionally people would be stopped on entry and detained awaiting removal, but at any one time there would usually be between 200–300 people in detention. This situation changed significantly in the 1990s. From 250 people in early 1993, the number of those detained increased to just over 2,260 ten years later (Schuster 2003a, 2003b). As the numbers increased, it was decided to build a facility to house detainees. The first purpose-built camp for migration detainees in the UK was opened in 1993 at Campsfield, Oxfordshire. That facility originally had 186 places, but later 100 more were added, reversing

New Labour's decision to close the center. The 1999 Immigration and Asylum Act stepped up the practice of detention, massively increasing the number of places. Since the Act came into force, four new purpose-built detention centers have opened: Oakington (400 places primarily for families), Harmondsworth (500 places), Yarl's Wood (900 places), and Colnbrook (326 places). Adding to the growing detention apparatus, Lindholme RAF base (110 places) was redesignated a removal center, Dungavel prison (200 places) became a detention center, and a closed induction center opened at Dover (20 places). There are also holding centers at Waterloo, Heathrow, and Manchester transit hubs. Despite government promises to end the practice, asylum-seekers continue to be housed in prisons. Moreover, NGOs report that removal from a detention center to a prison is a method sometimes used to punish detainees (Welch and Schuster 2005a, 2005b).

With respect to outsourcing, it is important to note that all the detention centers, except Haslar and Lindholme, are run by private security firms, such as Group 4 and Wackenhut. Haslar and Lindholme are prison establishments and run by the prison service (see PPRI 2010). Moreover, much like in the United States, various problems and abuses in private immigration detention are common, in part due to cost-cutting measures that include hiring poorly trained staff (Welch 2002). Disturbances at the Campsfield House and Yarl's Wood centers, alongside the practice of detaining children, have drawn intense criticism by human rights groups (11 Million 2009; Denton 2010; Molenaar and Neufeld 2003).

In Australia, mandatory detention for those arriving without proper documents has become the central policy for dealing with asylum-seekers since 1992. Soon thereafter, the privatization movement made inroads into the operation of immigration detention centers. In 1996, during the Howard administration, the government announced its decision to outsource immigration detention services, a plan so crassly committed to financial matters that there was no mention of wider ethical issues "such as public accountability for the actions of the state or whether it is morally defensible to detain someone for profit" (Grewcock 2009; see ANAO 2004: 45–46; Moyle 2000). The Australian version of privatization is not a home-grown enterprise but rather an offshoot of multinational security corporations (Welch and Turner 2008). From 1997 to 2004, Australia's mainland detention centers were run by ACM (Australasian Correctional Management, the operational arm of Australasian Correctional Services, ACS). That firm was a partnership between Thiess Constructions (the Australian construction giant) and the U.S.-based security company Wackenhut Corporation (Hooker 2005; Mares 2001: 69–78).

Especially because of well-publicized detainee abuses at Woomera, ACM faced harsh criticism by the Australian Human Rights and Equal Opportunity Commission (AHREOC 2004). ACM also was investigated by the Inquiry into Immigration Detention Procedures (Flood 2001). In 2003, ACM lost its contract with the Australian government (PPRI 2001). Between 2004 and 2009, the major corporate player in Australia's immigration detention network was Global Solutions Limited (GSL), a subsidiary of the British-based GSL (initially owned by Group 4 Falck) (ANAO 2004: 47). In May 2004, Group 4 Falck sold GSL to two European venture capital funds based on speculative data that the detention industry offered enormous "growth prospects" (Morton 2004). That *Field of Dreams* scenario ("if you build it, they will come") has not gone unnoticed by scholars. Grewcock (2009: 202) observes: "Such corporate interest in detention underscored both its potential profitability and the way commercialisation of immigration detention has contributed to a reinvention of the carceral relationship between the state and the detainee" (see Pickering 2005; Pickering and Weber 2006; Weber 2002; Welch 2007).

Eventually, GSL also faced criticism for reports of detainee abuse and mistreatment (AAP 2005; ASRC 2006; HRCOA 2005, SLCAC 2006; Palmer 2005). The Australian National Audit Office (2004) wrote that GSL's shortcomings were inherited from previous contractual regimes. Whereas auditors repeatedly referred to "the contract," much of that document is not public, protected under the "commercial-in-confidence clause" (Grewcock 2009; Harding 2001). The Palmer inquiry brought to light further impediments that conceal the inner workings of GSL, stating it "could never deliver to the Commonwealth the information on performance, service quality and risk management that DIMIA was confident it would" (2005: 70). In what amounts to a "gag order," private detention staff members are prohibited from publicly discussing information about their employment (SLCAC 2006: 215). In 2009, the Rudd government contracted Serco Australia (part of the London-based Serco Group) to operate the detention centers for five years. "British-based Serco (its name is short for "services company") is an outsourcing empire with 600 largely government sector contracts in 35 countries—including an estimated £2 billion (AU$4.1 billion) worth of contracts for prisons and security" (Denton 2010: 2). GSL (currently G4S) earned a separate contract to run immigration residential housing and transit services.

By 2010, with the detention apparatus fully privatized, human rights groups had begun monitoring Australia's next maneuver as it attempts to deal with asylum-seekers and so-called boat people. In what is described as a return to the Pacific Solution, the newly elected Gillard government has initiated talks with other nations in the region for offshore detention and processing. Gillard cited "border protection" as one area in which the Labor government under Rudd had "lost its way." Interestingly, one of Kevin Rudd's first tasks as Foreign Minister was to negotiate with East Timor to establish a processing centre for asylum-seekers—"a policy about which he had deep misgivings when prime minister" (Coorey 2010: 1). Indeed, those developments point not only to *new* modes of social control but to *international* ones as well.

Conclusion

In his sharp critique of the war on crime, Jonathan Simon (2007) reveals how a pervasive commitment to fight crime has significantly transformed American society. Rather than providing greater security, however, new forms of governance have exacerbated a fear of crime, which in turn generates a demand for tough-on-crime initiatives. This decidedly coercive approach has pulled the United States from its welfarist foundation toward what Simon calls a "penal state" characterized by an authoritarian executive, a passive legislature, and defensive judiciary (see Garland 2001). Indeed, the emergence of a strong executive, especially in the post-9/11 era, has produced greater administrative governance that bypasses the rule of law and due process, as previously noted in matters of immigration and terrorism (Agamben 2005; Ericson 2007). Simon emphasizes that governing through crime, illegal immigration, and terror is not the same as actually solving those social problems. Instead, such governance has become a way in which the state expresses its power along with its ambition to manage and control people. While resorting to tough strategies, government officials simultaneously go to great lengths to neglect the underlying sources of crime, immigration, and political violence (Bosworth and Guild 2008; Welch 2009).

Similar to Simon's analysis, Hardt and Negri also delve into the significance of war. By elaborating on notions of security, biopower, and legitimate violence, they suggest that war has become "the primary organizing principle of society" (2004:12). Other commentators have weighed in on the idea of perpetual war, proposing that rather than periods of the "world *at* war, we may have entered an era of the world *in* war" (Michalowski and Kramer 2006: 2; see Keen 2006; Welch, Bryan, and Wolff 1999). Since the 1970s, the United States has embarked on a series of wars on crime, drugs, illegal immigration, and terror. While demanding public support for the government's efforts to stay the course, elected leaders continue to pour funding into wars at the local and global levels, targeting street crime and terrorism as well as unauthorized migration and asylum-seeking. Consequently, such financing merely reinforces belligerent policies and fuels the markets of social control, most notably the detention-industrial complex aimed at cashing in on coercive practices. In challenging the new modes of social control and their emergent industries, scholars, activists, and concerned citizens ought to convince political leaders that criminalization strategies are not only unjust and costly but also produce more problems than they solve.

REFERENCES

11 Million. 2009. *The arrest and detention of children subject to immigration control.* London: Children's Commissioner for England.

Adams, Laura S. 2002. Divergence and the dynamic relationship between domestic and immigration law and international human rights. *Emory Law Journal* 51: 983–1002.

Agamben, Gorgio. 2005. *State of exception.* Translated by Kevin Attell. Chicago: University of Chicago Press.

American Civil Liberties Union. 1999. New immigrant law threatens people and principles: An interview with Lucas Guttentag, Director of the ACLU Immigrants' Rights Project (Reposted from, and with the permission of, TexLaw). www.aclu.org.

———. 2000. ACLU joins Fix '96 Campaign for justice for immigrants. www.aclu.org.

———. 2001. Know your rights: What to do if you're stopped by the police, the FBI, the INS, or the customs service. www.aclu.org.

———. 2010. Establishing a new normal: National security, civil liberties, and human rights under the Obama administration. New York: American Civil Liberties Union.

Amnesty International. 2003. Annual report. New York: Amnesty International.

ANAO (Australian National Audit Office). 2004. Management of the detention centre contracts—Part A. Audit Report, No. 54, 2003–2004. Canberra: Australian National Audit Office.

Asylum Seeker Resource Centre. 2006. Submission to the senate legal and constitutional references committee inquiry into the administration and operation of the Migration Act 1958. Melbourne: Asylum Seeker Resource Centre.

Australian Associated Press. 2005. Detention company fined over breaches. *The Age*, 1: October 17.

Australian Human Rights and Equal Opportunity Commission. 2004. A last resort? National inquiry into children in immigration detention. Sydney: Australian Human Rights and Equal Opportunity Commission.

Beck, Ulrich. 1992. *Risk society: Towards a new modernity.* London: Sage.

Beck, Ulrich, Anthony Giddens, and Scott Lash. 1994. *Reflexive modernity: Politics, tradition, and aesthetics in the modern social order.* Cambridge: Polity Press.

Beckett, Katherine, and Theodore Sasson. 2000. The war on crime as hegemonic strategy: a neo-Marxian theory of the new punitiveness in U.S. criminal justice policy. In *Of Crime and Criminality*, ed. S. Simpson. Thousand Oaks, CA: Pine Forge.

Bernstein, Nina. 2010. Border sweeps in north reach into US. *New York Times*, August 29: A1, 5.

Bonn, Scott 2010. *Mass deception: Moral panic and the U.S. war on Iraq*. New Brunswick, NJ and London: Rutgers University Press.

Bosworth, Mary, and Mhairi Guild. 2008. Governing through migration control. *British Journal of Criminology* 48: 703–19.

Bravin, Ames, Gregory Fields, Christopher Adams, and Russell Wartzman. 2001. Justice Department quickly moves to use new broad authority in detaining aliens. *Wall Street Journal*, September 26:1, 3.

Butler, Judith. 2004. *Precarious life: The powers of mourning and violence*. London: Verso.

Casimir, Lawrence. 2001. Asylum seekers are treated like criminals in the U.S. *New York Daily News*, February 16: 1, 4.

Christie, Nils. 1993. *Crime control as industry: Towards gulags, Western style?* London: Routledge.

Cohen, Stanley. 1972. *Folk devils and moral panics: The creation of mods and rockers*. London: Macgibbon and Kee.

———. 2002. *Folk devils and moral Panics: The creation of the mods and rockers*, 3rd edition. London: Routledge.

Cole, David. 1999. Terrorist scare: The government uses secret evidence to find aliens guilty by association. *Nation*, April 19: 26–28.

———. 2003. *Enemy aliens: Double standards and constitutional freedoms in the war on terror*. New York: New Press.

Cole, David, and James Dempsey. 2002. *Terrorism and the constitution: Sacrificing civil liberties in the name of national security*. New York: Free Press.

Coorey, Phillip. 2010. Rudd forced to back down on Timor. *Sydney Morning Herald*, September 13: 1.

Denton, Jenny 2010. Detention dividends. www.newmatilda.com. August 5.

Dietrich, Helmut. 2005. The desert front—EU refugee camps in North Africa? Statewatch News Online, March.

Ericson, Richard V. 2007. *Crime in an insecure world*. Cambridge: Polity.

Ericson, Richard V., and Kevin Haggerty. 1997. *Policing the risk society*. Toronto: University of Toronto Press.

Feeley, Malcolm, and Jonathan Simon. 1992. The new penology: Notes on the emerging strategy of corrections and its implications. *Criminology* 30(4): 449–74.

Flood, Phillip. 2001. Report into the inquiry into immigration detention procedures. Canberra: DIMA.

Foucault, Michel. 1977. *Discipline and punish: The birth of the prison*. Translated by Alan Sheridan. New York: Vintage.

Garland, David. 2001. *The culture of control: Crime and social order in contemporary society*. Chicago: University of Chicago Press.

Goode, Erich, and Nachman Ben-Yehuda. 1994. *Moral panics: The social construction of deviance*. Cambridge, MA: Blackwell.

Greenhouse, Linda. 2001. Justices permit immigrants to challenge deportations: 5-4 ruling may lead to judicial scrutiny of other actions by executive branch. *New York Times*, June 26: A1, A15.

Grewcock, Michael. 2009. *Border crimes: Australia's war on illicit migrants*. Sydney: Institute of Criminology.

Hall, Stuart, Chas Critcher, Tony Jefferson, John Clarke, and Brian Roberts. 1978. *Policing the crisis: Mugging, the state and law and order*. New York: Holmes and Meiser.

Harding, Richard. 2001. Standards and accountability in the administration of prisons and detention centres. A Speech to the International Correction and Prisons Association Conference. October 30, Perth.

Hardt, Michael, and Antonio Negri. 2004. *Multitude: War and democracy in the age of empire*. New York: Penguin Putnam.

Herman, Edward S., and Chomsky Noam. 2002, *Manufacturing consent: The political economic of the mass media*. New York: Pantheon Books.

Hooker, John 2005. The Baxter detention centre. NewMatilda.com, 23 February.

Human Rights Council of Australia. 2005. Children out of detention, Brotherhood of St. Laurence, Rights and accountability in development, and International Comission of Jurists. Submission to the Australian National Contact Point—Global Solutions Limited: Supplementary evidence on operations of GSL. Melbourne: Brotherhood of St. Laurence.

Human Rights Watch. 2002. Presumption of guilt: Human rights abuses of post September 11th detainees. New York: Human Rights Watch.

Immigration and Naturalization Service. 2001. 'This is INS' available at: http://www.ins. usdoj.gov/graphics/aboutins/thisisins/overview.htm.

Iyengar, Shanto, and Simon Jackman. 2010. Australian and American attitudes to illegal immigration: Media release (August 19). Sydney: United States Studies Centre, University of Sydney.

Jarecki, Eugene. 2006. *Why we fight*. Sony Pictures.

Kanstroom, Daniel. 1999. Crying wolf or a dying canary? *New York University Review of Law & Social Change* 25: 435–77.

———. 2000. Deportation, social control and punishment: Some thoughts about why hard laws make bad cases. *Harvard Law Review* 113: 1890–1935.

———. 2004. Criminalizing the undocumented: Ironic boundaries of the post-September 11th 'pale of the law.' *North Carolina International Law and Commerce Regulation* 29: 639–70.

Keen, David. 2006. *Endless war? Hidden functions of the 'war on terror.'* London: Pluto Press.

Klocker, Natascha, and Kevin Dunn. 2003. Who's driving the asylum debate? *Media International Australia* 109: 71–92.

Lawyers Committee for Human Rights. 2003. Imbalance of powers: How changes to U.S. law and policy since 9/11 erode human rights and civil liberties. New York: Lawyers Committee for Human Rights.

Lilly, Robert, and Mathieu Deflem. 1996. Profit and penality: An analysis of the corrections-commercial complex. *Crime & Delinquency* 42(1): 3–20.

Mares, Peter. 2001. *Borderline: Australia's treatment of refugees and asylum seekers*. Sydney: University of New South Wales Press.

McLuhan, Marshall. 1964. *Understanding Media: The First Extensions of Man*. New York: McGraw-Hill.

Medina, Michael I. 1997. The criminalization of immigration law: Employer sanctions and marriage fraud. *George Mason Law Review* 5: 669–731.

Melossi, Dario. 2003. In a peaceful life: Migration and the crime of modernity in Europe/ Italy. *Punishment & Society* 5(4): 371–98.

Michalowski, Raymond, and Ronald Kramer. 2006. *State-corporate crime: Wrongdoing at the intersection of business and government*. New Brunswick, NJ and London: Rutgers University Press.

Miller, Teresa A. 2003. Citizenship and severity: Recent immigration reforms and the new penology. *Georgetown Immigration Law Journal* 17(4): 661–66.

———. 2005. Blurring the boundaries between immigration and crime control after September 11th. *Boston College Third World Law Journal* 25(1): 81–123.

Molenaar, Bente, and Rodney Neufeld. 2003. The use of privatized detention centres for asylum seekers in Australia and the UK. In *Capitalist punishment: Prison and human rights*, ed. A. Coyle, A. Campbell, and R. Neufeld. London: Zed Books.

Morris, Helen. 1997. Zero tolerance: The increasing criminalization of immigration law. Interpreter Releases, August: 10–21.

Morton, Tom. 2004. The detention industry. Background Briefing. ABC Radio: 20 June.

Moyle, Paul. 2000. *Profiting from punishment, private prisons in Australia: Reform or regression*. Sydney: Pluto.

O'Malley, Pat. 2008. Experiments in risk and criminal justice. *Theoretical Criminology* 12(4): 451–69.

———. 2010. *Crime and risk*. London: Sage.

Palmer, Mick. 2005. *Report of the inquiry into the circumstances of the immigration detention of Cornelia Rau*. Canberra: DIMIA.

Pickering, Sharon. 2001. Common sense and original deviancy: News discourses and asylum seekers in Australia. *Journal of Refugee Studies* 14(2): 169–86.

———. 2005. *Refugees and state crime*. Sydney: The Federation Press.

Pickering, Sharon, and Leanne Weber. 2006. *Border, mobility and technologies of control*. New York: Springer.

PPRI (Prison Privatization Report International). 2001. Australia: ACM contract under scrutiny. Prison privatization report international, Number 39. London: Prison Reform Trust.

———. 2010. Prison privatisation report international. www.psriu.org, 15 September.

Refugee Council of Australia (RCOA). 2000. RCOA Discussion Paper on the Response to the 1999–2000 Boat Arrivals.

Reuters. 2001. US to listen in on some inmate-lawyer talks. November 13, 1–3.

Rothe, Dawn, and Stephen L. Muzzatti. 2004. Enemies everywhere: Terrorism, moral panic, and US civil society. *Critical Criminology* 12: 327–50.

Saxton, Alison. 2003. 'I certainly don't want people like that here': The discursive construction of 'asylum seekers'. *Media International Australia* 109: 109–20.

Schuster, Liza. 2003a. *The use and abuse of political asylum in Britain and Germany*. London: Frank Cass.

———. 2003b. Asylum seekers: Sangatte and the channel tunnel. *Parliamentary Affairs* 56(3): 506–22.

Senate Legal and Constitutional Affairs Committee. 2006. Administration and operation of the Migration Act 1958. Canberra: Senate Printing Unit.

Serco. 2009. Serco signs AUS$370m contract with Australian Government to transform immigration centres. Press release. June 29.

Simon, Jonathan. 2001. Sanctioning government: Explaining America's severity revolution. *University of Miami Law Review* 56: 217–54.

———. 2007. *Governing through crime: How the war on crime transformed American democracy*. New York: Oxford University Press.

Slattery, Kate. 2003. Drowning not waving: The 'children overboard' event and Australia's fear of the 'other'. *Media International Australia* 109: 93–108.

Stichter, Charlotte. 2002. Homeland security meets immigration: A review of recent government activity and pending legislation. *Immigration Briefings* 1 (October): 1–16.

Taylor, Charles. 2004. *Modern social imaginaries*. Durham, NC: Duke University Press.

Tebo, Margaret G. 2000. Locked up tight. *ABA Journal*, November: 1, 9.

Tharp, P. 2001. "Prison companies get hot." *New York Daily News*, October 4: 10.

Trucco, Lorenzo. 2005. Lampedusa—a test case for the subcontracting of EU border controls. Essays for civil liberties and democracy in Europe, Number 13. European Civil Liberties Network: www.ecln.org.

United States Studies Centre. 2010. Australians out-worry Americans on illegal immigration: A comparative study. Sydney: United States Studies Centre, University of Sydney.

Weber, Leanne. 2002. The detention of asylum seekers: 20 reasons why criminologists should care. *Current Issues in Criminal Justice* 14(1): 1–30.

Welch, Michael. 1996. The immigration crisis: Detention as an emerging mechanism of social control. *Social Justice: A Journal of Crime, Conflict & World Order* 23(3): 169–84.

———. 2000a. *Flag burning: Moral panic and the criminalization of protest*. New York: Aldine de Gruyter.

———. 2000b. The role of the Immigration and Naturalization Service in the prison industrial complex. *Social Justice: A Journal of Crime, Conflict & World Order* 27(3): 73–88.

———. 2002. *Detained: Immigration laws and the expanding I.N.S. jail complex*. Philadelphia: Temple University Press.

———. 2003a. Ironies of social control and the criminalization of immigrants. *Crime, Law & Social Change: An International Journal* 39: 319–37.

———. 2003b. Force and fraud: A radically coherent criticism of corrections as industry. *Contemporary Justice Review* 6(3): 227–40.

———. 2004. Quiet constructions in the war on terror: subjecting asylum seekers to unnecessary detention. *Social Justice: A Journal of Crime, Conflict & World Order* 31(1–2): 113–29.

———. 2006a. *Scapegoats of September 11th: Hate crimes & state crimes in the war on terror*. New Brunswick, NJ and London: Rutgers University Press.

———. 2006b. *Moral panic. Encyclopedia of activism and social justice*, ed. Gary L. Anderson and Kathryn Herr. Thousand Oaks, CA: Sage Publications.

———. 2006c. Immigration, criminalization, and counter-law: A Foucauldian analysis of laws against law. *Merging Immigration and Crime Control: An Interdisciplinary Workshop*, Baldy Center for Law and Social Policy, University at Buffalo Law School, Buffalo, New York, April 28.

———. 2007. Deadly consequences: Crime control discourse and unwelcome migrants. *Criminology and Public Policy* 6(2): 275–82.

———. 2008. Foucault in a post-9/11world: Excursions into security, territory, population. *Carceral Notebooks* 4: 225–40.

———. 2009. *Crimes of power and states of impunity: The U.S. response to terror*. New Brunswick, NJ and London: Rutgers University Press.

———. 2010a. Wall of noise and wall of boys: Hegemonic strategies for privatizing immigration detention in Australia. A workshop paper, Institute of Criminology, Law School, University of Sydney (Australia), September 1.

———. 2010b. Immigration detention and the sonics of social control. Faculty seminar, School of Law, University of New South Wales (Australia), September 13.

———. 2010c. Detained in occupied Iraq: Deciphering the narratives for neocolonial intern-
ment. *Punishment & Society: The International Journal of Penology* 12(2): 123–46.

———. 2011. War on terror, human rights, and critical criminology. In *The handbook of critical criminology*, ed. W. DeKeseredy and M. Dragiewicz. New York: Routledge.

Welch, Michael, Nicole Bryan, and Russell Wolff. 1999. Just war theory and drug control
policy: Militarization, morality, and the war on drugs. *Contemporary Justice Review* 2(1):
49–76.

Welch, Michael, and Liza Schuster. 2005a. Detention of asylum seekers in the UK and US:
Deciphering noisy and quiet constructions. *Punishment & Society: The International
Journal of Penology* 7(4): 397–417.

———. 2005b. Detention of asylum seekers in the US, UK, France, Germany, and Italy: A
critical view of the globalizing culture of control. *Criminal Justice: The International
Journal of Policy and Practice* 5(4): 331–55.

Welch, Michael, and Fatiniyah Turner. 2008. Private corrections, financial infrastructure,
and transportation: The new geo-economy of shipping prisoners. Special issue: Securing
the imperium: Criminal justice privatization and neoliberal globalization. *Social Justice:
A Journal of Crime, Conflict & World Order* 34(3–4): 56–77.

Young, Jock. 1971. The role of the police as amplifiers of deviancy, Negotiators of reality and
translators of fantasy. In *Images of deviancy*, ed. S. Cohen. Harmondsworth: Penguin.

Zatz, Marjorie. 1987. Chicano gangs and crime: The creation of a moral panic. *Contemporary
Crises* 11(2): 129–58.

Zatz, Marjorie, and Hillary Smith. 2008. Immigration, crime and justice: Rhetoric, reality
and ramifications of recent U.S immigration policies. Presented at the Law and Society
Review—University of California, Irvine conference, "The Paradoxes of Race, Law, and
Inequality in the United States," May 2–3.

3

Growing Tensions between Civic Membership and Enforcement in the Devolution of Immigration Control

DORIS MARIE PROVINE, MONICA VARSANYI, PAUL G. LEWIS, AND SCOTT H. DECKER

Like other nations that are responding to popular pressure to discourage unauthorized immigration, the United States is looking for new ways to step up enforcement. The ever-lengthening wall along the border with Mexico is the most obvious example of this commitment. While the wall incorporates innovative technological features, the enforcement strategy that it represents is familiar. What *is* new in U.S. immigration enforcement is the push toward formal partnerships between federal immigration authorities and local police. These relationships rely on the more intimate contact of local police with residents to assist in the detection and removal of unauthorized immigrants. Advocates describe these partnerships as a "force multiplier" to enhance interior enforcement by federal officials, but their significance is much greater.

Some raise concerns that strengthening relationships with federal immigration enforcement officials undermines a fragile social compact that has helped communities detect and resolve crimes. This compact gives residents without legal status who have lived and worked in the community for a period of time without incident a kind of informal social membership that enables them to seek the aid of police and offer evidence in criminal investigations. While the legal system does not recognize this compact, it resonates with a more general discussion of what being a member of a community means. It is why stories of long-term immigrants, particularly those with families, receive more sympathy and support than stories about transients or temporary residents who lack this social membership.[1]

The devolution of some federal enforcement authority to local police replaces this informal social membership with a narrow-gauge legal definition of belonging that is based on the premise that those who lack legal status threaten community safety, and that they may even be criminals who endanger national security. The fact that federal immigration enforcement now sits within the Department of Homeland Security (DHS), which was established one month after the September 11, 2001 deadly attacks on the Pentagon and World Trade Center, is also significant, especially in light of the agency's mission of "protecting the American people and their homeland."[2] Devolution of federal immigration-enforcement authority to the local level is occurring as national security is being defined more and more broadly to encompass threats within local communities.[3] Tolerance for people without status thus becomes tolerance for crime and insecurity. The framework within which communities used to think about security—street crime, lack of respect for community values, avoiding external dangers—has now become intertwined with concerns about legal status and fears of foreign people. As discussed at length in the previous chapter by Michael Welch, the result of this enhanced set of concerns is a sense of insecurity that justifies more exacting governmental controls.

This chapter explores the response of police leaders across the United States to the movement to devolve federal authority to enforce immigration laws at the local level, that is, to create shared responsibility for detecting and deporting unauthorized residents. Police chiefs and sheriffs are acutely aware of the potential for conflict between their commitment to community safety and the demand for order and "legibility" in an age of immigration. For local police, questions of how to define security, and how to foster it, are immediate and concrete, not abstract. With or without the guidance of public officials, police must craft their own response to the federal invitation to become more fully involved in enforcement of immigration laws. The first section of this chapter describes the trend toward devolution in immigration enforcement; this sets the stage for the remainder of the chapter, which describes how police are currently responding.

Devolution Gains Traction

The construction of unauthorized immigrants as bearers of crime is creating a moral panic about immigration control, much as Stanley Cohen described in the movement toward repression of the Mods and the Rockers in Britain more than a generation ago (Cohen 1972), and in line with the arguments made by other authors in this volume. The source of this construction, as in the past, is partly media hysteria, but it is a hysteria also driven by political opportunism and by the federal government's increasingly punitive response to pressure to "do something" about unauthorized immigration. The trend tends to be self-reinforcing. As Cohen observed, and as demonstrated in Welch's chapter in this volume, moral panics reduce our capacity to design wise public policy (Cohen 1972, 2002; also see Melossi 2000). Consistent empirical evidence that immigration, including unauthorized immigration, does not increase street crime or the threat of terrorism makes no difference in this situation. Nor is it easy to persuade skeptics that creating a safe space for residents who lack legal status may, in fact, make communities more secure than attempting to root them out.

The movement toward devolution appears to be unstoppable, as evidenced by the Obama administration's recent renewed commitment to internal immigration enforcement through the "Secure Communities" initiative (ICE 2009) and the expanding list of local partners trained by the Department of Homeland Security in immigration enforcement. Secure Communities has become the umbrella program that links federal enforcement to local policing through identification of individuals booked in local jails and transmission of that information to federal authorities. The plan is to extend the program to every jail in the United States, despite criticism that it is not targeting criminal aliens as promised, but rather low-level offenders and individuals who have no charges at all pending against them (Feltz and Baksh 2010; National Immigration Law Center 2009).

This trend toward devolution likely will not be derailed by the adoption of "comprehensive immigration reform," whatever its final dimensions. None of the current reform proposals contains a simple, ongoing program to regularize individuals who enter illegally or fall out of status. Such persons will continue to arrive, find work, and maintain relationships with family members who do have legal status. They will find work in informal labor markets (Calavita 2005; Massey, Durand, and Malone 2003; Marshall 1978: 169). Absent a re-conceptualization of the significance of lack of legal status, the presence of these individuals will continue to be controversial. One can thus reasonably anticipate there will be strong political pressure for the federal government to continue, and perhaps expand, interior enforcement, and to engage local police in this effort (Thatcher 2005; Kobach 2005).

Varied Local Responses

Our research, which is based on both survey and case-study evidence that will be described in more detail below, reveals a high degree of variation in local responses to federal devolution of immigration-enforcement responsibilities. We find a multi-layered, multi-jurisdictional patchwork of enforcement across the United States. The patchwork is sometimes evident even within municipal areas. This pattern of local practices and local policy-making suggests there is lively disagreement within the United States over how community safety can best be achieved. For some, community safety demands a trusting environment, in which all residents are accepted as members of the community deserving police services, regardless of legal status. Others disagree and seek to enlist local police in the federal enforcement effort to make it more effective. Many are standing on the sidelines of this debate, but elsewhere this conflict is being played out in city councils, state legislatures, police departments, and in the minds of individual officers, who often have enormous discretion in applying the law to persons with precarious legal status.

The Context: Unprecedented Immigration Flows

In the past several decades, the number of persons around the world living and working without legal authorization to remain in their adopted homes has grown to approximately 30–40 million people, with around 11 million estimated to be living in the United States and about 8 million living in the European Union (International Organization for Migration 2009; Passel and Cohn 2008, 2010). This trend has been fueled by a strong demand for immigrant labor (Massey et al. 2003) as well as war and other dislocations. Immigrant-receiving nations are attempting to cope with the inflow of residents without shutting themselves off from immigrant-fueled economic development or entirely neglecting their humanitarian commitments.

This results in an odd combination of legislative initiatives. National assemblies are adopting legislation designed to discourage those who come uninvited, while at the same time passing laws to encourage desired immigrants. They are doing this with new forms of visas and memberships, sometimes including citizenship. As the rules of exclusion have become progressively more elaborate and precise in countries like the United States, Canada, and Australia, it is clear that the "monopolization of the legitimate 'means of movement'" that national governments have traditionally claimed for themselves is becoming increasingly strained (Torpey 2000: 1; see also Cornelius et al. 2004; Dauvergne 2008).

There is no consensus about how many and what types of immigrants are required, or about how to integrate them into existing political and social structures. To cope with pressure to control entry despite porous borders, nation-states are turning to new sources of interior control, partnering with supra- and subnational units to deflect settlement. Local service providers and even quasi-private and private agencies, like hospitals, airlines, and foster-care agencies, have become involved in enforcement efforts (Guiraudon and Lahav 2000).

This movement toward engagement of multiple levels of governmental and quasi-governmental resources has been dubbed "immigration federalism" by scholars (Spiro 1997; see also Skerry 1995; Schuck 2007). The trend toward the rescaling of central authority is highly variable, depending on the configuration of institutions available for enlistment in the enforcement effort. In the European context, for example, the European Community now plays a significant part in setting national standards for entry and treatment of immigrants. Local political bodies are not major players in these developments. In the United States, immigration federalism generally involves the downward movement (i.e., devolution) of authority to state, county, and municipal governments to enforce federal law.

Immigration Federalism in the United States

The United States institutionalized immigration federalism in 1996, with the adoption of the Illegal Immigration Reform and Immigrant Responsibility Act (IIRIRA) and the Anti-terrorism and Effective Death Penalty Act (AEDPA). AEDPA gives local police the authority to arrest previously deported noncitizen felons. IIRIRA authorizes training of local and state police to enforce federal immigration laws through its "Section 287g" program that also authorizes memoranda of understanding between federal immigration authorities and cooperating local police agencies. The members of Congress who proposed or supported these programs justified them as a "force multiplier" in the effort to make federal immigration policy more effective in the nation's interior. They essentially ignored concerns expressed by some of their colleagues and by police agencies that enlisting local police in the enforcement effort would harm relationships with immigrants.

In April 2002, U.S. Attorney General John Ashcroft took an additional step, issuing a classified memo claiming that state and local police have inherent authority to make arrests for violation of civil immigration laws. This memo, released under a Freedom of Information Act request by the ACLU, overturned earlier interpretations of federal law that had denied local police such authority (Kobach 2005). At about the same time, the Justice Department began to enter immigration-related data, such as outstanding deportation orders, into the database routinely employed by local police, the National Criminal Information Center (NCIC) (Gladstein, Wagner, and Wishnie 2005). This meant that much information concerning civil violations of immigration law became part of a nationwide criminal justice database. The Secure Communities program expands this capacity by enlisting local jails in the information-gathering effort and at the same time, informing federal authorities of the location of individuals who may be deportable. The idea is to prevent the inadvertent release of anyone who might be eligible for deportation (ICE 2009).

These new laws and procedures are designed to create closer ties between local police departments and federal officials charged with immigration enforcement. They contain no safeguards against racial profiling or pretextual arrests designed to bring immigrants to the attention of federal authorities. Nor do they distinguish between the various and overlapping bodies that set policing policy in the United States, a silence that creates the potential for significant conflict if there is disagreement over the advisability of partnering to enforce federal immigration laws. Many large cities, for example, are opposed to enforcement partnerships, but they operate within a jurisdictional network that subordinates their policymaking powers to the state level. Sheriffs, who exercise significant power over their entire county, add an additional layer of complexity for cities reluctant to become involved in immigration enforcement (Provine 2010).

For more than a century, the federal government largely abstained from engaging localities in immigration enforcement. The federal government began to insist on sole responsibility to set immigration policy in the 1880s (Kanstroom 2007; Zolberg 2006). Bargains over admissions and enforcement were struck at the national level in an elite-dominated bargaining process from which localities were largely excluded (Money 1999; Tichenor 2002). Individual states and localities were sometimes involved in enforcement efforts, but only on an ad hoc basis (McDonald 1997). The relationship was reciprocal. Local police relied on federal authorities to deport foreign-born criminals, and federal authorities relied on local police to provide support for federally initiated immigration enforcement actions, such as Operation

Wetback (1954) (McDonald 1999, 2003; Ngai 2004). This more open-textured approach allowed room for localities to develop their own ideas about civic membership, some of which were more inclusive than others, but it did not generally result in local policymaking to enforce immigration law.

This informal, open-textured approach was also more compatible with what the federal government determined would be the primary role of the localities and states: to help integrate immigrants into the national social fabric. The difference in roles is evident in the jurisprudence of the U.S. Supreme Court, which long ago gave virtually unlimited power to the federal government to set immigration policy, while at the same time requiring the states to treat immigrants fairly and without discrimination (Varsanyi 2008a). This part of the old federalism bargain remains: The integration of immigrants remains primarily a local concern, with some federal financial backing. There is little attempt to achieve a uniform policy, and so there are large variations from place to place in the resources devoted to helping these new residents feel at home.

The 1996 federal legislation and subsequent federal action have re-written the enforcement side of this script. Federal interior enforcement efforts have dramatically increased, even as legal immigration has steadily increased (Migration Policy Institute Data Hub 2009). The Department of Homeland Security's Office of Immigration Statistics (OIS) reports that 393,289 aliens were removed in 2009, the sixth consecutive record high year (OIS 2009, 2010). And 2010 saw a slight increase in deportations, creating yet another record-breaking year. Local police have become increasingly involved in supporting these activities and in undertaking their own enforcement efforts, which are sometimes mandated by local authorities.

Localities must now decide how to balance their traditional role of integrating immigrants (immigrant policy) with the opportunity to root out residents who lack legal status. This represents a re-scaling of immigration policymaking to include local governments as immigration policymakers (Varsanyi 2008a). A city might, for example, decide on a policy of actively welcoming legal immigrants (following its traditional role in making immigrant policy), while at the same time authorizing police to proactively seek out unauthorized immigrants for possible deportation.

Local Responses to Immigration Federalism

The local level has not been silent in this series of developments. In the traditional immigrant-receiving states of California and Texas, pressure had been building since at least the 1980s to reduce the inflow of unauthorized immigrants. National attention began to focus on the issue with the 1994 passage, by large margins, of Proposition 187, a California initiative designed to deny many publicly funded social services, including public schooling, to persons who could not prove their legal status (Calavita 1996). A court quickly overturned this law as conflicting with the federal government's sole constitutional authority in setting immigration policy, but the anti-immigrant movement nevertheless gathered steam, and Congress began to focus on the potential role of local government in enforcement.

The anti-immigrant movement has grown in force as the number of people lacking legal documentation has continued to increase and as new arrivals have sought out cities, suburbs, and rural communities in parts of the country that have not traditionally hosted large immigrant populations (Zúñiga and Hernández-León 2005; Singer, Hardwick, and Brettell 2008). Unauthorized immigrants are increasingly bringing their families and setting up households, rather than working in the United States on a temporary basis or participating in seasonal labor migration (Massey et al. 2003). Evidence of the shift toward permanent migration in new places lies in the growth of the Mexican immigrant population (both legal and undocumented) in "new gateway" states between 1990 and 2000: in New York, Pennsylvania, Washington, and Wisconsin, 200–400 percent; 645 percent in Utah; 800 percent in Georgia; 1,000 percent in Arkansas and Minnesota; and over 1,800 percent in North Carolina, Tennessee, and Alabama (Zúñiga and Hernández-León 2005: xiv).

These demographic changes have been marked by controversy and occasional violence at the local level. The movement to make local residence more difficult for people lacking legal status gained new legitimacy in the wake of the terrorist attack of September 11, 2001 and the federal government's reaction to those events. Within a few years, state and local lawmakers began to adopt their own legislation, much of it designed to discourage immigrants from settling in their jurisdictions. The Immigrant Policy Project of the National Conference of State Legislatures (NCSL) reported that in 2010 more than 1,400 bills related to immigration and immigrants were considered by 46 states. State legislatures enacted 208 laws and adopted 138 resolutions, continuing an upward trend that began in 2005, when legislatures considered 300 bills and enacted 39 (NCSL 2011). Cities also have been active in drafting and adopting legislation. State and local laws include: requirements that landlords check legal status before renting; rules that prohibit public funding of day labor centers; restrictions on drivers' licenses; and legislation that creates state-level employment verification schemes, that criminalize human smuggling, and that require public officials to check legal status in the course of routine activities (Esbenshade 2007; Varsanyi 2008a, 2008b). An increasing number of state and local governments are also asking law enforcement to take a more active role in identifying and arresting immigrants for civil immigration violations.

What emerges from this collection of actions is a nationwide re-visioning of immigration enforcement driven by federal law and policy, as well as by politics at the local level. This development has been marked by a patchwork of local practices that are often inconsistent or even in conflict with each other. The adjoining municipalities of New Haven and East Haven, Connecticut, for example, are polar opposites in their response to unauthorized immigration. In Arizona, state lawmakers have attempted to coerce cities within the state into proactive enforcement policies (Provine 2010). Whether that effort is successful will be determined by litigation brought by cities, local police officers, and the federal government.

There is a logic to these developments. Despite its rhetoric of inclusion inscribed on the Statue of Liberty, the United States has always treated immigration as a potential threat (Higham 1955; Zolberg 2006; Kanstroom 2007; Tichenor 2002; Neuman 1996). The nation has gone through periods of reluctant inclusion as well as xenophobia and nativism. Policy in this realm has never been stable for long periods of time. What has recently changed in this picture, as noted earlier, is the willingness of the federal government to more proactively and systematically share enforcement authority with subnational units of government. Given the current anxiety about unauthorized immigration, the federal government's effort to enlist local police in the work of enforcement in the nation's interior should not be surprising.

The rapidity with which the movement to devolve immigration authority has occurred reveals there are few timeless truths where federalism is concerned. As Grodzins (1966: 32) stated in the mid-1960s, "It is difficult to find any governmental activity that does not involve all three of the so-called levels of the federal system." Though "immigration policy [has been] a lagging indicator of general trends towards devolved governance" (Spiro 2001: 73), we are now witnessing a reconfiguration of long-standing relationships in this realm. But this reconfiguration raises serious concerns. Grodzins emphasized the necessity for intergovernmental cooperation to achieve broader goals (see also Broughton 1943; Elazar 1966). Yet in the realm of immigration enforcement, increased cooperation may disrupt fragile trust, carefully nurtured over the years, between local law enforcement and immigrant communities. Policing immigration is not like the distribution of federal services or even regulatory enforcement. It involves highly discretionary decision making by "street-level bureaucrats" that carries enormous consequences for vulnerable people.

The Response of Local Police Agencies

To get a better sense of how local police executives are responding to the push to become involved in enforcement of federal immigration laws, in November 2007, our research team distributed a detailed questionnaire to police chiefs in large and medium-sized U.S. cities. The effort began with a list of all 492 municipalities that were represented in the U.S. Census Bureau's American Community Survey (ACS) of 2005. The ACS represents all communities nationwide with populations of 65,000 or above.[4] We removed from this list 40 communities that lacked their own locally governed police departments (generally due to contractual relationships with their county sheriff), for a total universe of 452 incorporated communities whose police chiefs received an invitation to complete the survey. The chiefs, who were promised anonymity of their responses, had the option of completing the survey on paper and returning it by mail or answering the survey on a secure website. After several rounds of reminders by mail and/or email, we received completions from 237 cities, for a response rate of 52 percent.[5]

The survey revealed that police chiefs see differences between views in their department and those that prevail in the communities they serve. Respondents described immigration as more controversial in their communities than in their departments, and also more cut-and-dried. They also saw their communities as less concerned than their police department about the implications for community safety, and also less concerned with gaining the trust of unauthorized immigrants. Table 3.1 illustrates these differences by contrasting the understanding of chiefs about sentiments in their own department with those in the locality in which they serve.

A majority of respondents saw elected officials in their jurisdiction as supportive of their current level of enforcement, with a small percentage (9 percent) saying that officials wanted police to be more involved, and a still smaller share (4 percent) reporting that their city government sought less police involvement in immigration enforcement. Twelve percent reported that officials in their city had no interest in this issue.

City policies on immigration policing followed a similar pattern, with nearly half (46 percent) stating that their local government has no official policy at all. A small minority (4 percent) noted that their local government had officially enunciated a policy to protect unauthorized

Table 3.1 Police Chiefs' View of Community versus Police Department Attitudes

Immigration is a controversial topic	Agree or strongly agree (%)
In this locality	58
In my department	30
People believe that it is relatively easy to determine who is in this country without authorization	
In this locality	47
In my department	25
Victimization of immigrants is considered a serious problem	
In this locality	23
In my department	31
Gaining the trust of unauthorized immigrants is a priority	
In this locality	24
In my department	51

immigrants from local police enforcement in non-criminal situations ("sanctuary" policies), while 15 percent reported an unwritten "don't ask, don't tell" policy regarding immigration status. At the other end of the spectrum, 12 percent noted that their local government expects police to take a proactive role to deter unauthorized immigration in all activities, while 18 percent said their local government was developing a policy to encourage local participation in targeted situations, such as human smuggling and trafficking.

Another source of relevant legislation is ordinances focused on the working or living conditions of unauthorized immigrants. Just over two-thirds of respondents reported there were formal or informal day-labor hiring sites in their community, and of these, 45 percent indicated they enforce local and state ordinances related to day-labor activities. However, most (78 percent) stated they do not maintain a police presence at these sites.

The chiefs responding to this survey had not, in general, accepted the invitation for a formal enforcement relationship with the Immigration and Customs Enforcement (ICE) branch of the federal Department of Homeland Security. Only 3 percent had a Memorandum of Understanding with ICE (a 287g agreement) to help manage incarcerated inmates, and 3 percent had an agreement to work with ICE on investigations and arrests for (civil) immigration violations. The vast majority (74 percent) answered that they contact ICE when holding suspected unauthorized immigrants for criminal violations, but have no formal agreement with the agency. Thirteen percent responded that they "do not participate or assist in ICE immigration-enforcement activities."

Among the group of police departments that do not assist ICE in immigration enforcement, most (68 percent) had not considered the issue. Of those that had, the most frequent concerns reportedly leading to the decision to not become involved were local opposition and the potential to decrease public safety. Responses to a question about the flow of information between ICE and the department were consistent with this pattern. Nearly a third (32 percent) said they have little or no communication with ICE. Those who do have a working relationship with ICE generally express satisfaction with it. Yet, it is evident that even departments that work with ICE regularly do not send all potential cases to federal authorities. For instance, an overwhelming 83 percent said they do not contact ICE when they resolve day-labor violations.

In general, these chiefs claimed they maintain a high degree of independence from all federal and local law enforcement authorities. Half said that federal law enforcement has no impact on their ability to interact with local immigrants in the ways they deem appropriate. The response rates were even higher for the lack of impact of state police (74 percent), county sheriffs and county police (61 percent), and neighboring municipal police forces (65 percent). When they did note an impact, it was more often evaluated as positive, rather than negative, suggesting the respondent's sense of capacity to act was usually not reduced by the presence of other policing agencies with powers that overlapped those of the respondent department.

It is clear from these results that police departments retain significant discretion over how to respond to individuals they believe to be immigrants, a finding supported by other research (Lewis and Ramakrishnan 2007). Most of the responding police departments have not clearly committed themselves to any particular policy with respect to interactions with unauthorized immigrants. Only 39 percent said they have a written departmental policy, with an additional 9 percent noting they have an unwritten policy. Most, however, stated their department has no policy (51 percent). Fewer than half of the responding departments (46 percent) offer training to officers for incidents or calls involving unauthorized immigrants.

The reluctance to create policy at the local level may help explain why major national-level police organizations—the International Association of Chiefs of Police, the Police Foundation, and the Police Executive Research Forum—have been concerned about the lack of federal guidance that has accompanied the repeated federal invitation to become more involved in immigration enforcement. The Secure Communities program now being implemented by the federal government appears to be bringing these concerns to a head. The governors of New York, Massachusetts, and Illinois have already attempted to withdraw and others may follow suit unless the program is redesigned to actually target criminals, as the federal government promised in rolling out Secure Communities.

Clearly, many departments are relying on individual officers to make their own decisions regarding possible unauthorized immigrants. How do they make these decisions? What criteria are they using? Chiefs believe their officers to be exercising a nuanced approach in these situations (see table 3.2). The pattern is of less frequent consultation with ICE when violations are minor or the person is interviewed as a witness or crime victim, though even here, some individuals get reported to federal immigration officials. Overall, though, reporting becomes more frequent in cases of more serious wrongdoing.

Table 3.2 Reported Practices When Encountering Possible Unauthorized Immigrants

Scenario: A suspected unauthorized immigrant is . . .	% of police departments where officers would check immigration status, report to ICE, or both
Arrested for a violent crime	87
Detained for parole violation or failure to appear in court	69
Arrested for domestic violence	64
Interviewed as possible victim of human trafficking	59
Arrested for a nonviolent crime, assuming no prior record	51
Stopped for a traffic violation	21
Interviewed as crime victim, complainant, or witness	15

Community Policing

Principles of community policing may play a role in decisions about whether or not to report suspected unauthorized immigrants to federal authorities. Community policing stresses the importance of maintaining lines of communication and trust with all elements of a locality in order to gain information about criminal activity and to make residents comfortable in reporting crime (Greene 2001; Herbert 2006). As an approach to safety and security, community policing has become the predominant approach to policing in U.S. municipalities.

This level of support was evident in our survey results. A sizeable majority of respondents expressed enthusiasm about bike patrols, regular neighborhood meetings, foot patrols, visits to schools, churches, and neighborhood organizations, providing citizen access to crime statistics and maps, holding public hearings, coordinating with nongovernmental organizations, and having officers who are proficient in foreign languages. Sixty-nine percent count ability to speak a second language in favor of officers and applicants for positions on the force, and usually offer extra pay and salary bonuses. Most of the responding chiefs believe the current level of foreign-language proficiency in their department is not adequate given the need to communicate with all community members.

A majority of respondents expressed the belief that unauthorized immigrants are more vulnerable to theft and robbery than other residents. Chiefs also tend to see all types of immigrants as less likely to report crimes to the police than other residents, both when they are witnesses and when they are victims. The steps some departments are taking to accommodate immigrants include acceptance of consular identification cards such as the Mexican matrícula consular; our survey indicates that 74 percent accept them while only 14 percent refuse to do so. A significant minority (21 percent) have personnel specifically assigned to identify and respond to cases of human trafficking or smuggling.

What emerges from this snapshot of perceptions of chiefs is a layering of responsibility that locates a great deal of discretionary authority at the bottom of the enforcement hierarchy—where it usually is in police work—in the hands of individual officers. An individual officer, often acting alone, must determine whether or not to stop an individual, whether or not to accept the personal identification offered, whether or not to hold individuals and for what violations, and whether or not to report the matter to federal officials. Crucial decisions are made, not just by patrol officers but also by jailers and by federal officials, who may or may not exercise their right to intervene when informed of an immigrant appearing to lack legal status. As the Secure Communities program takes effect in more and more jurisdictions, the discretion of the officer on patrol will become more significant. An arrest and booking will mean certain notification to federal immigration authorities of the presence of someone who may be subject to deportation.

Our survey suggests that municipalities have not, in general, acted forcefully to direct their police departments toward greater or lesser engagement with immigration enforcement. Nor have departments seized the opportunity to engage in policymaking in this area. A strong commitment to community policing, as well as the heated politics of unauthorized immigration, help to explain the reluctance of municipalities to engage in this area.

Conclusion

The belief that public safety is best secured by promoting the trust of residents appears to be holding its own in some localities. Nearly one-fifth of cities in this survey were described by their chiefs as "sanctuary" or "don't ask, don't tell" cities. Most have no policy of their own, leaving the matter to their police departments. Although local police departments are at an early stage in formulating policy in this area, their own pragmatic concerns—backed up by a long-standing professional commitment to community policing—favor inclusiveness. This involves respect for nonlegal conceptions of community membership. Our results are reflected in statements released by various national policing organizations. For example, the Immigration Committee of the Major Cities Chiefs observed, "Local enforcement of federal immigration laws raises many daunting and complex legal, logistical and resource issues for local agencies and the diverse communities they serve" (Major Cities Chiefs 2006: 3). And more recently, the Police Executive Research Forum (PERF) issued a statement that "civil immigration enforcement by local police undermines their core public safety mission, diverts scarce resources, increases their exposure to liability and litigation, and exacerbates fear in our communities" (PERF 2008).

At the same time, however, many community members in the municipalities in which these police forces operate appear to see the matter somewhat differently. Chiefs, we found, perceived a tendency in the community at large to underestimate the difficulty of adding immigration enforcement to the police officer's traditional role. Given the considerable controversy within communities about which approach is appropriate, it is not surprising that municipal officials have proven reluctant to commit themselves to a specific policy. In many cases, a kind of de facto immigration policy is emerging from the practices of individual police officers. Chiefs report a pattern of enforcement practices that suggest that their officers may be making decisions that reflect professional values. The tendency to report immigration status more frequently when there is serious criminal activity than when there is not also suggests that police officers recognize a form of social membership in their communities.

This survey clearly points to a multi-layered, jurisdiction-crossing system of authority to make immigration policy, combined with widespread reluctance at the local level to set policy into concrete terms. This reluctance puts municipal police departments and individual officers in a uniquely powerful position. As enforcers of the law, police officers are also arbiters of what the law actually means. Their own conception of effective policing tends to conflict with the priorities that the federal government and states like Arizona seek to impose upon them. That view, based on experience in reacting to urban disturbances in the 1960s, is by now conventional wisdom in policing circles and helps to explain why organizations of police officials have been among the most outspoken opponents of federal/local partnerships in immigration control.

As our research indicates, the invitation to partner with federal authorities puts police in the awkward position of being charged with law enforcement but imbued with values that suggest the wisdom of sometimes not enforcing the law. The federal government's commitment to devolution of authority to enforce federal immigration law has not been responsive to these concerns, nor has it been sensitive to the potential for abuse of local police powers. Racial profiling, excessive surveillance, and pretextual arrests all have been noted as risks in this new era of local enforcement. The federal government has simultaneously extended its reach into law enforcement, while reducing its oversight of the overall enforcement process.

The effort to enlist local police in the federal immigration-enforcement effort exposes a dividing line in American politics over whose authority should govern the meaning of membership in society. Interior enforcement targeted at anyone who comes into contact with local police reflects a government-centered view of membership in which the state's own stamp of legitimacy is the sole criterion of membership. Community policing, in contrast, valorizes civil society's own norms in the process of enforcement. This division of opinion helps to explain why those who advocate a state-centered framing of membership are undisturbed by the deportation of even long-settled residents if proper procedures are followed. For those who defend a civil-society view, deportation of long-standing residents is disturbing, particularly if the process claims to be just.

NOTES

This survey was funded with support from a seed grant from the North-American Center for Transborder Studies at Arizona State University. The analysis and subsequent field-work were supported by the National Science Foundation under grant no. SES-0819082. Any opinions, findings, and conclusions or recommendations expressed in this material are those of the authors and do not necessarily reflect the views of the National Science Foundation.

1. Consider, for example, the DREAM Act, which enjoys broad public support and was approved by the U.S. House of Representatives in 2010. It failed to become law only because of cloture rules in the Senate that prevented its consideration, despite the Senate majority's approval. The DREAM Act provides provisional legal status to young people who came to the United States before the age of 16 and who have at least five years of U.S. residency and no criminal record. They would be permitted to enroll in college or join the military, and upon completion of two years in either, would earn permanent residency status. Polls suggest that 70 percent of American citizens favor the DREAM Act.

2. The DHS absorbed the former Immigration and Naturalization Service (INS) on March 1, 2003. Brief Documentary History of the Department of Homeland Security, 2001–2008. History Office, Office of Homeland Security, http://www.dhs.gov/xlibrary/assets/brief_documentary_history_of_dhs_2001_2008.pdf, and see Department of Homeland Security, *Department Subcomponents and Agencies*, http://www.dhs.gov/xabout/structure/ (retrieved on 9/16/2010).

3. Tom Barry usefully points out the "mission creep" of the DHS, which is pushing the linkage between security from foreign threats and communities. He notes recent DHS initiatives like the Secure Communities program, which builds on the idea of protection from foreign terrorists to facilitate the removal of unauthorized workers. Tom Barry, "Border Security, Homeland Security, & Now "Community Security," Tuesday August 4, 2009 edition of *Border Lines* at http://borderlinesblog.blogspot.com/2009/08/border-security-homeland-security-now.html, retrieved on August 5, 2009.

4. In examining the population data, however, we noted the ACS's inclusion of several cities with populations slightly below this intended minimum threshold of 65,000. Eight of these smaller cities ultimately responded to our survey.

5. In planning and carrying out the survey so as to try to maximize response, we followed Dillman's (2007) tailored design method.

REFERENCES

Broughton, J. M. 1943. "The Future of the States." State Government 16 (March).
Calavita, Kitty. 1996. "The New Politics of Immigration: 'Balanced Budget Conservatism' and Prop. 187." *Social Problems* 43. Reprinted in *Presidential Series, Social Problems, Law, and Society,* ed. A. Stout, R. Dello Buono, and W. Chambliss, 263–88. Lanham, MD: Rowman and Littlefield, 2004.
———. 2005. *Immigrants at the Margins: Law, Race, and Exclusion in Southern Europe.* New York: Cambridge.
Cohen, Stanley. 1972, 2002. *Folk Devils and Moral Panics.* London: MacGibsonn and Lee. New York: Routledge.
Cornelius, W. A., T. Tsuda, P. L. Martin, and J. F. Hollifield. 2004. *Controlling Immigration: A Global Perspective,* 2nd ed. Stanford: Stanford University Press.
Dauvergne, Catherine. 2008. *Making People Illegal: What Globalization Means for Migration and Law.* New York: Cambridge.
Dillman, Don A. 2007. *Mail and Internet Surveys: The Tailored Design Method,* 2nd ed. Hoboken, NJ: John Wiley & Sons.
Elazar, Daniel. 1966. *American Federalism: A View from the States.* New York: Crowell.

Esbenshade, Jill. 2007. *Division and Dislocation: Regulating Immigration Through Local Housing Ordinances*. Washington, DC: American Immigration Law Foundation.

Feltz, Rence, and Stokely Baksh. 2010. "Immigration crackdown creates insecure communities," Need to Know (PBS), http://www.pbs.org/wnet/need-to-know/security/video-immigration-crackdown-creates-insecure-communities (retrieved 9/16/2010).

Gladstein, H., A. Lai, J. Wagner, and M. Wishnie. 2005. "Blurring the Lines: A Profile of State and Local Police Enforcement of Immigration Law Using the National Crime Information Center Database, 2002–2004." Washington, DC: *Migration Policy Institute*. Accessed July 2007. www.migrationpolicy.org/pubs/MPI_report_Blurring_the_Lines_120805.pdf.

Greene, Jack R. 2001. "Community Policing." In *Criminal Justice 2000*, ed. Julie Horney, 299–370. Washington, DC: National Institute of Justice.

Grodzins, Martin. 1966. *The American System*. Chicago: Rand McNally.

Guiraudon, Virginie, and Gallya Lahav. 2000. "A Reappraisal of the State Sovereignty Debate." *Comparative Political Studies* 33: 163–95.

Herbert, Steve. 2006. *Citizens, Cops, and Power*. Chicago: University of Chicago Press.

Higham, John. 1955. *Strangers in the Land: Patterns of American Nativism, 1860-1925*. New Brunswick, NJ: Rutgers Univ. Press.

Immigration and Customs Enforcement. 2009. http://www.ice.gov/pi/news/factsheets/secure_communities.htm.

International Organization for Migration. 2009. "Facts and Figures: Regional and Country Figures." http://www.iom.int/jahia/Jahia/about-migration/facts-and-figures/regional-and-country-figures/cache/offence.

Kanstroom, D. 2007. *Deportation Nation: Outsiders in American History*. Cambridge, MA: Harvard University Press.

Kobach, Kris W. 2005. "The Quintessential Force Multiplier: The Inherent Authority of Local Police to Make Immigration Arrests." *Albany Law Review* 69: 179–236.

Lewis, Paul G., and S. Karthick Ramakrishnan. 2007. "Police Practices in Immigrant-Destination Cities: Political Control or Bureaucratic Professionalism?" *Urban Affairs Review* 42(6): 874–900.

Major Cities Chiefs. 2006. "M.C.C. Immigration Committee Recommendations for Enforcement of Immigration Laws by Local Police Agencies." http://www.houstontx.gov/police/pdfs/mcc_position.pdf.

Marshall, F. Ray. 1978. "Economic Factors Influencing the International Migration of Workers." In *Views Across the Border*, ed. Stanley Ross, 163–80. Albuquerque: University of New Mexico Press.

Massey, D., J. Durand, and N. J. Malone. 2003. *Beyond Smoke and Mirrors: Mexican Immigration in an Era of Economic Integration*. New York: Russell Sage Foundation.

McDonald, William F. 1997. "Crime and Illegal Immigration: Emerging Local State and Federal Partnerships." *National Institutes of Justice Journal* 232: 2–10.

———. 1999. *The Changing Boundaries of Law Enforcement: State and Local Law Enforcement, Illegal Immigration, and Transnational Crime Control* (Final Report). Washington, DC: National Institute of Justice.

———. 2003. "The Emerging Paradigm for Policing Multi-ethnic Societies: Glimpses from the American Experience." *Police and Society* 7: 231–53.

Melossi, Dario. 2000. "Changing Representations of the Criminal." *British Journal of Criminology* 40(2): 296–320.

Migration Policy Institute Data Hub. 2009. *Legal Immigration to the United States: Fiscal Years 1820 to 2007*. Accessed August 2009. http://www.migrationinformation.org/DataHub/charts/historic.1.shtml.

Money, Jeannette. 1999. *Fences and Neighbors: The Political Geography of Immigration Control*. Ithaca, NY: Cornell University Press.

National Conference of State Legislators (NCSL). 2011. *2010 Immigration-Related Laws and Resolutions in the States (January–December 31, 2010)*. Accessed June 16, 2011, http://www.ncsl.org/default.aspx?tabid=21857.

National Immigration Law Center (2009). *More Questions than Answers about Secure Communities Program*. Accessed September 2010. http://www.nilc.org/immlawpolicy/Local-Law/secure-communities-2009-03-23.pdf .

Neuman, Gerald L. 1996. *Strangers to the Constitution*. Princeton, NJ: Princeton University Press.

Ngai, Mae M. 2004. *Impossible Subjects: Illegal Aliens and the Making of Modern America*. Princeton, NJ: Princeton University Press.

Office of Immigration Statistics (Department of Homeland Security). 2009, 2010. *Annual Report: Immigration Enforcement Actions: 2008–2009*. Washington, DC: Department of Homeland Security. Accessed September 2010. http://www.dhs.gov/files/statistics/immigration.shtm.

Passel, Jeffrey S. and D'Vera Cohn. 2008, 2010. "U.S. Unauthorized Immigration Flows Are Down Sharply Since Mid-Decade." Washington, DC: *Pew Hispanic Center*. Accessed September 2010. http://pewhispanic.org/reports/report.php?ReportID=126.

Police Executives Research Forum (PERF). 2008. *Police Chiefs and Sheriffs Speak Out on Local Immigration Enforcement*. Washington, DC.

Provine, Doris Marie. 2010. "Local Immigration Policy and Global Ambitions in Vancouver and Phoenix." In *Taking Local Control: Immigration Policy Activism in U.S. Cities and States*, ed. M. Varsanyi, 217-235. Stanford, CA: Stanford University Press.

Schuck, Peter. 2007. "Taking Immigration Federalism Seriously." *University of Chicago Legal Forum* 57.

Singer, Audrey, W. S. Hardwick, and C. Brettell, eds. 2008. *Twenty-First Century Gateways: Immigrant Incorporation in Suburban America*. Washington, DC: Brookings Institution.

Skerry, Peter. 1995. "Many Borders to Cross: Is Immigration the Exclusive Responsibility of the Federal Government?" *Publius* 25(3): 71–85.

Spiro, Peter J. 1997. "Learning to live with immigration federalism." *Connecticut Law Review* 29: 1627–36.

———. 2001. "Federalism and Immigration: Models and Trends." *International Social Science Journal* 53(167): 67–73.

Thatcher, David. 2005. "The Local Role in Homeland Security." *Law & Society Review* 39(3): 635–76.

Tichenor, Daniel J. 2002. *Dividing Lines: The Politics of Immigration Control in America*. Princeton, NJ: Princeton University Press.

Torpey, J. 2000. *The Invention of the Passport: Surveillance, Citizenship and the State*. Cambridge, MA: Cambridge University Press.

Varsanyi, M. W. 2008a. "Rescaling the 'Alien,' Rescaling Personhood: Neoliberalism, Immigration and the State. *Annals of the Association of American Geographers* 98(4): 877–96.

Varsanyi, M. W. 2008b. "Immigration Policing through the Backdoor: City Ordinances, the 'Right to the City,' and the Exclusion of Undocumented Day Laborers." *Urban Geography* 29(1): 29–52.

Zolberg, Aristide R. 2006. *A Nation by Design: Immigration Policy in the Fashioning of America.* New York: Russell Sage.

Zúñiga, Víctor, and Rubén Hernández-León, eds. 2005. *New Destinations: Mexican Immigration in the United States.* New York: Russell Sage Foundation.

4

No Surprises

The Evolution of Anti-Immigration Legislation in Arizona

KYRSTEN SINEMA

On April 23, 2010, Arizona Governor Jan Brewer signed SB 1070, the Support Our Law Enforcement and Safe Neighborhoods Act, into law. Within days, national attention focused on Arizona, with countless pundits, media commentators, and engaged activists from around the country and the world wondering aloud how SB 1070 seemingly appeared out of nowhere. For months following the governor's approval, national and international media focused on the new law, its implications and impact, and the resulting lawsuits borne from the controversial proposal. Between April and July 2010, national news media discussed SB 1070 nearly every day. For much of the nation, the question posed to Arizonans was "where did this come from, and how did it all happen so quickly?"

Astute students of Arizona's history and the long-standing relationship between anti-immigrant legislation architect State Senator Russell Pearce and national anti-immigration organizations such as the American Legislative Exchange Council (ALEC) and Federation for American Immigration Reform (FAIR) recognize the years of planning and careful execution that led to SB 1070. Beginning in the early 2000s, then-State Representative Russell Pearce, with the support and assistance of national organizations, began a patient, strategic, and focused effort to integrate anti-immigrant legislation into Arizona's system of state laws. What began as a seemingly singular obsession on the part of one Arizona lawmaker developed into a statewide and national effort growing in power, stature, and effectiveness. This chapter traces the development of anti-immigrant legislation in Arizona, highlighting the steady, organized movement from the initial introduction of anti-immigrant legislation to the passage of SB 1070 and beyond. The evolution demonstrates that Arizona's strategic movement from introduction of ideas to the passage of legislation was carefully crafted and executed by a coalition of state-elected officials and national activists, with the intent to utilize Arizona as a model for other states' actions. The chapter also reflects on the political left's failure to accurately gauge the seriousness of anti-immigrant proposals and the lack of strategic response to the steady progression of such legislation. Finally, the chapter evaluates the impact of Arizona's anti-immigration laws on other states and looks ahead to the movement's next steps in Arizona and beyond. For illustration purposes, in the Appendix I include a table of the major anti-immigrant legislation introduced in Arizona from 2003 to 2011, highlighting the development of ideas and concepts over the years.[1]

The Making of a Moral Entrepreneur

Russell Pearce was elected to the Arizona House of Representatives in November 2000, representing the conservative Phoenix suburb of western and central Mesa. Prior to his election, Pearce served as the chief deputy at the Maricopa County Sheriff's Office, spending 35 years as an officer in that department. He also served for several years as the Arizona director of Highway Safety and then director of the Arizona Motor Vehicle Division. Pearce was discharged from the Motor Vehicle Division in August 1999, after a state investigation indicated that he had tampered with driving records (Moeser 1999). He began his campaign for the Arizona House of Representatives shortly thereafter, and was elected in November 2000. During his first term in the Arizona House, Pearce focused largely on traffic, courts, justice of the peace, and criminal justice issues. He did not introduce legislation related to immigration during his first two-year term, although he co-sponsored a Memorial to Congress in 2002 requesting that the federal government increase funds for border control in Arizona (HM 2003, 2002).

After his first successful re-election campaign in November 2002, Pearce began focusing more of his attention on illegal immigration. In January

2003, he introduced two measures relating to illegal immigration (see appendix). The first, HB 2243, required local law enforcement to enforce all federal immigration laws, public K-12 schools to determine the legal status of all students and report undocumented students to local immigration authorities, and institutions of higher learning in Arizona to deny enrollment to students lacking legal status in the country (HB 2243, 2003). The second measure, HB 2246, required that all Arizonans provide proof of citizenship in order to register to vote (HB 2246, 2003). While neither bill moved forward in the Legislature, both began to lay the groundwork for future legislation and ballot initiatives. More significantly, Pearce's career as a moral entrepreneur was launched.

Howard Becker coined the term "moral entrepreneur" in the 1960s to define individuals who create and enforce rules to implement their deeply held moral beliefs. According to Becker, these individuals believe so deeply in a profoundly disturbing "evil" in the community that new rules must be established and enforced to correct the moral wrong (Becker 1963). Moral entrepreneurs fall into two categories: rule creators (moral crusaders) and rule enforcers. Rule creators are those who believe that new rules must be created, as existing rules do not and cannot adequately address the evil occurring in the community. As Becker states, the moral crusader believes that "nothing can be right in the world until rules are made to correct it. He operates with an absolute ethic; what he sees is truly and totally evil with no qualification. Any means is justified to do away with it" (1963: 148). Russell Pearce fits Becker's profile perfectly; his legislation sought from the beginning to create stringent rules that punished those here unlawfully, without exceptions. In Pearce's world, the federal government was doing nothing to address this moral dilemma. He would have to do it for them.

Pearce's moral entrepreneurship grew from the introduction of two proposals in 2003 to a career-long obsession with illegal immigration-related measures in the Arizona Legislature. His almost singular focus on illegal immigration has transformed both state laws regarding immigration and the political landscape in the state. While many of Pearce's ideas have yet to be implemented, including his first piece of anti-immigrant legislation, HB 2243, numerous other proposals have been enacted into law and are now the subject of copycat legislation around the nation.

No one except Pearce can fully understand or explain why he chose illegal immigration as his bailiwick. Arizona was in a state of rapid change in the early 2000s, with a marked spike of immigrants moving to Arizona (largely from Mexico, but also from other countries). Communities that formerly had been largely Anglo began to see Latino families move into neighborhoods, shop at the local groceries, and work in industries such as service, tourism, and construction (all major growth industries in Arizona at the time). While the media and the community at large weren't paying much attention to the issue of immigration in Arizona, it was a heated topic in nearby California, and national efforts to restrict immigration were ramping up after the passage of Prop 187 and national efforts around English-only laws. For those looking to find a vanguard issue in which to launch a moral entrepreneur's campaign, illegal immigration was a savvy choice.

In particular, Pearce's role as a moral entrepreneur has fueled the anti-immigrant wave across state legislatures. States far from any national border, with minute immigrant populations, are latching on to Pearce's proposals and attempting to replicate them in their own communities. With the help of organizations like FAIR (Federation for American Immigration Reform) and ALEC (American Legislative Exchange Council), Pearce's most virulently anti-immigrant legislation such as SB 1070 and the birthright citizenship measures have been introduced in more than 20 states nationwide.

FAIR's Entry to Arizona

In 2003, Representative Pearce sponsored House Bill 2246, a measure that would require Arizona citizens to provide proof of citizenship in order to register to vote and to vote in local and state elections. The bill failed on a roll call vote in the House Judiciary Committee, with two Republicans joining Democrats in opposition (HB 2246, 2003). The 2003 legislation session represented Pearce's first real attempt to pass an anti-immigrant measure, and after the bill failed in the Legislature, Pearce began working with FAIR to place the issue on the next general ballot.

Founded in 1979 by Jon Tanton, a wealthy environmentalist who opposes both unlawful and lawful immigration, FAIR seeks to stop all illegal immigration to the country, temporarily halt lawful immigration "except spouses and minor children of U.S. citizens and a limited number of refugees," and then eventually permit no more than 300,000 immigrants and refugees to enter the United States per year (FAIR 2011). FAIR works to advance anti-immigrant measures at both the state and federal levels.

In addition to these legislative efforts, Arizona is one of 24 states in the nation that permits popular initiatives to be placed on the ballot during general elections (BISC 2011). Historically, the ballot initiative process has been used by interest groups in Arizona to address issues that the Legislature has not addressed, or to advance specific policy agendas. Prior to 2004, several anti-immigration initiatives passed in Arizona, including English for the

Children, approved in 2000, which prohibited dual-language learning programs and bilingual education, and a 1988 constitutional provision establishing English as the Official Language in the state, which was later struck down as unconstitutional (Prop 203, 2000; Prop 106, 1988). The 1988 provision was sponsored and funded by FAIR's Jon Tanton, also the founder of ProEnglish, a group dedicated to establishing English as the official language in the country (Johnson 2009).

Shortly after the 2003 legislative session ended, Representative Pearce began working with FAIR on a citizen initiative to require proof of citizenship in order to register to vote and requiring voters to provide identification in order to receive a ballot. The initiative also required individuals applying for public benefits to provide proof of citizenship upon application, and for government officials to report violations of the law to federal immigration authorities (Prop 200, 2004). It was easy for Pearce to connect with FAIR—they had a history in the state with the passage of the English-only law five years earlier, and they were surely watching Arizona in the early 2000s as Pearce began working on anti-immigrant legislation.

With the assistance of FAIR, the initiative titled the "Arizona Taxpayer and Citizen Protection Act," commonly referred to as Prop 200, qualified for the November 2004 ballot in Arizona. FAIR contributed $450,000 to Arizona's Prop 200, by far the largest contribution recorded by the campaign committee that year (Arizona Secretary of State 2010). The initiative passed with 56 percent approval. At the time Prop 200 was on the ballot, Senators Jon Kyl and John McCain, the entire Arizona Congressional delegation, the Arizona Republican Party, the Arizona Democratic Party, the Arizona Chamber of Commerce, and then-Governor Janet Napolitano all vocally opposed the initiative (Prop 200, 2004).

Prop 200 represented the introduction of FAIR's influence in Arizona and reintroduced Tanton to the state in a broader anti-immigrant context. The organization also attempted to qualify for the November 2004 ballot in Nevada, Colorado, and California, but those attempts all failed. Since 2004, FAIR's influence has increased and the organization now works with lawmakers across the country to advance state-based anti-immigration measures.

Post-Prop 200 in Arizona

Fresh from his ballot victory in November 2004, Representative Pearce introduced House Concurrent Resolution (HCR) 2030 at the start of the 2005 legislative session. This ballot referendum sought to amend the Arizona Constitution to make English the official language of the state. A previously passed constitutional amendment (1988) had been ruled unconstitutional by the state Supreme Court in 1998, and the 2005 referendum sought to replace the unconstitutional language with new, conforming language. The referendum was held in the Senate Rules committee and did not advance (HCR 2030, 2005).

In 2006, Representative Pearce introduced the HCR again, this time as HCR 2036. The referendum required that English be recognized as the official language of the state, that all official actions in the state be conducted in English, and provided a right of legal action to any citizen of the state in the event that a state official violates the constitutional amendment. The measure passed both chambers in the Legislature and appeared on the November 2006 ballot as Proposition 103 (HCR 2036, 2006). The measure received 74 percent approval on the ballot and went into effect shortly thereafter (Prop 103, 2006).

Three additional measures ultimately appeared on the November 2006 ballot. The first was introduced by Senator Dean Martin and was patterned after Russell Pearce's 2003 legislation. HCR 1031 sought to restrict programs such as adult education, family literacy, and childcare assistance to legal residents and citizens. The measure also stated that undocumented persons could not qualify for in-state tuition at public colleges and universities, and could not receive scholarships, tuition waivers, grants, or financial aid. The measure required the State Board of Education, the Department of Economic Security, and public community colleges and universities to report annually to the state legislature the number of undocumented persons who applied to participate in the various programs herein (SCR 1031, 2006). This referral passed both chambers of the Legislature, was referred to the ballot and became Prop 300, Public Program Eligibility. Prop 300 passed in November 2006 with 71 percent support (Prop 300, 2006).

In 2006, Senator John Huppenthal introduced SB 1057, which was amended in the House Appropriations Committee to state that persons unlawfully present in the United States shall not have legal standing to file civil action in any Arizona court, save to recover actual damages (SB 1057, 2006). This legislation was held in the House prior to floor action, while Senate Concurrent Resolution (SCR) 1001, a measure proposing an amendment to the Arizona Constitution to prohibit unlawfully present persons from recovering punitive damages in civil actions within Arizona courts, passed both chambers and was referred to the November 2006 ballot (SCR 1001, 2006). SCR became Proposition 102 on the November 2006 ballot (Prop 102, 2006) and passed with 74 percent of the voters' support (Prop 102, results 2006).

The final measure on the November 2006 ballot actually started in 2005. Representative Pearce sponsored a ballot referral, HCR 2028, which sought to amend the Arizona Constitution to state that a person suspected of committing a serious felony and who entered or remained in the country unlawfully was not eligible for bail. HCR 2028 was passed by both chambers in 2005 and referred to the November 2006 ballot as a constitutional amendment known as Prop 100 (HCR 2028, 2005; Prop 100, 2006). Prop 100 passed the November 2006 ballot with 78 percent support from the voters (Prop 100, results 2006).

After the 2006 election, the Legislature saw the increasing popularity of anti-immigration legislation in Arizona and forged ahead. By this time, it was clear to the Legislature that the public supported anti-immigrant measures, at least when presented with no clear sign of any positive solutions to the growing immigration crisis Arizona was experiencing. As such, the political pressure to approve anti-immigrant measures increased exponentially, with Republicans, in particular, concerned about primary election challenges from the right as political payback for failure to support these measures. With growing public pressure to "do something" about immigration and thinly veiled threats from the political right about repercussions for those who opposed anti-immigrant measures, most legislative Republicans began voting for Pearce's measures.

As the session started in 2007, Russell Pearce introduced HB 2779, the Fair and Legal Employment Act (HB 2779, 2007), prohibiting employers from knowingly hiring an undocumented person for labor. The bill imposed a variety of civil penalties for first and subsequent violations, including suspension of a business's license to operate. The bill also created a state crime of identity theft for knowingly taking, purchasing, manufacturing, possessing, or using any personal identifying information belonging to another person with the intent to obtain employment. Finally, the bill created a state mandate that employers use e-verify to ensure that all hires are legally authorized to work in the United States. The bill passed both chambers and was signed into law by Governor Janet Napolitano.

Passage of the employer sanctions bill marked a huge victory for Pearce, as his legislative proposals in previous years had been defeated, including his 2006 proposed ballot referendum HCR 2044, which was passed by the House but held in the Senate. That referendum would have created a state-based employer sanction system in Arizona (HCR 2044, 2006). The referendum would require all employers in Arizona to comply with federal laws regarding employment eligibility verification and create state sanctions for failure to comply, including civil fines, criminal punishment, and revocation of a business's license to operate within the state of Arizona. The failed 2006 ballot referral formed the basis for the successful 2007 legislation.

In 2008, Representative Russell Pearce introduced legislation amending the 2007 law regarding employer sanctions. HB 2745 made a number of adjustments to the law, including clarification of the use of e-verify by Arizona businesses and requiring all government contractors and subcontractors to utilize this system. The bill passed both chambers and was signed into law by Governor Janet Napolitano (HB 2745, 2008).

The Rise of SB 1070

SB 1070 passed the Legislature in 2010 and was signed into law by Governor Jan Brewer (SB 1070, 2010). One week after the passage of SB 1070, the Legislature passed, and Governor Brewer signed, HB 2162. This was a "trailer" bill, meaning that it made clarifying adjustments to SB 1070 (HB 2162, 2010). This omnibus legislation, the subject of current federal litigation, made numerous changes to state law regarding the mandated local law enforcement of federal immigration laws, the unlawful solicitation of labor, unlawful harboring and transporting of unlawfully present persons, and the impoundment of vehicles operated by undocumented persons.

Yet the roots of SB 1070 go back as early as 2003, when then-Representative Russell Pearce sought to change Arizona law to require all local law enforcement agencies to enforce federal immigration laws in all arrests of persons suspected of being in the United States unlawfully. In 2003, HB 2243 was never even heard in committee (HB 2243, 2003).

In 2005, Representative Pearce introduced HB 2386, legislation that authorized local law enforcement officers to apprehend, detain, and/or remove unlawfully present persons from the United States, including transporting suspected individuals across state lines to detention centers. This legislation was never heard in committee (HB 2386, 2005). However, Senator Karen Johnson introduced similar legislation in the Senate that session, SB 1306 (SB 1306, 2005). SB 1306 passed both chambers and was vetoed by Governor Janet Napolitano (SB 1306, letter 2005).

Governor Napolitano vetoed three additional measures that included provisions later seen in SB 1070. In 2006, Representative Russell Pearce introduced HB 2577, an omnibus bill that sought to make major changes to immigration policy in Arizona (HB 2577, 2006). The legislation required that local law enforcement officials enforce all federal immigration laws, denied punitive damages awards to any undocumented persons suing in a civil court in Arizona, made trespassing a state crime, denied adult education classes and childcare assistance to undocumented persons, denied financial assistance in public colleges or universities to undocumented persons, created an employer sanctions law that punished employers for knowingly hiring undocumented workers, created a border enforcement security team, and appropriated funds for border security. HB 2577 passed both chambers of the Arizona Legislature and was vetoed by Governor Janet Napolitano. In her veto letter, Napolitano stated that the legislation was unconstitutional and did not meet appropriate standards to hold employers accountable for illegal hiring practices (HB 2577, letter 2006).

Also in 2006, Senator Barbara Leff introduced legislation that created a state crime of "trespassing." Senate Bill 1157 punished individuals present in Arizona without lawful presence in the United States with a class one misdemeanor for a first offense, class six felony for a subsequent offense, and class two felony if the person also possessed drugs or weapons (SB 1157, 2006). The legislation also permitted the arresting officer to deport the detainee or turn the individual over to the appropriate federal agency. The bill passed both chambers and was vetoed by Governor Janet Napolitano. In her veto letter, Napolitano noted that the legislation was unconstitutional, and that law enforcement organizations such as the Arizona Police Association and the Arizona Conference of Police and Sheriffs opposed the bill (SB 1157, letter 2006).

In 2008, Representative John Nelson introduced HB 2807, legislation that required local law enforcement agencies to train law enforcement officials in the implementation of federal immigration laws, or to embed ICE officers within the police force (HB 2807, 2008). The bill was vetoed by Governor Janet Napolitano. She expressed concern that the bill shifted the cost of training local law enforcement officers to enforce federal immigration laws from the federal government to the state government (HB 2807, letter 2008).

In 2009, Representative John Kavanagh introduced legislation that also served as a precursor for SB 1070. HB 2280 required all local law enforcement officials to enforce all federal immigration laws at all times. The bill also created a state crime of trespassing and created civil and criminal penalties for any undocumented person who entered or remained on public or private land in Arizona. The bill passed the House and Senate but failed on the House floor during final read on the eve of the Legislature's *sine die* (HB 2280, 2009).

Finally, in 2010, the Legislature passed SB 1070. SB 1070 included most of the ideas previously vetoed by Governor Napolitano, as well as the enforcement measures in Representative Kavanagh's failed 2009 legislation. While the rest of the country and the world were shocked by SB 1070, as this discussion reveals, it represented nothing new to Arizona's Legislature. The body had been considering these measures for years.

SB 1070, like the 2004 ballot initiative Protect Arizona Now, was heavily influenced by FAIR. Kris Kobach, newly elected Kansas Secretary of State, counsel to the Immigration Law Reform Institute, and former law professor at the University of Missouri–Kansas School of Law, drafted SB 1070 and several previously passed anti-immigration proposals in Arizona. The Immigration Law Reform Institute is the legal advocacy arm of FAIR and Kobach has worked for the Institute for years, drafting legislation, litigating immigration measures, and assisting state legislators like Russell Pearce in efforts to pass anti-immigrant legislation (ILRI 2010). For example, Kobach previously represented FAIR in a Kansas lawsuit regarding tuition rates for undocumented college students (Maines and Rothschild 2006). He drafted SB 1070 (and earlier versions proposed by Senator Russell Pearce in 2007, 2008, and 2009) and suggested edits to the "trailer" bill to SB 1070, HB 2162, less than one week after SB 1070 was passed (Sinema 2010). Kobach's suggested edits were subsequently adopted by Senator Russell Pearce and are currently law in Arizona.

Post-SB 1070 in Arizona

Following the passage of SB 1070, advocates around the nation declared a boycott of Arizona, and the state lost up to $150 million in revenue due to the loss of conferences, tourism, and residents and businesses leaving the state (Oppel 2011). As a result of the economic black eye Arizona developed post-1070, the Arizona Chamber of Commerce and other business leaders and groups in the state stepped up to oppose the passage of further anti-immigrant measures in the state legislature. In 2011, newly elected Senate President Pearce shepherded five major anti-immigrant measures in the Senate, intending to pass them in the same manner as SB 1070. Instead, all five bills were defeated by the Senate during the final vote.

The five measures all recycle ideas Pearce has promoted in the past, without success. Two sought to redefine the Fourteenth Amendment to deny citizenship recognition to children whose parents lack legal status in the country, or who live in the United States on immigrant visas but are not legal permanent residents. The measures also deny citizenship recognition to children born in Arizona whose parents hold dual citizenship in the United States and another country (SB 1309, 2011). A third measure sought to require hospitals to determine the citizenship status of all persons seeking emergency and non-emergency medical attention in any Arizona hospital, and further required hospitals to notify local law enforcement and immigration authorities if any person seeking medical attention could not prove his or her legal status in the country (SB 1405, 2011). A fourth bill sought to require public K-12 schools to determine which students were citizens, legally present non-citizens, and students present in the country without lawful status and conduct research on the adverse impact of educating students who are not lawfully present in the country. It also would have required school districts to calculate the costs of educating non-citizen students lawfully present and the costs of educating students who are not lawfully present, and would have allowed the Superintendent of Public Instruction to withhold a school district's state funds for non-compliance (SB 1407, 2011). The final measure represented a compilation of 16 pieces of legislation formerly introduced in the Arizona Legislature by Senate President Russell Pearce. This "omnibus" legislation combined bills sponsored by Pearce between 2006 to 2010 into one piece of legislation, and added several new restrictive immigration measures: restricting eligibility for federal, state, and local benefits; prohibiting undocumented persons from operating vehicles; requiring proof of citizenship for K-12 school enrollment; prohibiting undocumented individuals from enrolling in community colleges or universities; expanding the e-verify program to all employers in the state; prohibiting the recognition of consular cards as valid identification; requiring proof of citizenship for title and registration of a vehicle; withholding housing assistance dollars to households in which undocumented persons reside; and revoking the certification of peace officers who fail to enforce all provisions of the law (SB 1611, 2011). Like the other four bills, this measure was defeated by the Senate on a Third Read vote.

Many have questioned how and why the Senate, led by the champion President Russell Pearce, defeated these measures, particularly given the meteoric rise of anti-immigration measures in the state over the last seven years. The Arizona Chamber of Commerce, joined by a multitude of other business organizations and business leaders, began lobbying against these five measures as early as January 2011. As a result of national boycott efforts, the exodus of between 100,000 and 200,000 Arizona residents, and the loss of economic relocation to the state, the Arizona business community chose to focus its legislative efforts on stopping further passage of anti-immigrant measures in 2011. As noted in the *New York Times*, their efforts were well-placed, swaying a number of conservative legislators who had previously supported employer sanctions measures and SB 1070 to vote against the five immigration measures in March 2011 (Oppel 2011).

The Failure of the Political Left

Arizona's large immigrant population is not a new phenomenon. While states like Tennessee, Georgia, and North Carolina have experienced rapid, even explosive immigrant population growth, Arizona's sizeable immigrant population has existed for decades. It is undeniable that the size of its immigration population increased after the implementation of federal initiatives such as Operation Hold the Line (1993) and Operation Gatekeeper (1994) in the southwest, effectively closing off corridors of travel between Mexico and California, Nevada, and New Mexico, and funneling immigrant traffic through the deadly Arizona desert (Nevins 2010). The federal government believed that unlawful immigration would decrease when the only corridor of travel was via Arizona. Prior to the implementation of Operation Gatekeeper, deaths in the Arizona desert numbered around 200 per year. After implementation, deaths more than doubled to between 400 and 500 per year (USGAO 2006). The federal government underestimated migrants' economic desperation, assuming that the treacherous route would act as a deterrent. Instead, migration through the Arizona desert increased dramatically.

It is estimated that nearly half of all illegal entries into the United States occurred in Arizona between 1993 and 2004, and that roughly half of those entrants settled in Arizona (U.S. Border Patrol 2005). This led to a rapid increase in the number of new immigrants in Arizona from 1993 to the present. For the most part, Arizona's existing Latino and immigrant communities did not anticipate or respond to this explosive growth.

Although Arizona has long been a diverse state, with a Latino population of over 25 percent (now at 30 percent) and a Native American population of roughly 12 percent, Arizona historically has been segregated. First segregated via local, state, and federal policies, Arizona remained largely segregated via de facto behavior following the advent of civil rights laws. Housing, education, and the workplace remained largely segregated for many years. Only since the early 1990s have central, northern, and rural Arizona (beyond the border region) experienced an influx of integration in housing developments, suburban and extra-urban communities, and the workplace. Today in Maricopa County, one finds *carnicerías* in areas that 20 years ago were almost exclusively Anglo. While the face of Arizona's community changed rapidly, community leaders did not. Instead of noting the rapid changes and initiating discussion, leaders and politicians ignored them. Meanwhile, average Arizonans began to feel discomfort about the change they did not seek and were not prepared to manage.

The political left reacted in an anemic way; social services were provided at minimal levels for newly arriving families, but little cultural exchange or discussion ensued in the affected communities. Meanwhile, the extreme right noticed the change and reacted forcefully. With Arizonans expressing outrage over small changes like choices of English or Spanish in automated phone answering services and traditional Mexican food choices in the local grocery, the right saw an opportunity to capitalize on the frustration ordinary Arizonans felt.

While the left continued to call for comprehensive federal immigration reform as the only solution, the right saw an opportunity to "fill" the hole left by the federal government's failure to act. Thus, state-based anti-immigrant legislation was born in Arizona. As the left told voters to be patient and wait for reform, the right told voters that reform could happen right here, right now, and they offered solutions by the dozens.

The left responded by decrying state-based enforcement-only decisions as false solutions and pointing out the state's lack of authority to implement reform. These overly technical responses to a very emotional situation alienated Arizona voters, who began to express support for enforcement-only solutions. Research has shown that voters actually prefer comprehensive reform solutions to state-based enforcement-only solutions, but that they will support whatever is offered to them. Because no comprehensive measures have been offered by Congress, voters are continuing to support state-based enforcement measures (Sharry 2010).

The left's failure to adequately understand voters' fears and concerns about the changing nature of their communities and to offer proactive local measures to "fill the void" left by the federal government's failure to act created the space that the political right needed to move voters to support more extreme measures like SB 1070. Today, the left is just beginning to catch up in these two areas. One effort, the Welcoming America project, seeks to address community concerns about immigration and immigrants before Arizona-style legislation can take hold by organizing community conversations about immigration, creating a positive narrative about immigration, and providing opportunities for immigrants to integrate peacefully and rapidly into their new communities (Welcoming America 2011).

The second effort, headed by the Progressive States Network and Progressive States Action, seeks to assist state legislators in introducing and passing pro-immigrant legislation in states across the country (Progressive States Action 2011). These measures would create wage-enforcement laws, support in-state tuition for undocumented students, promote community policing efforts that build trust between police and immigrant communities, support immigrant-owned businesses, and more. As a whole, they aim to redefine immigrants and immigration in states, moving away from punitive measures that dehumanize and criminalize immigrants and toward policies that emphasize the benefits immigrants bring to communities and the rights of workers.

While these fledgling efforts are making a difference in states just beginning to feel the impact of illegal immigration, the left's failure to implement creative and proactive solutions in the past has left voids in states like Arizona, which created space for the development and acceptance of anti-immigrant legislation.

Arizona's Influence on Other State Legislatures

While Arizona pioneered much of the anti-immigration legislation in the United States, many states have followed suit, adopting Arizona-style laws in whole or in part. As of June 2010, "44 state legislatures passed 191 laws and adopted 128 resolutions. Five bills were vetoed, for a total of 314 enacted laws and resolutions, a 21 percent increase over 2009. An additional ten bills were pending governor's approval" (NCSL 2010). This represents an increase of nearly 50 more enacted bills from 2009. Additionally, while state legislators are introducing more legislation, a greater number of bills and resolutions are passing state chambers and moving to enactment by governors.

This trend has continued since 2005, when a significant number of states began introducing and moving anti-immigrant legislation. The National Conference on State Legislatures notes that "[s]tate laws related to immigration have increased dramatically in recent years." To wit, in 2005, 300 bills were introduced, 38 were enacted, and 6 bills were vetoed. In just the first half of 2010, the number of bills introduced is more than five times that of 2005 (NCSL 2010). It is anticipated that the increase of bill and resolution introduction and passage will continue to grow until and unless Congress enacts a comprehensive package of federal immigration reform laws.

A number of state legislatures introduced so-called copycat bills following the passage of SB 1070, including Pennsylvania, Rhode Island, Minnesota, South Carolina, and Michigan (among others) (NCSL 2010; Miller 2010). As of December 2010, none of those proposals had passed. However, 18 states introduced Arizona-style SB 1070s in the 2011 legislative cycle, and several of those states have passed and implemented the law (Miller 2010). Notable examples of states with proposals include Mississippi, South Carolina, Georgia, Tennessee, and Utah (Raghunathan 2010). Georgia and Alabama successfully passed measures similar to Arizona's SB 1070. The Alabama law has been largely upheld by a federal court judge, while an appeal is moving forward to block other portions of the law (Robertson 2011). Meanwhile, the Arizona law remains largely inert, as the Ninth Circuit has upheld initial injunctions halting the implementation of the major components of the law (Fischer 2011).

Continued Collaboration with ALEC and FAIR

As noted earlier, Russell Pearce, prime architect of Arizona's anti-immigrant legislation throughout the last decade, has long worked in partnership with two national organizations—the American Legislative Exchange Council (ALEC) and Federation for American Immigration Reform (FAIR). Together, these organizations provide ideas, drafting assistance, legislative support, and grassroots networking to anti-immigrant legislators across the country. Their greatest successes have been in Arizona, with a model that "exports" Arizona's successful legislation to other states in rapid, coordinated succession. A recent set of stories by National Public Radio highlights the close relationship between legislators and ALEC, which allows state legislators to easily and quickly adapt Arizona-style legislation to other legislative bodies (Sullivan 2010a, 2010b).

ALEC, a national legislative support organization, provides assistance to conservative state legislators throughout the country, largely through corporate funded conferences held several times a year (see Sullivan 2010b) and via their website and staff support services. Notably, their website provides "model" legislation for any of the more than 7,000 state legislators in the United States to download and adapt for use in their own legislatures. A review of ALEC's model immigration legislation reveals Arizona as the avant-garde state in the area of homeland security; much of the legislation posted on the website is patterned closely after Arizona's already enacted laws (ALEC 2010).

What's Next

FAIR has organized a 14-state effort in 2011 to challenge the Fourteenth Amendment and its application to children born in the United States to undocumented persons (Rau 2010). Specifically, the multi-state legislative effort seeks to spur litigation in federal court so anti-immigrant activists and legislators can argue that the Fourteenth Amendment does not apply to U.S.-born children of undocumented persons residing in the United States. As of press time, none of those measures had passed in any state legislature, including Arizona.

Senator Pearce previously sponsored HCM 2005 in the 2007 legislative cycle—a memorial to Congress that urged the federal government to enact legislation that would clarify the Fourteenth Amendment of the U.S. Constitution as denying citizenship to children of undocumented immigrants born on U.S. soil (HCM 2005, 2007). That memorial passed two House committees and was held from full consideration by the Arizona House of Representatives. In 2008, Senator Karen Johnson introduced the memorial again as SCM 1003 (SCM 1003, 2008). The memorial was held in committee. Senator Johnson also introduced a voter referendum in 2008 that, if passed, would have issued separate birth certificates to children born in Arizona to undocumented persons (SCR 1016, 2008). The referendum was held in committee. Since that time, Pearce and FAIR modified their approach from sending a message to Congress urging them to take action to a more aggressive approach seeking to spur litigation in federal court on the question of the Fourteenth Amendment's application to the children born in the United States to undocumented immigrants.

While there is little debate among legal scholars about the valid application of the Fourteenth Amendment to persons born in the United States, and while such legislation stands no real chance of implementation due to constitutional barriers, the legislation plays two critical roles in the development of anti-immigration sentiment in the country: (1) the discussion seeks to impede movement at the national level toward comprehensive immigration reform; and (2) the legislation spurs state-sponsored litigation in federal court, providing a long-term opportunity for media exposure and the opportunity to shape public opinion about the children of undocumented persons in the United States. To wit, a recent poll conducted in Arizona reported that 67 percent of Arizonans do not believe that children born in the United States to undocumented residents should be eligible for citizenship (Phoenix Business Journal 2010). High-profile politicians such as Senator Jon Kyl and Arizona Governor Jan Brewer have publicly indicated support for such legislation (Phoenix Business Journal 2010).

While none of the 14 states considering these Fourteenth Amendment challenges have passed their legislation, the attempts surely will not end this year. As noted, Arizona has been pursuing this issue since 2007 and Congress has now joined the fray by introducing federal legislation seeking to redefine the application of the Fourteenth Amendment (H.R. 140, 2011).

Conclusion

The proliferation of anti-immigration legislation in Arizona and in the United States was not organic; SB 1070 did not suddenly appear in Arizona's legislature—just as the Fourteenth Amendment legislation introduced by Senator Russell Pearce in Arizona, by Representative Steve King in Congress, and in 13 other state legislatures is not a new or even a novel concept. Instead, these and a variety of other anti-immigrant measures have been carefully cultivated, tested, altered, developed, and implemented, first in Arizona and then in states around the country. Russell Pearce's development as a moral entrepreneur radically changed the political landscape in Arizona and has subsequently impacted public policy development in states across the country. Without a champion like Pearce at the state legislative level, anti-immigrant legislation may not have developed so quickly or effectively in the southwest, and almost certainly would not have spread so efficiently to other state legislatures. While Tanton and FAIR provide resources and support to local anti-immigrant measures, it was the "fertile ground" of Arizona's legislature in the form of a moral crusader that created the growth and development of this legislation.

As shown in this chapter, a careful review of anti-immigrant legislation in Arizona's recent history demonstrates the development and growing sophistication of anti-immigrant activists' and legislators' tactics, strategy, and messaging points. Arizona's history is public record, available for all to see. The lessons learned from Arizona's story are clear: anti-immigrant legislation develops steadily and strategically over time, with the architects of such legislation making adjustments through the years, and allowing legislation to "simmer" for some time while the public adjusts to ideas regarding immigration that were previously considered unacceptable. By being persistent, strategic, and patient, Senator Russell Pearce and his allies at ALEC and FAIR eventually passed a record number of anti-immigrant measures in Arizona, including SB 1070. The left's failure to anticipate or strategically respond to these measures created a void in Arizona that allowed anti-immigrant legislation to flourish. Only by taking action to work strategically in Arizona and around the country to combat these measures and create an alternative narrative around immigration can other states avoid Arizona's fate.

APPENDIX: IMMIGRATION-RELATED LEGISLATIVE ACTIVITY IN ARIZONA, 2003-2011

2003

VOTING RIGHTS AND CITIZENSHIP

2246 (Pearce) – failed in House Judiciary. Required proof of citizenship in order to register to vote.

PUBLIC BENEFITS

2243 (Pearce) – bill was not heard. Required all emergency medical service institutions in the state to report all suspected unlawfully present persons seeking care to federal immigration authorities.

EDUCATION

HB 2243 (Pearce) – bill was not heard. Required law enforcement to enforce all federal immigration laws; also stated that public institutions of higher learning shall not admit or enroll students who are not legally present in the United States, and that the public institutions must determine the status of all applicants and enrollees and report undocumented persons to federal immigration authorities.

LOCAL ENFORCEMENT OF FEDERAL IMMIGRATION LAW

2243 (Pearce) – bill not heard. Required all local law enforcement agencies to enforce federal immigration laws in all arrests of persons suspected to be present in the United States unlawfully.

2004

VOTING RIGHTS AND CITIZENSHIP

Prop 200 –Arizona Taxpayer and Citizen Protection Act. Required proof of citizenship in order to register to vote and required voters to provide identification in order to receive a ballot. In addition, the initiative required individuals applying for public benefits to provide proof of citizenship upon application and required government officials to report violations of the law to federal immigration authorities.

EMPLOYMENT AND EMPLOYER SANCTIONS

2448 (Pearce) – held in House committee. Requires the Attorney General to suspend a company's business license for six months upon determination that the company violated federal statutes regarding illegal hiring.

2005

PUBLIC BENEFITS

2394 (Pearce) – bill was not heard. Required the state Medicaid program, AHCCCS, to verify the immigration status of all applicants and report individuals who reside in the state unlawfully to federal immigration authorities.

2395 (Pearce) – bill was not heard. Required the Department of Economic Security to verify the immigration status of all persons applying for traditional welfare assistance programs.

EDUCATION

2030 (Nichols) – passed and vetoed. Prohibited undocumented students from qualifying for in-state tuition, financial assistance, or scholarships at public community colleges or universities in the state. Also restricted Family Literacy and adult education classes to lawfully present persons, and mandated that child care assistance only be provided to families in which all persons are lawfully present in the United States.

ENGLISH AS THE OFFICIAL LANGUAGE

HCR 2030 (Pearce) – passed the House, held in the Senate Rules committee. This ballot referendum sought to amend the Arizona Constitution to make English the official language of the state. A previously passed constitutional amendment (1998) had recently been ruled unconstitutional by state courts, and this referendum sought to replace the unconstitutional language with new, conforming language.

CRIMINAL JUSTICE AND THE COURTS

2259 (Gray) – passed and signed by Governor Napolitano. Created longer prison sentences for individuals convicted of a felony offense if the defendant was also in violation of any federal immigration law. Specifically, the legislation created five new "aggravating factors" that, if present, a court could consider when imposing a defendant's prison sentence. The aggravating factors included: the unlawful bringing of aliens into the United States, bringing in and harboring certain aliens, improper entry by an alien, re-entry of removed aliens, and importation of alien for immoral purposes. In practice, this allows judges to consider a person's legal status in the United States as a factor in enhancing a defendant's penalty for an unrelated criminal act.

2709 (Jones) – passed and vetoed by Governor Napolitano. Required the Arizona Department of

Administration to contract with a private prison corporation to build and maintain a private prison facility in Mexico to house Mexican nationals arrested and convicted of criminal offenses in Arizona.

2389 (Pearce) – passed House and Senate Judiciary. Created a non-bailable offense if a person charged with a class 1, 2, or 3 felony has also entered or remained in the United States without authorization.

HCR 2028 (Pearce) – referred to the ballot and passed. Amended the Arizona Constitution to state that a person suspected of committing a serious felony offense and who entered or remained in the country unlawfully was not eligible for bail. Known as Prop 100.

Proposition 100 passed the November 2006 ballot with 78% support from the voters.

EMPLOYMENT AND EMPLOYER SANCTIONS

2384 (Pearce) – bill was not heard. Required businesses who had been sanctioned by the federal government for violating federal employer sanctions laws to first post a notice of the federal sanction, and on subsequent offenses, face suspension and loss of one's business license.

DAY LABORERS

2592 (Rosati) – passed and signed into law by Governor Napolitano. Prohibited local governments from constructing or maintaining work centers if the work center assists unlawfully present persons in obtaining employment in Arizona.

LOCAL ENFORCEMENT OF FEDERAL IMMIGRATION LAW

2386 (Pearce) – bill not heard. Authorized local law enforcement officers to apprehend, detain, and/or remove unlawfully present persons from the United States including transporting suspected individuals across state lines to detention centers.

1306 (Johnson) – passed both chambers, vetoed by Governor Napolitano. Identical to 2386.

2006

PUBLIC BENEFITS

2448 (Burges) – Passed and signed into law. Required AHCCCS to verify all applicants' citizenship status prior to accepting or enrolling applicants in the state's Medicaid program. The bill also required employees to report persons unlawfully present to federal immigration authorities, and imposed a class two misdemeanor for the failure to report.

EDUCATION

2068, 2069 (Gray) – bills were not heard. Stated that undocumented students were not eligible for in-state tuition and could not qualify or accept scholarships, tuition waivers, grants, or financial aid.

2597, 2598 (Boone) – bills were not heard. These bills were nearly identical to Representative Gray's bills 2068 and 2069.

HCR 1031 (Martin) – passed and became law. A measure referred to the voters that sought to restrict programs such as adult education, family literacy, and child care assistance to legal residents and citizens. The measure also stated that undocumented persons could not qualify for in-state tuition at public colleges and universities, and could not receive scholarships, tuition waivers, grants, or financial aid. The measure required the State Board of Education, the Department of Economic Security, and public community colleges and universities to report annually to the state legislature the number of undocumented persons who applied to participate in the various programs herein. The measure was referred to the ballot and became Prop 300, Public Program Eligibility; it passed in November 2006 with 71% support.

ENGLISH AS THE OFFICIAL LANGUAGE

HCR 2036 (Pearce) – passed both chambers, passed at the ballot. Required that English be recognized as the official language of the state, that all official actions in the state be conducted in English, and provides a right of legal action to any citizen of the state in the event that a state official violate the constitutional amendment. Appeared on the November 2006 ballot as Proposition 103. The measure received 74% approval on the November 2006 ballot and went into effect shortly thereafter.

CRIMINAL JUSTICE AND THE COURTS

2761 (Jones) – passed two House committees but was held in the House Rules Committee. Bill repeated effort to place prisons in Mexico, attempt vetoed by Governor Napolitano in 2005.

1057 (Huppenthal) – held in House. This bill was amended in the House Appropriations Committee to state that persons unlawfully present in the United States shall not have legal standing to file civil action in any Arizona court, save to recover actual damages.

SCR 1001 (Huppenthal) – referred by the Legislature to the ballot, passed with 74% support. The measure proposed an amendment to the Arizona Constitution to prohibit unlawfully present persons from recovering punitive damages in civil actions within Arizona courts.

HCR 2028 sought to amend the Arizona Constitution to state that a person suspected of committing a serious felony offense and who entered or remained in the country unlawfully was not eligible for bail.

HB 2580 (Pearce) – passed and signed by Governor Napolitano. The conforming legislation to accompany Proposition 100. The legislation was nearly identical to HB 2389 from 2005, and was designed to go into effect only if Arizona voters approved Proposition 100 in November 2006.

EMPLOYMENT AND EMPLOYER SANCTIONS

HCR 2044 (Pearce) – passed House, held in Senate. A referendum to the Arizona ballot that would create a state-based employer sanction system in Arizona. The referendum, if passed by the voters, would require all employers in Arizona to comply with federal laws regarding employment eligibility verification and create state sanctions for a failure to comply, including civil fines, criminal punishment, and revocation of a business's license to operate within the state of Arizona.

TRESPASSING

2582 (Pearce) – passed House, held in Senate. Created a state crime of trespassing, punishable to any person found in violation of federal trespassing statutes. The legislation also allowed law enforcement officers to detain and remove unlawfully present persons, including the transport of said persons across state lines to federal detention centers. The bill also created a Border Security Council to make grants to local governments for border security.

1157 (Gray) – passed both chambers, vetoed by Governor Napolitano. Punished individuals present in Arizona without lawful presence in the United States with a class one misdemeanor for a first offense, class six felony for a subsequent offense, and class 2 felony if the person also possessed drugs or weapons. Created state crime of trespassing.

LOCAL ENFORCEMENT OF FEDERAL IMMIGRATION LAW

2071 (Gray) – bill not heard. Stated when law enforcement officers detain an individual for suspected criminal activity, they can question that person's immigration status.

2837 (Pearce) – failed on a final vote in the House. Stated that any local government that enacts a stated or implied "sanctuary" policy involving any aid or assistance to undocumented persons or any reduction of enforcement of federal immigration laws would be deprived of state shared revenues.

OMNIBUS LEGISLATION

2577 (Pearce) – passed both chambers, vetoed by Governor Napolitano. Sought to make major changes to immigration policy in Arizona. The legislation required that local law enforcement officials enforce all federal immigration laws, denied punitive damages awards to any undocumented persons suing in a civil court in Arizona, created a state crime of trespassing, denied adult education classes and childcare assistance to undocumented persons, denied financial assistance in public colleges or universities to undocumented persons, created an employer sanctions law that punished employers for knowingly hiring undocumented workers, created a border enforcement security team, and appropriated funds for border security.

2007

PUBLIC BENEFITS

2471 (Pearce) – bill was not heard. Denied public benefits including access to K-12 education, higher education, grants, loans, professional licenses and employment, retirement benefits, public welfare benefits, healthcare, public housing, and disability benefits to all persons born in the country to one or more undocumented parents living in the United States.

CRIMINAL JUSTICE AND THE COURTS

1265 (Gray) – passed and signed into law by Governor Napolitano. Made a number of clarifications to HB 2580 and the implementation of recently-passed Prop 100.

EMPLOYMENT AND EMPLOYER SANCTIONS

2779 (Pearce) – passed and signed into law by Governor Napolitano. The Fair and Legal Employment Act created a state violation for any employer who knowingly hires an undocumented person for labor. The bill imposed a variety of civil penalties for first and subsequent violations, including suspension of a business's license to operate. The bill also created a state crime of identity theft, stating that a person commits identity theft if s/he knowingly takes, purchases, manufactures, possesses, or uses any personal identifying information belonging to another person with the intent to obtain employment.

DAY LABORERS

2589 (Kavanagh) – passed and was vetoed by Governor Napolitano. Sought to criminalize individuals who stand in specific locations for the purposes of soliciting employment or labor.

TRESPASSING

HCR 2022 (Pearce) – passed House committee then held. A referendum to the voters that would prohibit any undocumented person from entering private or public land. The measure punished individuals present in Arizona without lawful presence in the United States with a class one misdemeanor for a first offense, class six felony for a subsequent offense, and class 2 felony if the person also possessed drugs or weapons.

LOCAL ENFORCEMENT OF FEDERAL IMMIGRATION LAW

2461 (Pearce) – bill not heard. Required all local law enforcement officers to inquire into the legal status of persons detained for suspected violations of state law or municipal ordinances. The legislation provided that the Attorney General or the Arizona House Judiciary Committee could determine, by a majority vote, whether a local law enforcement agency was violating the requirements of the legislation. If such a violation were found, the agency would be denied state funding until the Attorney General determined that the agency had come into compliance.

2751 (Pearce) – passed three House committees, then held. Required all local law enforcement agencies to fully comply with and fully support the enforcement of federal immigration laws. The legislation also created an Arizona Border Enforcement Security Team and appropriated $25 million from the state general fund to make grants to local agencies for border security.

HCR 2049 (Pearce) – passed House committee, held before floor vote. Changed state law via a voter referendum to require all local law enforcement agencies to fully comply with and enforce all federal immigration laws.

2008

EDUCATION

HCR 2043 (Pearce) – bill was not heard. A voter referendum that would prohibit any person not providing written proof of legal residency within the United States from attending any public education institution in the state.

EMPLOYMENT AND EMPLOYER SANCTIONS

2745 (Pearce) – passed and signed into law by Governor Napolitano. Made a number of adjustments to the employer sanctions law of 2008, including clarification of the use of e-verify by Arizona businesses. The bill also required all government contractors and subcontractors to utilize e-verify.

2750 (Pearce) – bill was not heard. Prohibits undocumented workers from applying for or receiving workers' compensation when injured at the workplace.

DAY LABORERS

2412 (Kavanagh) – passed the House, failed in the Senate. Redefined criminal trespass to include knowingly standing in a public street, highway, or adjacent areas for the purposes of soliciting employment.

TRESPASSING

HCR 2039 (Pearce) – passed committee, held in the House. A ballot referendum that, in addition to requiring law enforcement officers to fully implement all federal immigration laws, created a state crime of trespassing and imposed civil and criminal penalties for any undocumented person to enter or remain on public or private land in Arizona.

COMMERCIAL TRANSACTIONS AND CONTRACTS

2625 (Pearce) – passed committee, held in House. Prohibit landlords from knowingly or recklessly renting or leasing any property or dwelling to an undocumented person. Landlords who violate the provisions of this legislation would be subject to civil penalties.

2631 (Pearce) – bill not heard. Required applicants for marriage licenses in Arizona to provide proof of citizenship and valid social security identification.

LOCAL ENFORCEMENT OF FEDERAL IMMIGRATION LAW

2807 (Nelson) – passed both chambers, vetoed by Governor Napolitano. Required local law enforcement agencies to train law enforcement officials in the implementation of federal immigration laws, or to imbed ICE officers with the police force.

HCR 2064 (Nelson) – passed committee, held before floor vote. Voter referendum of same language as 2807.

2009

EDUCATION

1172 (Pearce) – bill was not heard. Required that the Department of Education collect data from school districts on the populations of undocumented students in their jurisdiction. The report must include an estimated cost of educating students who are undocumented. The legislation also gave the Superintendent of Public Instruction the ability to withhold a school district's state aid if the school district is non-compliant with this legislation.

EMPLOYMENT AND EMPLOYER SANCTIONS

1334 (Pearce) – bill was not heard. Prohibits undocumented workers from applying for or receiving workers' compensation when injured at the workplace.

1177 (Pearce) – bill was not heard. Prohibited an unlawfully present person from applying for work, soliciting work in a public place, or performing work as an employee or independent contractor.

DAY LABORERS

2533 (Kavanagh) passed the House, held in the Senate. Created a state crime for any person to stand in or along a street, highway or sidewalk to solicit employment from any person occupying a motor vehicle.

TRESPASSING

2280 (Kavanagh) – passed House and Senate, failed on final read. Required all local law enforcement officials to enforce all federal immigration laws at all times. The bill also created a state crime of trespassing and created civil and criminal penalties for any undocumented person who entered or remained on public or private land in Arizona.

1159 (Pearce) – bill was not heard. Created a state crime of trespassing and imposed civil and criminal penalties for any undocumented person to enter or remain on public or private land in Arizona. An identical measure, SCR 1010 (Pearce) was also not heard.

LOCAL ENFORCEMENT OF FEDERAL IMMIGRATION LAW

2331 (Boone) – passed House, held in the Senate. Prohibited local governments from enacting ordinances or resolutions that prohibited the lawful enforcement of federal immigration laws.

2280 (Kavanagh) – passed House and Senate, failed on final read. Required all local law enforcement officials to enforce all federal immigration laws.

2010

Education

1097 (Pearce) – passed the Senate and was held in a House Committee. Largely replicated SB 1172 from 2009.

Omnibus Legislation

1070 (Pearce) – passed both chambers, signed by Governor Brewer. Made numerous changes to state law regarding the mandated local law enforcement of federal immigration laws, the unlawful solicitation of labor, unlawful harboring and transporting of unlawfully present persons, and the impoundment of vehicle operated by undocumented persons.

2162 (Nichols) – passed both chambers, signed by Governor Brewer. Made limited adjustments to SB 1070.

2011

VOTING RIGHTS AND CITIZENSHIP

1308/1309 (Gould) –defeated by Senate. These bills seek to define Arizona citizenship as an individual born in the United States to parents who are citizens or legal permanent residents. Seeks to prevent the 14th Amendment birthright citizenship from applying to the children of undocumented persons.

2561/2562 (Kavanagh) – not heard in committee. Identical to 1308 and 1309.

PUBLIC BENEFITS

1222 (Biggs) – passed Senate, held in the House. Requires recipients of HUD public housing to demonstrate lawful presence; creates more restrictive regulations than federal law and excludes some lawful immigrants from the federal housing benefit.

1405 (Smith) – defeated by Senate. Requires hospitals to determine citizenship status of all patients and requires personnel to notify local immigration authorities if a patient is unlawfully present in the country.

EDUCATION

1407 (Smith) –defeated by Senate. Requires the Department of Education to collect data on populations of students who are enrolled in school districts and who are aliens who cannot prove lawful residence in the United States. Requires school districts to submit an annual report on this data, including research on the adverse impact of the enrollment of illegal students, and a detailed estimate of the total cost to the taxpayers for the education of undocumented students.

CRIMINAL JUSTICE AND THE COURTS

2191 (Weiers) – passed both chambers, signed by Governor. Retroactive measure that prohibits undocumented persons from receiving punitive damages in any civil action in the state.

EMPLOYMENT AND EMPLOYER SANCTIONS

1490 (Gould) – passed Senate, held in House. Prohibits counties from issuing food handler's cards to individuals who cannot provide documents indicating citizenship or alien status which prove an individual's legal presence in the United States.

2102 (Kavanagh) – passed House and Senate, signed by Governor. States that fingerprint clearance cards for employment be restricted to individuals who can prove lawful presence in the United States.

OMNIBUS LEGISLATION

1117 (Pearce) – passed both chambers and signed by Governor Brewer. Permits the leaders of the House and the Senate to participate in legal challenges to SB 1070 without seeking authorization from the Legislature. 2537 (Adams) – identical measure to 1117.

1611 (Pearce) – defeated by Senate. This "omnibus" legislation combines a number of former Pearce-sponsored bills from 2006 to 2010 into one piece of legislation, and adds new restrictive immigration measures. The measure restricts eligibility for federal, state and local benefits, prohibits undocumented persons from operating vehicles, requires proof of citizenship for K-12 school enrollment, prohibits undocumented individuals from enrolling in community colleges or universities, expands the e-verify program to all employers in the state, prohibits the recognition of consular cards as identification, requires proof of citizenship for title and registration of a vehicle, includes the provisions of 1222 (from 2011), revokes the certification of peace officers who fail to enforce all provisions of the law.

NOTE

1. This chapter does not discuss all anti-immigrant legislation introduced in Arizona during this time. Instead, it covers a sampling in an attempt to provide a broader picture of the types of legislation introduced in the Arizona Legislature. For a complete listing of anti-immigrant legislation introduced from 2003 to 2011, visit www.azleg.gov or contact the author of this chapter. Well over 100 bills on immigration have been introduced, debated, and voted on in Arizona over the last nine years.

REFERENCES

Arizona House Bill 2162. 2010.
http://www.azleg.gov/DocumentsForBill.asp?Bill_Number=2162&Session_Id=93&image.
    x=0&image.y=0.
Arizona House Bill 2243. 2003.
http://www.azleg.gov/DocumentsForBill.asp?Bill_Number=2243&Session_Id=76&image.
    x=0&image.y=0.
Arizona House Bill 2246. 2003.
http://www.azleg.gov/DocumentsForBill.asp?Bill_Number=2246&Session_Id=76&image.
    x=0&image.y=0.
Arizona House Bill 2280. 2009.
http://www.azleg.gov/DocumentsForBill.asp?Bill_Number=2280&Session_Id=87&image.
    x=0&image.y=0.
Arizona House Bill 2386. 2005.
http://www.azleg.gov/DocumentsForBill.asp?Bill_Number=2386&Session_Id=82&image.
    x=0&image.y=0.
Arizona House Bill 2577. 2006.
http://www.azleg.gov/DocumentsForBill.asp?Bill_Number=2577&Session_Id=83&image.
    x=0&image.y=0.
Arizona House Bill 2577 Governor's Veto Letter. 2006.
http://www.azleg.gov/GovernorLetters.asp.
Arizona House Bill 2745. 2008. http://www.azleg.gov/DocumentsForBill.asp?Bill_
    Number=2745&Session_Id=86&image.x=0&image.y=0.
Arizona House Bill 2779. 2007. http://www.azleg.gov/DocumentsForBill.asp?Bill_
    Number=2779&Session_Id=85&image.x=0&image.y=0.
Arizona House Bill 2807. 2008. http://www.azleg.gov/DocumentsForBill.asp?Bill_
    Number=2807&Session_Id=86&image.x=0&image.y=0.
Arizona House Bill 2807. Governor's Veto Letter. 2008. http://www.azleg.gov/GovernorLet-
    ters.asp.
Arizona House Concurrent Memorial 2005. 2007. http://www.azleg.gov/DocumentsForBill.
    asp?Bill_Number=HCM2005&Session_Id=85&image.x=0&image.y=0.

Arizona House Concurrent Resolution 2028. 2005. http://www.azleg.gov/DocumentsFor-Bill.asp?Bill_Number=HCR2028&Session_Id=82&image.x=0&image.y=0.

Arizona House Concurrent Resolution 2030. 2005. http://www.azleg.gov/DocumentsFor-Bill.asp?Bill_Number=HCR2030&Session_Id=82&image.x=0&image.y=0.

Arizona House Concurrent Resolution 2036. 2006. http://www.azleg.gov/DocumentsFor-Bill.asp?Bill_Number=HCR2036&Session_Id=83&image.x=0&image.y=0.

Arizona House Concurrent Resolution 2044. 2006. http://www.azleg.gov/DocumentsFor-Bill.asp?Bill_Number=HCR2044&Session_Id=83&image.x=0&image.y=0.

Arizona House Memorial 2003. 2002. http://www.azleg.gov/DocumentsForBill.asp?Bill_Number=HM2003&Session_ID=71.

Arizona Secretary of State Website, 2000. http://www.azsos.gov/election/2000/info/pub-pamphlet/english/prop204.htm (accessed January 20, 2012).

Arizona Senate Bill 1057. 2006. http://www.azleg.gov/DocumentsForBill.asp?Bill_Number=1057&Session_Id=83&image.x=0&image.y=0.

Arizona Senate Bill 1070. 2010. http://www.azleg.gov/DocumentsForBill.asp?Bill_Number=1070&Session_Id=9&image.x=0&image.y=0.

Arizona Senate Bill 1157. 2006. http://www.azleg.gov/DocumentsForBill.asp?Bill_Number=1157&Session_Id=83&image.x=0&image.y=0.

Arizona Senate Bill 1157 Governor's Veto Letter. 2006. http://www.azleg.gov/GovernorLet-ters.asp.

Arizona Senate Bill 1306. 2005. http://www.azleg.gov/DocumentsForBill.asp?Bill_Number=1306&Session_Id=82&image.x=0&image.y=0.

Arizona Senate Bill 1306 Governor's Veto Letter. 2005. http://www.azleg.gov/Governor-Letters.asp.

Arizona Senate Bill 1309. 2011. http://www.azleg.gov/DocumentsForBill.asp?Bill_Number=1309&Session_Id=102&image.x=0&image.y=0.

Arizona Senate Bill 1405. 2011. http://www.azleg.gov/DocumentsForBill.asp?Bill_Number=1405&Session_Id=102&image.x=0&image.y=0.

Arizona Senate Bill 1407. 2011. http://www.azleg.gov/DocumentsForBill.asp?Bill_Number=1407&Session_Id=102&image.x=0&image.y=0.

Arizona Senate Bill 1611. 2011. Available at http://azleg.gov/DocumentsForBill.asp?Bill_Number=1611&Session_Id=102&image.x=0&image.y=0.

Arizona Senate Concurrent Resolution 1001. 2006. http://www.azleg.gov/DocumentsFor-Bill.asp?Bill_Number=SCR1001&Session_Id=83&image.x=0&image.y=0.

Arizona Senate Concurrent Resolution 1016. 2008. http://www.azleg.gov/DocumentsFor-Bill.asp?Bill_Number=SCR1016&Session_Id=86&image.x=0&image.y=0.

Arizona Senate Concurrent Resolution 1031. 2006. http://www.azleg.gov/DocumentsFor-Bill.asp?Bill_Number=SCR1031&Session_Id=83&image.x=0&image.y=0.

Ballot Initiative Strategies Center. 2011. http://www.ballot.org/pages/an_overview_of_ballot_measures.

Becker, Howard S. 1963. *Outsiders: Studies in the Sociology of Deviance.* New York: Free Press.

Birthright Citizenship Act of 2011. H.R. 140, 2011. http://thomas.loc.gov/cgi-bin/thomas.

FAIR Website, 2011. http://www.fairus.org/site/PageNavigator/about.html (accessed January 20, 2012).

Federation for American Immigration Reform. 2010. http://www.fairus.org/site/PageNavigator/about/.H.R. 140 (January 5, 2011).

Fischer, Howard. Ninth Circuit: Arizona Cannot Enforce Key Parts of SB 1070. East Valley Tribune, April 11, 2011. http://www.eastvalleytribune.com/arizona/article_f3379bf4-6462-11e0-875e-001cc4c002e0.html.

Immigration Law Reform Institute. 2010. http://www.irli.org/.

Johnson, Alex. 2009. "Pro-English measures being revived across U.S. Congress: States consider new proposals to declare an 'official language.'" MSNBC, June 15, http://www.msnbc.msn.com/id/31176525/ns/us_news-life/.

Maines, Sophia and Scott Rothschild. 2006. "Immigration Tuition Law on Trial." *Lawrence Journal and World News*, September 28, http://www2.ljworld.com/news/2006/sep/28/immigrant_tuition_law_trial/.

Moeser, Chris. 1999. "3 ADOT officials are fired." *The Arizona Republic*, August 21.

National Conference of State Legislators (NCSL). 2010. *2010 Immigration-Related Laws and Resolutions in the States (January-June 2010)*, http://www.ncsl.org/default.aspx?tabid=20881.

Nevins, Joseph. 2010. *Operation Gatekeeper and Beyond: The War on "Illegals" and the Remaking of the U.S.-Mexico Boundary*. Routledge: New York.

Oppel, Richard A. 2011. "Arizona, Bowing to Business, Softens Stand on Immigration." *New York Times*, March 18; http://www.nytimes.com/2011/03/19/us/19immigration.html.

Phoenix Business Journal. 2010. "Rasmussen poll: Immigrant babies should not get citizenship." August 2, http://www.bizjournals.com/phoenix/stories/2010/08/02/daily10.html.

Progressive States Action. 2001. http://www.progressivestatesaction.org/campaigns/immigration.

Proposition 100, Bailable Offenses Election Results. 2006. http://www.azsos.gov/results/2006/general/BM100.htm.

Proposition 102, Standing in Civil Actions Election Results. 2006. http://www.azsos.gov/results/2006/general/BM102.htm.

Proposition 103, English as the Official Language Election Results. 2006. http://www.azsos.gov/results/2006/general/BM103.htm.

Proposition 106, English as the Official Language, 1988. http://www.languagepolicy.net/archives/art28.htm.

Proposition 200, the Arizona Taxpayer and Citizen Protection Act. 2004. http://www.azsos.gov/election/2004/general/I-03-2004.htm.

Proposition 203, English for the Children. 2000. http://www.azsos.gov/election/2000/info/PubPamphlet/english/prop203.htm.

Proposition 300, Public Programs Eligibility Election Results. 2006. http://www.azsos.gov/results/2006/general/BM300.htm.

Raghunathan, Suman. 2010. Personal Interview with author, October 29. Raghunathan is the Immigration Policy Specialist at the Progressive States Network.

Rau, Alia. 2010. "Pearce legislation takes aim at Fourteenth Amendment." *Arizona Republic*, October 20, http://www.azcentral.com/arizonarepublic/local/articles/2010/10/20/20101020pearceplan1020.html.

Robertson, Campbell. Alabama Wins in Ruling on Its Immigration Law. *New York Times*, Sept 28, 2011. http://www.nytimes.com/2011/09/29/us/alabama-immigration-law-upheld.html.

Senate Concurrent Memorial 1003, 2008. http://www.azleg.gov/DocumentsForBill.asp?Bill_Number=SCM1003&Session_Id=86&image.x=0&image.y=0.

Sharry, Frank. 2010. "Shocker: Most Backers of Arizona Law Support Humane Immigration Reform." *Huffington Post*, June 2, http://www.huffingtonpost.com/frank-sharry/shocker-most-backers-of-a_b_597481.html.

Sinema, Kyrsten. 2010. Email from Kris Kobach to Senator Russell Pearce in which Kobach instructs Senator Pearce to amend language of HB 2162 to include civil code violations. On file with author.

Sullivan, Laura. 2010a. "Prison Economics Help Drive Ariz. Immigration Law." *National Public Radio*, October 28, http://www.npr.org/templates/story/story.php?storyId=130833741.

Sullivan, Laura. 2010b. "Shaping State Laws With Little Scrutiny." *National Public Radio*, October 29, http://www.npr.org/templates/story/story.php?storyId=130891396.

U.S. Government Accountability Office. August 2006. "*GAO-06-770 Illegal Immigration: Border-Crossing Deaths Have Doubled Since 1995.*" http://www.gao.gov/new.items/d06770.pdf.

U.S. Border Patrol. 2005. "Apprehension Statistics 1993–2004: Data Presented in Actual Numbers and as a Percentage of Total Southwest Apprehensions," http://www.lawg.org/docs/apprehension stats.pdf.

Welcoming America. 2011. http://www.welcomingamerica.org/.

PART II

Consequences for Individuals and Communities

5

Unearthing and Confronting the Social Skeletons of Immigration Status in Our Criminal Justice System

EVELYN H. CRUZ

The need for competent representation of noncitizens[1] in criminal proceedings has never been more critical. As documented extensively in the first section of the volume, in the last 20 years, domestic immigration laws have become more complex and severe. Additionally, the line between criminal proceedings and immigration proceedings has blurred. Today, what is decided in the criminal case may very well seal the noncitizen's fate in the removal process. And, in the name of efficiency, law enforcement agencies are pressing the judicial system to combine criminal and immigration proceedings into one simultaneous administration in which one tribunal decides both the criminal and immigration fates of the noncitizen defendant (Taylor and Wright 2002: 1151–57).

For criminal tribunals, the convergence of criminal and immigration law in the courtroom challenges the judge who "bears the 'heavy responsibility' for presiding over a 'fair' proceeding, which includes not only what occurs at trial itself, but outcomes produced by the common result of settlement"(Pearce 2004: 978 n.48). The noncitizen status of the defendant alters the stakes of the criminal proceedings and, if ignored, fosters distrust of the judicial system.

Noncitizen criminal defendants find themselves on unequal footing with U.S. citizen defendants. Noncitizens are often subjected to disparate treatment in bail and sentencing because of their immigration status (*Ruvalcaba v. Nevada* 2006). The threat of removal looms large in the criminal proceedings. These inequalities lead to disillusionment with the American legal system and its effectiveness.

There is a social ripple effect to the noncitizen's encounters with the judicial system. Mixed-status families are a fact of life in immigrant communities. Over half of the 16 million Latino children in the United States have at least one immigrant parent (Fry and Passel 2009). Of all new lawful permanent residents, 65 percent obtain status based on a family relationship with a U.S. citizen or lawful permanent resident of the United States (USDHS 2009). A majority of Latinos, even in the absence of criminal proceedings, worry about deportation—their own or that of a family member. As a result, the despair and disillusionment that noncitizen defendants feel toward the legal system spills over to the entire population (Lopez and Minushkin 2008b).

In February 2009, the U.S. Supreme Court granted a *writ of certiorari* to *Padilla v. Commonwealth of Kentucky* to consider whether criminal defense counsel must inform a client of the immigration consequences of a plea; and whether a noncitizen may be allowed to set aside a plea when defense counsel has grossly misadvised the defendant on the immigration consequences of the plea (*Padilla v. Kentucky* 2009). Behind the legal issue lies a larger policy question—whether it is appropriate for our criminal justice system to continue to ignore the primacy citizenship status plays in immigrant communities' relationships to the judicial system. The Supreme Court's answer was a resounding no.

The Supreme Court's decision on *Padilla v. Kentucky* was handed down March 31, 2010. Placing the concern of immigration consequences of criminal convictions in its proper context, retiring Justice Stevens wrote,

> The importance of accurate legal advice for noncitizens accused of crimes has never been more important. These changes confirm our view, that as a matter of federal law, deportation is an integral part—indeed, sometimes the most important part—of the penalty that may be imposed on noncitizen defendants who plead guilty to specific crimes. (*Padilla v. Kentucky* 2010: 1481)

Through *Padilla v. Kentucky*, the Supreme Court took the opportunity to accept the reality that expertise and advice on immigration consequences are part and parcel of a defense attorney's duty to a noncitizen client. Specifically, the Court acknowledged that the immigration consequences of a criminal conviction and an individual's status as a noncitizen are not collateral, but rather are an essential part of a defendant's decision to accept a plea agreement (Chin and Holmes 2002). But *Padilla v. Kentucky* also presents the opportunity for the criminal legal system to advance due process protection to noncitizen defendants in criminal proceedings beyond *Padilla*, and include advances in holistic[2] and preventive law practice (Hardaway 1997).

This chapter reviews the current due process protections afforded to noncitizens in criminal proceedings and the impact current practices have on immigrant communities. The narrative provides an additional example for the volume's conversation on the impact of policies and practices driven primarily by immigration control goals. I illustrate the phenomenon by drawing on two poignant examples: The federal criminal prosecutions of undocumented workers in Postville, and the related experiences of criminal defense attorneys in Arizona assisting noncitizen defendants. What I find is that noncitizens without immigration status often carry a sense of guilt arising from their unlawful status, which affects their choices and interactions with the criminal courts. Unfortunately, the sense of guilt is amplified by inequalities in charges, punishment, and redemption in criminal proceedings. Noncitizen criminal defendants are not the only ones suspicious of the criminal justice system; the recent upsurge of immigration enforcement has led to an increased distrust of the U.S. justice system by immigrant communities in general (Menjívar and Bejarano 2004).

The ramifications of these phenomena have been immediate and profound. Latino confidence in the criminal justice system has declined as policies that fuse criminal and immigration laws grow. For these reasons, both attorneys and the courts must be sensitive to preserving the due process rights of vulnerable populations including noncitizens. The recent *Padilla v. Kentucky* decision supporting noncitizens' right to meaningful representation will bolster trust of noncitizens in our legal institutions by requiring attorneys to acknowledge the primacy immigration status plays in the decision making of noncitizen criminal defendants.

The Criminal Justice System Noncitizens Face
Criminal Prosecution of Noncitizens by the Federal Government: Postville

On May 12, 2008, the Department of Justice (DOJ), in collaboration with the Department of Homeland Security's Immigration and Customs Enforcement (ICE), arrested nearly 400 undocumented workers at a meat processing plant in Postville, Iowa (Speper 2008). Of those arrested, 306 were turned over to the U.S. Attorney for the Northern District of Iowa to face criminal charges under 18 U.S.C. §1546(a) (possession /use of a fraudulent immigration document) and 42 U.S.C. §408(a)(7) (false representation of a social security number). In addition, the government threatened defendants with 18 U.S.C. §1028A(a) (aggravated identity theft).

The criminal charges were considerable, carrying potential sentences of several years. Just as significant, a guilty plea automatically made the individual ineligible for several forms of immigration relief, including family visa petitions, asylum, and cancellation of removal, which account for over 80 percent of the available relief to individuals living without immigration status in the United States (USDHS 2008). Moreover, even if some hope of immigration relief might have remained after conviction, it vanished when the individual waived the right to defend against removal from the United States. The only good news for the 300 or so individuals was that since they were defendants in criminal proceedings, they were entitled to appointed criminal defense counsel, albeit not necessarily counsel with immigration expertise, time, or fluency in the noncitizen's native language (Camayd-Freixas 2008).

The Postville defendants, who were simultaneously prosecuted for crimes and processed for immigration removal, were all offered the same standard plea of a five-month sentence for misuse of false documents and a removal agreement that read as follows:

> Stipulated judicial order of removal: The parties agree defendant is subject to removal from the United States. Defendant waives the right to notice and a hearing before an immigration judge and stipulates to entry of a judicial order of removal from the United States. ("*Sample Plea Agreement*" 2008: 1)

Time played a pivotal role in the Postville proceedings. ICE, the Federal Prosecutor's Office, and the District Court had coordinated a plan to swiftly adjudicate the cases (Schau 2008). A 60-acre cattle fairground was rented, a manual for public defenders was produced, and a standard plea agreement was drafted. The court convened a meeting of local defense attorneys and interpreters, asking them to keep their calendars open for mid-May and to tell no one of the request. The Postville defendants were arraigned in groups of ten, given seven days to accept a plea, and sentenced less than two weeks after arrest (Moyers 2009).

The aggressive prosecutorial practices and assembly line judicial proceedings virtually compelled the defendants' acquiescence to the criminal charges. They were segregated from their families and support system and rushed through the criminal judicial system. As one of the interpreters, Professor Camayd-Freixas, noted in frustration, "They needed much more time and individualized legal counsel than could be remotely provided by this fast-tracking process under the average ratio of 17 clients per attorney" (Camayd-Freixas 2008: 7). Many of the Postville defendants were immigrants from Guatemala and Mexico, countries where judicial corruption and governmental abuses are well documented (U.S. State Department 2009). The Postville adjudications likely elicited the same distrust defendants had for the judicial system of their home country.

Both Dr. Camayd-Freixas, and then judicial clerk Moyers, note in their written accounts of the events that the defendants appeared worried, fearful, overwhelmed, and embarrassed at the proceedings and when meeting with defense counsel (Camayd-Freixas 2008; Moyers 2009). The defense attorneys noted in post-representation interviews that all of their Postville clients had at least a generalized sense of culpability arising from their possession and use of fraudulent identification documents or means of identification and, as such, felt they had no right to redemption. However, the reality was that the mere use of fake documents did not close the door on their ability to secure immigration relief. Immigration statutes provide for waiver of document fraud convictions. But convictions for the harsher identity theft charge are more problematic. Noncitizens convicted of identity theft are only eligible for removal protection under the Convention Against Torture, which disallows the return of deportees to a country where they will face government torture. So, although a number of defendants had a vested interest in fighting their charges, and ultimately removal from the United States, many felt their status as undocumented sealed their ultimate fate. Consequently, as then judicial law clerk Peter R. Moyers observes, "The accelerated plea process was also a result of the uniform sense of guilt among the defendants" (Moyers 2009: 678).

Criminal Prosecution of Noncitizens by States: Arizona

Events like Postville, fortunately, do not happen every day. However, noncitizen defendants regularly face similar challenges in criminal courts across the country. The state of Arizona, for instance, subjects noncitizens to immigration status checks, bail restrictions, and stepped-up prosecution (Ariz. Const. Art. II Sec. 22).

In addition to the host of acts that typically lead to criminal prosecution, it is not unusual for undocumented noncitizens in Arizona to face prosecution for charges linked to their immigration status. Beginning in 2006, Arizona law enforcement began experimenting with using criminal statutes to prosecute undocumented aliens in the hopes that a hostile environment would force them from the state. The first law enacted made smuggling a state crime (Ariz. Code Anno. §13-2319). Although most county attorney offices have used the statute to prosecute human smuggling rings, Maricopa County Attorney Andrew Thomas began charging immigrants arrested in the company of smugglers with "conspiracy to smuggle" (*Arizona v. Barragan-Serra* 2008). In 2008, the Arizona legislature enacted an employer sanctions law. Under the statute, employers who fail to confirm the lawful status of employees could face loss of their business license (Ariz. Code Anno. §§ 23-211, 23-212). The Maricopa County Sheriff has utilized the statute to conduct raids at local businesses in order to arrest employees in possession of fake documents and prosecute them for forgery and identity theft charges. Few, if any, employers have had their business license revoked under the statute (Harris 2009). Most recently, as discussed at length in Sinema's chapter, the Arizona legislature enacted SB 1070, creating a number of additional state crimes targeting aliens. Although much of the statute has been enjoined by the federal district court, provisions prohibiting the blocking of traffic when hiring undocumented day laborers, and harboring and transporting of undocumented aliens when in violation of a criminal law, are still in effect and may lead to the prosecution of even more undocumented persons.

Arizona also has employed federal law in its quest to use the state criminal system for immigration enforcement. Congress enacted 8 USC §1357(g) as part of the Illegal Immigration Reform and Immigrant Responsibility Act of 1996. The statute authorized ICE "to enter into written agreements under which state or local enforcement agencies may perform, at their own expense and under the supervision of ICE officers, certain functions of an immigration officer in relation to the investigation, apprehension, or detention of aliens in the United States" (8 USC 1357(g)). The "287(g) Program," as it is commonly known, permits state and local officers to tap into the ICE database, to issue Notice to Appear (NTA) orders which initiate the immigration removal process, and to participate in federal criminal task forces.

Several counties in Arizona participate in the 287(g) program (ICE 2010). Noncitizens, and those who are not readily identified as citizens, must be interviewed by an officer about their immigration status. This interview often occurs before the defendant is seen by the judge, and in many cases before he or she is able to meet with an attorney. According to one criminal law attorney practicing in Tucson who was interviewed for this chapter,

When the court determines that they have an alien the name is hyphenated. Once the hyphenated tag is attached a number of things occur. . . . the U.S. Marshall notifies ICE so a detainer is placed on all hyphenated defendants. Judges and pretrial services assume the detainer is the equivalent of an arrest warrant and refuse to accept that it is only an investigatory detainer limited in time and with an unclear impact on the defendant's future.

In 2006, Arizona voters passed Proposition 100, which limits the availability of bail for defendants suspected of being unlawfully in the country and charged with a felony. In addition, noncitizens who are eligible for bail face different treatment depending on the county in which they are located. In Pima County, defense attorneys report that, "Once the detainer is in place there is an unwritten rule that the hyphenated defendant will not get a bond, and in order to get a bond a much higher threshold needs to be met." Defense attorneys in Maricopa find that courts often agree to release noncitizen defendants who are not subject to Proposition 100 without requiring bail. However, a release from state detention does not automatically signify the individual is free to go, as they are transferred to ICE custody where they face a federal bond process.

Once in court, the immigration consequences of the charges often dictate the litigation choices, regardless of the nature of the charges (misdemeanor or felony). A practicing Arizona criminal law attorney explains,

Immigration status is often the *most* important factor in a criminal defendant's analysis of his case. Quite often they are charged with crimes that, in and of themselves, are relatively minor [such as misdemeanor DUI], however they choose to fight the charge in order to give them a chance to obtain or preserve their immigration status. Quite often, also, they are charged with immigration damaging crimes that are not so bad for citizens [for example, shoplifting or prostitution]. The incentive is even higher in those instances to fight the criminal case. In either event, the desire to remain within the U.S., even in the face of severe odds, often compels noncitizens to fight their criminal cases with as much vigor as they can muster.

The noncitizen's status regularly affects the disposition of the case. Defense attorneys complain that prosecutors often do not offer undocumented defendants diversion programs because they believe these individuals will not able to complete the program before deportation. Moreover, diversion is not as beneficial for noncitizens because they will still have a conviction for immigration purposes. Defendants have little power in negotiating a plea to charges that carry lesser immigration consequences.

The Criminal Bar's Obligations to Noncitizen Defendants

The Supreme Court recognizes that the Sixth Amendment guarantees the right to effective assistance of counsel. Furthermore, the Federal Rules of Criminal Procedure mandate courts to set aside convictions where ineffective assistance of counsel prevented a defendant from receiving a fair trial or entering a voluntary plea. The test developed requires the defendant to demonstrate that: (1) the counsel's assistance was not within the range of competence demanded of attorneys in criminal cases; and (2) a reasonable probability exists that he/she would not have pleaded guilty had his or her counsel been competent. The Supreme Court, however, did not provide a framework or guidelines defining the minimum level of competency required of counsel, choosing instead to leave the establishment of such standards to the legal profession.

State standards of professional conduct throughout the country require that attorneys provide competent representation to a client. The attorney must have the necessary knowledge and skill to address the client's legal problem. The rules permit attorneys to limit the scope of representation they provide, and consequently the spectrum of expertise required from the attorney. In most respects, this narrowing creates few problems when legal issues can be segregated, but unfortunately, immigration and criminal law are not easily separated. A criminal law attorney's attempt to limit the scope of representation to criminal law advice raises ethical concerns because of the direct impact criminal convictions have on immigration relief and vice versa. Decisions such as what information is placed on the record, which criminal code section is pled, and which exact sentence is served have strategic value in a criminal case, but these considerations may have completely different value in a noncitizen defendant's subsequent immigration case. For instance, a sentence of 364 days is not dissimilar to a sentence of 365 days in the criminal context; however, for immigration purposes, one day may mean the difference between having no immigration relief and having a chance to remain in the country. Under 8 U.S.C. 101(a)(43)(F), a conviction for a crime of violence with a sentence of one year renders an individual an "aggravated felon" and ineligible for most immigration relief. If, however, an individual is sentenced to less than one year for the same crime, he or she is not deemed an aggravated felon. Although the individual may remain removable under the immigration statute, the fact that he/she is not an aggravated felon will significantly improve his/her ability to obtain immigration relief.

The need for defense counsel with immigration expertise is essential in plea agreement negotiations. Federal prosecutors are directed to use immigration as a bargaining chip in plea negotiation. If the individual's attorney is not well-versed in the immigration consequences of criminal convictions, immigration removal proceedings, or available immigration remedies, the noncitizen is disadvantaged in the consideration of the plea.

Consequently, the American Bar Association Standards for Criminal Justice explicitly define competency to include knowledge and skill to identify and advise clients of the immigration consequences of a guilty plea or conviction (ABA 1999). While the standards are not binding, "the standards do, however, represent the considered consensus views of prosecutors, defenders, and judges, and constitute a realistic and balanced approach to criminal justice that has proven effective over time" (ABA 1999: 3).

Attempting to maintain a divide between immigration and criminal legal representation is inconsistent with the legislative landscape. Congress and some states have significantly altered the treatment of noncitizens in criminal proceedings. Statutes have been amended to require that noncitizens face additional immigration consequences upon conviction. Often there is specific language that removes any doubt that conviction of a given particular crime may lead to an initiation of removal proceedings. Even in those situations involving criminal convictions that do not have a clearly defined immigration consequence, courts are often bound to sentencing and bail statutes that factor in citizenship status (Taylor and Wright 2002). For the criminal attorneys in the trenches, the legislative changes mean that boundaries between zones of representation are fading. It has become difficult to distinguish between necessary and optional legal advice.

In *Padilla v. Kentucky*, the Supreme Court concluded that, given the intimate relationship between immigration and criminal penalties, it was difficult to divorce one from the other, and therefore impractical to view the immigration consequences as either direct or collateral to the criminal conviction. Rather, the proper inquiry was to examine whether the attorney's representation fell below the objective standard of reasonableness (*Padilla v. Kentucky* 2010).

Citing *Strickland v. Washington*, the court noted that prevailing professional norms were critical to said assessment. Moreover, given that a large number of legal professional organizations and criminal practice authorities agree that criminal defense attorneys need to advise noncitizen defendants on the risk of deportation, the Court reasoned it was not unexpected to require attorneys to provide noncitizen clients advice regarding the immigration consequences of the criminal case (*Padilla v. Kentucky* 2010).

Requiring criminal law attorneys to have immigration law expertise is controversial, however. The more knowledge is demanded of the attorney, the more potential malpractice liability exists. Immigration law has grown extremely complex in the last 20 years, especially with regard to criminal law. Burdening criminal defense attorneys, many of whom work in understaffed public defenders' offices, with the additional duty of knowing immigration law creates resource allocation problems. Public defenders cannot handle the same volume of cases if they have to navigate criminal and immigration laws.

Leading up to the decision, the Solicitor General had proposed the Court limit the defense counsel's responsibility to merely not providing erroneous advice, thereby tailoring the holding to Mr. Padilla's factual circumstances. Justices Alito and Roberts fervently agreed in their concurring opinion. Justice Alito considered it unreasonable to expect criminal law attorneys to possess expertise in immigration law, especially in light of immigration law's complexity (*Padilla v. Kentucky* 2010). Justice Alito instead proposed it was more reasonable to expect an attorney to refrain from providing advice outside his or her field of practice.

The majority, however, were not persuaded by such concerns. After all, the inclusion of proper immigration advice in criminal proceedings is consistent with current criminal alien suppression trends, is already a part of the client advocacy culture, and is necessary to maintain the proper function and acceptance of the criminal justice system. Even the Supreme Court in *St. Cyr* recognized the important role immigration consequences play in a noncitizen's decision to plea, and concurred with the Ninth Circuit's *Magana-Pizano* opinion "that an alien charged with a crime . . . would factor the immigration consequences of conviction in deciding whether to plead or proceed to trial is well-documented" (*Magana-Pizano v. INS* 1999: 612). Moreover, Justice Stevens noted,

> A holding limited to affirmative misadvice would invite two absurd results. First, it would give counsel an incentive to remain silent on matters of great importance, even when answers are readily available. Silence under these circumstances would be fundamentally at odds with the critical obligation of counsel to advise the client of "the advantages and disadvantages of a plea agreement". . . Second, it would deny a class of clients least able to represent themselves the most rudimentary advice on deportation even when it is readily available. (*Padilla v. Kentucky* 2010: 1484; *INS v. St. Cyr* 2001)

While Justice Stevens was confident that a majority of the criminal bar had adopted the practice of informing noncitizen defendants of the immigration consequences of criminal convictions, the reality of a mandatory duty to do so raised eyebrows among practitioners. Fortunately, just days after the decision, Manuel D. Vargas of the Immigrant Defense Project drafted and disseminated an excellent practice advisory that provided information on the *Padilla v. Kentucky* decision and an extensive list of resources for practitioners (Vargas 2010). Over the next several years, these resources should lead to a steady rise in the quality of the criminal bar's ability to evaluate immigration consequences of criminal convictions.

Steamroller Prosecution

The Supreme Court has said that the prosecutor's duty in a criminal prosecution is not to win but to seek justice (*Berger v. U.S.* 1935). Under the ABA Model Rules of Professional Conduct, prosecutors have a special duty to criminal defendants:

> A prosecutor has the responsibility of a minister of justice and not simply that of an advocate. This responsibility carries with it specific obligations to see that the defendant is accorded prosecutorial justice, that guilt is decided upon the basis of sufficient evidence, and that special precautions are taken to prevent and to rectify the convictions of innocent persons. (Model Rules 2009:§3.8 comment 1)

What's more, prosecutors have broad discretion to decide what charges to bring, negotiate plea bargains, or even to dismiss charges. Consequently, Justice Stevens proposed that "informed consideration of possible deportation can only benefit both the State and noncitizen defendants during the plea-bargaining process. By bringing deportation consequences into this process, the defense and prosecution may well be able to reach agreements that better satisfy the interest of both parties" (*Padilla v. Kentucky* 2010: 1486).

The Supreme Court did not discourage prosecutors from factoring the noncitizen status of the defendant into the plea bargain process: "the threat of deportation may provide the defendant with a powerful incentive to plead guilty to an offence that does not mandate that [deportation] penalty in exchange for a dismissal of a charge that does" (*Padilla v. Kentucky* 2010: 1486).

However, deportation as a bargaining chip in the plea process is not the same as having deportation constitute the goal of the plea process. This was the case in Postville. The prosecutors were specifically seeking to remove noncitizen defendants regardless of other options. The prosecutors could have turned the defendants over to ICE for removal proceedings instead of seeking a plea that included a criminal conviction and automatic removal. In Postville, prosecutors pursued the most damaging criminal charges they could muster by charging, or threatening to charge, the workers with felonies for document fraud and/or identity theft. In Arizona, defense attorneys also encounter state prosecutors who choose to prosecute noncitizens for charges that impede their ability to remain in the United States. As this defense attorney noted in our interview,

> It did not used to make a difference for prosecutors until County Attorney Thomas' office and the types of pleas offered became more limited. It was obvious that Thomas did not want people to try to obtain any immigration benefit. So, if a deviation or charge was requested to keep folks from having inadmissible offenses, they were denied.

Despite the constraints in the plea agreement negotiations, noncitizen defendants in Arizona hesitate to press their luck with the jury. Arizona defense attorneys acknowledge that,

> Even if the prosecutor does not allege or mention any issue regarding status, they know a Maricopa jury is clearly not the most unbiased. If a person is using an interpreter and looks Latino, a jury is likely to make certain presumptions about the noncitizens that he would not make of Anglo defendants. This is an unfortunate side issue, but undocumented defendants know it can make a difference in a close case.

The Judge's Responsibility to Protect the Due Process Rights of Noncitizen Defendants

The courts have found that, at a minimum, in immigration proceedings, which are civil, noncitizens must be given notice of the fact that they are facing removal from the United States, that they have an opportunity to defend their right to remain in the country, and that they are entitled to an impartial forum. In criminal proceedings, the Constitution does not segregate defendants by immigration status and therefore noncitizen defendants should expect the same due process protection as any other defendant. As Justice Stevens explains, "It is our responsibility under the Constitution to ensure that no criminal defendant—whether a citizen or not—is left to the 'mercies of incompetent counsel'" (*Padilla v. Kentucky* 2010: 1486). However, equal treatment does not always mean the same treatment. Judges must be cognizant of the codependency between immigration and criminal laws in our justice system. The plea agreement process presents an illustration.

As noted earlier, it is the prosecutor—not the judge—who controls what charges and plea deals are offered to defendants. Yet the judge is not completely powerless in the plea process. In *Brady v. United States*, the Supreme Court mandated criminal tribunals to accept a guilty plea only from defendants "fully aware of the direct consequences, including the actual value of any commitments made to him by the court, prosecutor, or his own counsel" (*Brady v. U.S.* 1970: 755). Judges are required to determine whether a defendant's guilty plea is voluntary, knowing, and intelligent. In accepting a plea, a defendant gives up critical rights, so the judge must ensure that defendants are neither coerced nor misinformed in the choice.

It is crucial that a warning about consequences be given as soon as possible because the likelihood of successfully withdrawing a plea depends on the timing of the withdrawal. For instance, withdrawal is generally permitted before the court accepts the plea. But if the defendant seeks to withdraw the plea after the court has accepted it, the court requires a "fair and just reason" for withdrawal. Guilty pleas cannot be withdrawn once a sentence has been imposed. Once a trial has ended, pleas can be withdrawn through direct appeal or collateral attack, and only where necessary to correct a miscarriage of justice.

The Supreme Court in *Brady* did not bind tribunals to make certain the defendant was aware of all the consequences of a guilty plea, and it did not clearly delineate what it meant by "direct consequences." As a result, lower courts have categorized consequences either as direct or collateral. In *Padilla v. Kentucky*, the court made it clear that the immigration consequences of a criminal conviction are direct consequences of a guilty plea. It follows that when accepting a plea from a noncitizen, the trial court must confirm that the accused understand these consequences.

Interestingly, in his *Padilla v. Kentucky* concurrence, Justice Alito alludes to the utility of noncitizen warnings by the court as a possible solution to the problem. Such warnings, he believes, "can ensure that a defendant receives needed information without putting a large number of criminal convictions at risk" (*Padilla v. Kentucky* 2010: Concurring at 1491). Justice Alito further predicted that the Court's holding in *Padilla v. Kentucky* would derail efforts to require criminal courts to provide noncitizen warnings.

Other than acknowledging in a footnote that a number of jurisdictions require courts to provide noncitizen warnings, Justice Stevens did not address Justice Alito's concern. However, his silence should not be interpreted to mean the Court finds that noncitizen warnings are superfluous after *Padilla v. Kentucky*. Rather, Justice Stevens seems to be limiting the court's attention to the role of counsel in the criminal process and not closing the door on the utility of noncitizen warnings.

A growing number of state jurisdictions, including Arizona, require by statute that judges alert noncitizen defendants of the possibility that the conviction may result in immigration consequences. Arizona Rule 17.2 requires judges to read the following statement to all defendants:

> If you are not a citizen of the United States, pleading guilty or no contest to a crime may affect your immigration status. Admitting guilt may result in deportation even if the charge is later dismissed. Your plea or admission of guilt could result in your deportation or removal, could prevent you from ever being able to get legal status in the United States, or could prevent you from becoming a United States citizen. (Ariz. R. Crim Pro 2009: 17.2(f))

A generic warning from the judge alone will not provide the necessary protections for noncitizen defendants. To be confident of a decision, the defendant will need time to consult with an attorney, hoping that the attorney competently advises the defendant on all consequences of the proposed plea. Nevertheless, the inclusion of a noncitizen warning in criminal proceedings, or at the very least an acknowledgment by the court of the value that obtaining or preserving legal immigration status has on a defendant's decision making, is a crucial step in improving the delivery of due process to noncitizens—bringing to full circle the interconnection between the tribunal and advocates and providing a true forum where litigants feel that they have a meaningful voice (Petrucci, Wexler, and Winick 2003).

Dr. Camayd-Freixas, who served as a court-appointed interpreter for the Postville defendants, observes that one judge took the time to explain to a Postville defendant that he could not depart from the plea agreement because to do so would expose the defendant to a trial, forcing the defendant to remain in jail, which the defendant indicated he did not want. Beyond that, the judge acknowledged the defendants' humanity, noting, "I appreciate the fact that you are very hard working people who have come here to do no harm. And I thank you for coming to this country to work hard. Unfortunately, you broke a law in the process, and now I have the obligation to give you this sentence" (Camayd-Freixas 2008: 8). The judge displayed care, compassion, and a desire for the defendants to understand the judicial process. In turn the defendants, "thanked him, and I saw their faces change from shame to admiration, their dignity restored" (Camayd-Freixas 2008: 8).

Neither Rule 11 nor judicial precedent required the Postville judges to inform the defendants of the immigration ramifications of guilty pleas, even though the plea included an order of removal and despite the fact that deportation was a condition of probation. However, the judge's actions reflect an honest adherence to the ideal that a plea be voluntary, knowing, and intelligent (*Brady v. U.S.* 1970). And, although it remains the duty of the criminal defense counsel to provide defendants with the necessary legal advice, there is value in judges taking an active role in acknowledging the defendant's humanity. Judges are, after all, the face of the legal system (Petrucci et al. 2003).

Our Nation's Responsibility to Provide Fair and Transparent Adjudications

Society demands from our criminal court system a reasoned and impartial decision through a fair and transparent court process, comforting us that justice has prevailed and proving that our tribunals are fair. Petrucci and colleagues (2003) point out, "As viewed by litigants and the general public, the fairness of court processes depends on the extent to which judicial officers are neutral and unbiased, respectful, allow those affected to participate meaningfully in the decision-making process, and, most importantly, are trustworthy" (152).

The goal of a more transparent and accessible justice system has gained substantial momentum among legal professionals in the past several years and it is most visible in the creation of problem solving courts, outreach programs, and professional development continuing education courses that emphasize empathy and care (Stolle, Wexler, and Winick 2000). Winick and Wexler (2000) promote a revamping of the legal process to include more disclosures, information, and opportunities for meaningful litigant participation. Several scholars have promoted techniques aimed at addressing clients' legal needs with dignity and encouraging attorneys to bear witness to their clients' humanity and psychological well-being as the criminal court system meanders down its path.

Judicial clerk Moyers writes in his Postville article, "It is unreasonably optimistic to expect each and every client, i.e., a less educated, non-English speaker, to grasp the nuances of an unfamiliar criminal justice system, as well as its interaction with prevailing immigration law" (Moyers 2009: 675). I disagree. Providing clients a transparent view of the process, the options, and the ramifications is precisely what attorneys do. Moreover, it is what a number of attorneys attempted to accomplish by Moyers' own accounts in

Postville. The oppressively rushed nature of the proceedings crippled their efforts.

By all accounts, noncitizen defendants in these proceedings exhibit psychological reactions to the criminal proceedings. For more than 20 years, a group of legal scholars working under the umbrella of therapeutic jurisprudence has explored the positive and negative psychological consequences of the legal process on litigants. Therapeutic jurisprudence maintains that when attorneys fail to acknowledge their clients' negative emotional reactions to the judicial process, the clients are inclined to regard the lawyer as indifferent and part of a criminal system bent on punishment. By contrast, when attorneys are sensitive to these emotions and seek to address the clients' psychological soft spots, clients see the attorneys as allies and become more responsive to their legal assistance (Stolle et al. 2000).

Social cognition literature demonstrates that the more information litigants possess, the better they are able to adjust to the stressful circumstances and address the challenges (Fiske and Taylor 1984). Individuals feel better about making decisions when they have a degree of control and self-determination. Litigants are more likely to accept the resolution of their cases if they believe they had an opportunity to be heard by an impartial tribunal (Warren 2000). Without reassurances of fair proceedings, and with little time to compose themselves, noncitizen defendants' acquiescence to the prosecution and a conviction is destined.

Postville was the antithesis of transparency and self-determination. In Postville, the foregone conclusion that individuals who were illegally in the country were deportable justified expedited criminal procedures, despite legitimate concerns over the validity of the charges. However, the manipulation of the judicial system to expedite proceedings resulted in a failure to provide defendants with a sense of judicial transparency and a real opportunity to be heard.

Both the planning and execution of the proceedings cast into doubt the fairness and transparency of the trial, which damaged the perception of our legal system. As Robert R. Rigg, a Drake University law professor and president of the Iowa Association of Criminal Defense Lawyers points out, "Postville left a bitter taste for a lot of people . . . It paints a pretty bleak picture of American criminal justice, and I don't think it's the type of thing the judiciary or main Justice wants to replicate" (Schau 2008: 797).

To a lesser extent, state criminal courts are perpetuating the inequality of noncitizen defendants in the criminal justice system. The noncitizen status is exploited for reasons not connected to crime prevention. Defense attorneys object that noncitizens are subjected to charges normally not raised against citizens, and the prosecutor prioritizes removal from the United States over fair punishment, all of which undermine confidence in the criminal justice system.

Conclusions

In the Postville case, the noncitizen status of the defendants affected decisions made by all the parties involved in the criminal process. The experiences of noncitizen defendants in Arizona follow a similar path. Without knowledge of the immigration consequences of a conviction, or the individual's eligibility for immigration relief in general, defense counsel may not be able to diffuse the fears that cloud the noncitizen's judgment, resulting in hasty plea decisions. Tribunals may undercut the noncitizen's opportunity for a fair hearing by devaluing criminal procedures in light of imminent immigration consequences. Even the prosecutor may cut corners to move the case faster since the criminal charge is just a means to an end—exile of the noncitizen.

Ignorance and marginalization of immigration law in the adjudication of a criminal case involving a noncitizen can be catastrophic. It can lead to a devaluation of the criminal proceedings or to heightened immigration consequences from the proceedings, or both. The first is illustrated by the Postville raid and the second by Arizona's criminal justice system. Tribunals and criminal law attorneys must also recognize that noncitizens will often assume that their legal status will compromise their access to an impartial tribunal, especially where there are statutes that treat noncitizen defendants differently from U.S. citizens. Regrettably, in Postville and in Arizona, this assumption has proven true.

Requiring the criminal bar to provide noncitizen defendants meaningful advice regarding the immigration consequences of conviction is critical in an era of stepped-up immigration enforcement (what the chapters in the first section of this volume refer to as new modes of social control) and the merging of criminal and immigration proceedings. The *Padilla v. Kentucky* decision sends a strong message to our criminal justice system not to ignore the primacy citizenship status plays in the process.

To immigrant families and communities there is nothing "collateral" about permanent exile of a loved one. A Pew Hispanic Center survey conducted in 2009 revealed that 35 percent of native-born Latinos worry about the deportation of a loved one. The study also found that such anxiety correlated with their view that life for Hispanics had deteriorated and that anti-immigrant sentiment was on the rise (Lopez and Livingston 2009). Trust in our administration of criminal justice is fundamental to preserving society's confidence in our government as the "good shepherd" of our constitutionally guaranteed due process rights. A Supreme Court decision in *Padilla* holding that immigration law is merely a collateral consequence of a criminal conviction would have further damaged the relationship between the Latino community and our criminal justice system.

Regrettably, the existing erosion of confidence in our criminal system by Latinos and other immigrants will not be rebuilt by simply giving noncitizen defendants good legal advice. They need criminal proceedings that segregate their rights as criminal defendants from their status as noncitizen. Ultimately, no matter how relevant the criminal case is to the future immigration status of the defendant, it is first a question of whether the prosecution can show culpability for a crime irrespective of the immigrant status of the defendant. Perhaps restoring this piece of the puzzle is the crucial next step.

NOTES

Portions of this chapter first appeared in my earlier article, "Competent Voices: Noncitizen Defendants and the Right to Know the Immigration Consequences of Plea Agreements," 13 *Harvard Latino Law Review* 47 (Spring 2010), and those portions are used with permission by the journal. This chapter was made possible by a generous summer grant from the Sandra Day O'Connor College of Law.

1. I use the term "noncitizen" to include individuals in the United States who are not U.S. citizens by birth, derivation, or naturalization. A noncitizen could be residing in the United States legally or illegally. When speaking about a noncitizen that lacks immigration status, I use the word "undocumented." The alternative term "alien," which is used by the Immigration and Nationality Act to describe noncitizens, is avoided whenever possible.

2. Holistic practice has been defined as legal advocacy that aims to address not just the legal issue at hand but the underlying problems that create them. Preventive law practice is defined as a proactive approach to lawyering where the attorney assists the client in addressing present and future issues simultaneously.

BIBLIOGRAPHY

ABA Crim. Just. 1999. Section 14-3.2(f), cmt.75, 3d ed.

Adele, Bernhard. 2002. "Take Courage: What the Courts can do to Improve the Delivery of Criminal Defense Services." *University of Pittsburg Law Review* 63: 293–302.

Antiterrorism and Effective Death Penalty Act of 1996. 1996. Pub. L. No. 104-132, 110 Stat. 1214.

Bennett, Mark. 2010. "*Padilla v. Kentucky,*" Defending People: The Tao of Criminal Defense Trial Lawyering. (March 31), http://bennettandbennett.com/blog/2010/03/padilla-v-kentucky.html.

Camayd-Freixas, Erik. 2008. "Interpreting After the Largest ICE Raid in US History: A Personal Account." June 13, http://docs.google.com/gview?a=v&q=cache:EwwctGJS_hQJ:graphics8.

nytimes.com/images/2008/07/14/opinion/14ed-camayd.pdf+camayd-freixas+essay&hl=en&gl=us (accessed August 19, 2009).

Chin, Gabriel J. and Richard W. Holmes. 2002. "Effective Assistance of Counsel and the Consequences of Guilty Pleas." *Cornell Law Review* 87: 697–726.

Fiske, Susan T. and Shelley Taylor. 1984. *Social Cognition*. New York: McGraw-Hill.

Francis, John. 2003. "Failure to Advise Non-Citizens of Immigration Consequences of Criminal Convictions: Should This Be Grounds to Withdraw a Guilty Plea?" *University of Michigan Journal of Law Reform* 36: 691, 697–705.

Fry, Richard and Jefferey S. Passel. 2009. "Latino Children: A Majority Are U.S.-Born Off-spring of Immigrants." May 28, http://www.hispanicpew.org.

Hardaway, Robert M. 1997. *Preventative Law: Materials on Non Adversarial Legal Process*. Cincinnati, OH: American Publishing.

Harris, Craig. 2009. "Funds Reveal How Maricopa, Other Counties Differ on Law." *Arizona Republic*, November 18. http://www.azcentral.com/news/articles/2009/11/08/20091108sactions1108-new.html.

Lopez, Mark H. and Gretchen Livingston. 2009."Hispanics and the Criminal Justice System: Low Confidence, High Exposure."*Pew Hispanic Center*. April 7, www.pewhispanic.org.

Lopez, Mark H. and Susan Minushkin. 2008a. "Hispanics See Their Situation in the U.S. Deteriorating; Oppose Key Immigration Enforcement Measures." *Pew Hispanic Center*. September 18, http:// www.hispanicpew.org.

Lopez, Mark H. and Susan Minushkin. 2008b. "Situation of Hispanics in the U.S., Immigration Enforcement, and Latino Opinion." *Pew Hispanic Center*. September 18, http://www.hispanicpew.org.

Menjívar, Cecilia and Cynthia L. Bejarano. 2004. "Latino Immigrants' Perceptions of Crime and Police Authorities in the United States: A Case Study from the Phoenix Metropolitan Area." *Ethnic and Racial Studies* 27:120.

Monger, Randall and Nancy Rytina. 2009. "Department of Homeland Security, Annual Flow Report: U.S. Legal Permanent Residents: 2008." March, http://www.dhs.gov/xlibrary/assets/statistics/publications/lpr_fr_2008.pdf (accessed February 12, 2010).

Moyers, Peter R. 2009. "Butchering Statutes: The Postville Raid and the Misinterpretation of Federal Criminal Law." *Seattle University Law Review* 32: 651.

National Lawyer's Guild. *Immigration Law and Crimes*. 2006. Eagan: West.

Padilla v. Kentucky. 2009. Brief for the United States of America as Amicus Curiae Supporting Affirmance at 10, No. 08-651, August 17.

Pearce, Russell G. 2004. "Representing Inequality in the Market for Justice: Why Access to Lawyers Will Never Solve the Problem and Why Rethinking the Role of Judges Will Help." *Fordham Law Review* 73, no. 48: 969–76.

Petrucci, Carrie J., David B. Wexler, and Bruce J. Winick, eds. 2003. *The Judge-Defendant Interaction: Toward a Shared Respect Process in Judging in a Therapeutic Key: Therapeutic Jurisprudence and the Courts*. Durham: Carolina Academic Press.

Pinnard, Micheal. 2004. "Incorporating Collateral Consequences and Reentry into Criminal Defense Lawyering" *Fordham Urban Law Journal* 31, no. 6: 1067, 1068.

Roberts, Jenny. 2008. "The Mythical Divide Between Collateral and Direct Consequences of Criminal Convictions: Involuntary Commitment of 'Sexually Violent Predators.'" *Minnesota Law Review* 93: 670, 684–85.

"*Sample Plea Agreement.*" 2008. United States Attorney, Northern District of Iowa. 13 May. Available: http://www.fd.org/ImmigrationRaids/PostvillePlea.pdf (accessed Aug. 19, 2009).

Schau, Jessica. 2008. "Justices to Weigh-in on Fallout in Recent Workplace Raids." *Georgetown Immigration Law Journal* 22 (Summer): 795–97.

Speper, Jerry. 2008. "300 Arrested in ICE raid at Iowa Plant." *Washington Times*, May 13.

Steinberg, Robert and David Feige. 2004. "Cultural Revolution: Transforming the Public Defender's Office." *New York University Review of Law & Social Change* 29: 123–24.

Stolle, Dennis P., David B. Wexler, and Bruce J. Winick, eds. 2000. *Therapeutic Jurisprudence: Law as a Helping Profession.* Durham: Carolina Academic Press.

Taylor, Margaret H. and Ronald F. Wright. 2002. "The Sentencing Judge as Immigration Judge." *Emory Law Journal* 51: 1131, 1151–57.

United States Department of Homeland Security (USDHS). 2007. *ICE 2007 Annual Report.* Washington, DC: Office of Immigration Statistics.

United States Department of Homeland Security (USDHS). 2008. *Yearbook of Immigration Statistics.* Washington, DC: Office of Immigration Statistics, http://www.dhs.gov/files/statistics/publications/YrBk08En.shtm.

United States Department of Homeland Security (USDHS). 2009. *Annual Flow Report.* Washington, DC: Office of Immigration Statistics. (March), www.dhs.gov.

U.S. Immigration and Customs Enforcement (ICE). 2010. Delegation of Immigration Authority Section 287(g) Immigration and Nationality Act. Washington, DC: USCIS Office of State and Local Coordination (August 2), http://ice.gov/pi/news/factsheets/section287_g.htm.

U.S. State Department. 2009a. *2008 Human Rights Report Guatemala.* http://www.state.gov/g/drl/rls/hrrpt/2008/wha/119161.htm (last visited Aug. 20, 2009).

U.S. State Department. 2009b. *2008 Human Rights Report Mexico.* http://www.state.gov/g/drl/rls/hrrpt/2008/wha/119161.htm (last visited Aug. 20, 2009).

Vargas, Manuel D. 2010. "A defending Immigrants Partnership Advisory: Duty of Criminal Defense Counsel Representing an Immigrant Defendant after *Padilla v. Kentucky.*" (April 6), available: http://www.immigrantdefenseproject.org/docs/2010/10-Padilla_Practice_Advisory.pdf.

Warren, Roger K. 2000. "Public Trust and Procedural Justice." *Supreme Court Review* 37: 12, 14–16.

Wexler, David B. 1990. *Therapeutic Jurisprudence: The Law as a Therapeutic Agent.* Durham: Carolina Academic Press.

Winick, Bruce J. 1999. "Redefining the Role of the Criminal Defense Lawyer at Plea Bargaining and Sentencing: A Therapeutic Jurisprudence/Preventive Law Model." *Psychology, Public Policy, and Law* 5: 1034, 1039–42.

CASES

Arizona v. Barragan-Serra, AZ App. Div. One CR07-0048 (July 17, 2008)

Berger v. U.S. 295 U.S. 78 (1935).

Brady v. U.S. 397 U.S. 742 (1970)

Flores-Figueroa v. U.S. 129 S. Ct. 1886 (2009)

Hill v. Lockhart 474 U.S. 52, 57. 474 (1985)

Hirsh v. INS 308 F.2d 562, 566 (9th Cir. 1962)

INS v. St. Cyr 533 U.S. 289, 322 (2001)

Landon v. Plasencia, 459 U.S. 21 (1982)

Magana-Pizano v. IN, 200 F.3d 603, 612 (9th Cir. 1999)

New Jersey v. Nunez-Valdez 975 A.2d 418 (N.J. 2009)

Newman v. U.S. 382 (D.C. Cir. 1967)

Padilla v. Kentucky, 253 S. W. 3d 482 (KY 2008), *cert. granted*, 08-651, 2009 U.S. LEXIS 1453 (U.S. Feb 23, 2009)

Padilla v. Kentucky 559 U.S. (2010), 130 S. Ct. 1473, 2010 Lexis 2928, No. 08-651 (March 31, 2010)

People v. Pozo 746 P.2d 523 (Colo. 1987)

Reno v. Flores 507 U.S. 292, 342 n.27 (1993)

Ruvalcaba v. Nevada 122 Nev. 961, 965 Nev. Sup. Ct. 2006

Strickland v. Washington 466 U.S. 668, 692 (1984)

U.S. v. Igbonwa 120 F.3d 437, 442-45 (3rd Cir. 1997)

U.S. v. Jacobo-Zavala 241 F.3d 1009, (8th Cir. 2001)

U.S. v. LaBonte 520 U.S. 751, 762 (1997)

Zadvydas v. Davis 533 U.S. 678, 723 (2001)

STATUTES

Ariz. Const. art. II § 22 (2009)

Ariz. Const. art. II § 22(a)(4) (2009)

Ariz. R. Crim. Pro. 17.2(f) (2009)

Ariz. Code Anno. §13-2319 (2009)

Ariz. Code Anno. §23-211 (2009)

Ariz. Code Anno. §23-212 (2009)

Fed. R. Crim. P. 11 (2009) Fed. R. Crim. P. 11(15) (2009)

Fed. R. Crim. P. 11(b)(1) (2009)

Fed. R. Crim. P. 11(d)(1) (2009)

Fed. R. Crim. P. 11(d)(2) (2009)

Illegal Immigration Reform and Immigrant Responsibility Act of 1996, Pub. L. No. 104-208, 110 Stat. 3009 (1996)

Immigration Act of 1990, Pub. L. 104-649, 104 Stat.

Model Rules of Prof'l Conduct R. 1.1 (2009)

Model Rules of Prof'l Conduct R. 1.4(b) (2009)

Model Rules of Prof'l Conduct R. 3.8 (2009)

U.S. Const. amend. V

U.S. Const. amend. VI

8 U.S.C. §1357(g) (2)

8 U.S.C.A. §1101(a)(43)(A) (2010)

8 U.S.C.A. §1158 (2009)

8 U.S.C.A. §1181(a)(2)(D) (2010)

8 U.S.C.A. §1182 (2009)

8 U.S.C.A. §1227(a)(2)(E) (2008)

8 U.S.C.A. §1228(c) (2000)

8 U.S.C.A. §1229 (2008)
8 U.S.C.A. §1229(b) (2006)
18 U.S.C.A. §1028A(a)(1) (2009)
18 U.S.C.A. §1546(a) (2009)
18 U.S.C.A. § 3563(b)(21) (2000)
18 U.S.C.A. §1028A(a)(1)(2004)
28 U.S.C.A. §1827 (1996)
42 U.S.C.A. §408(a) (2004)

6

The Ruptures of Return

Deportation's Confounding Effects

M. KATHLEEN DINGEMAN-CERDA AND SUSAN BIBLER COUTIN

During a 2008 interview conducted in El Salvador, Victor Castillo recounted his experience of deportation from the United States. Victor first migrated with legal documentation to the United States in 1967 at the age of four.[1] After his U.S. citizen stepfather adopted him at the age of eight, Victor assumed that he, too, became a citizen. He grew up in the United States, where he attended school. But when his family moved to a neighborhood where gangs were prevalent, Victor also joined a gang and became addicted to drugs. In 2004, after several drug-related convictions, Victor was stripped of his legal permanent residency and deported to El Salvador. Shortly thereafter, he re-entered the United States without authorization and was soon deported a second time. In El Salvador, at age 45, without family or significant social connections, Victor could not get a job, and desperately missed his wife and children in the United States. With great anguish, Victor described the devastating rejection he had experienced: "I was ready to serve my country, I was a registered voter, I voted for governor of CA, I voted for presidents, my whole life was over there, my wife, my kids. I was a total American; I was

American in my heart, my mind. And for them to just uproot me and just throw me [away]. . . . I've been *banished* from my country. . . . And they said forever!"

This sense of deportation-as-exile was shared by Freddy Mendoza, who first migrated during the onset of the Salvadoran civil war in 1980 at the age of five. He grew up in the United States with Spanish-speaking parents who, to promote Freddy's upward mobility, spoke only English in the household. When Freddy turned 17, his mother became a naturalized citizen and started the process to adjust the legal status of her children. However, before Freddy's petition was filed, he was deported for a non-gang-related criminal offense. Like Victor, he immediately re-migrated to the United States, where he completed a general equivalency diploma (GED), worked in catering, attended community college, and entertained dreams of becoming a French chef. These dreams were interrupted in 2008 when Freddy was arrested for public intoxication, detained, and deported a second time. In El Salvador, he struggled to communicate in Spanish with native speakers, was frequently confused with gang members, and lived off of credit cards paid for by his parents in the United States. Freddy, a self-reported "typical American," explained with great frustration, "I never really worried about my legal status [in the U.S.] because of the way I was raised. The way my mom raised me, I just never felt that I didn't belong. . . . I always thought that I belonged there. I never felt that I could ever be taken away from that place, you know. It was my home."

Victor's and Freddy's experiences suggest that in the current era, forced removal—or deportation—has effects that confound three of its ostensible goals. First, despite popular and legal rhetoric depicting deportation as the unproblematic return of noncitizens *to* their homelands, deportees frequently experience removal as an exile *from* their home. This sense of exile is often reinforced by the reactions of fellow citizens in their countries-of-origin, who perceive and treat deportees as outsiders, foreigners, and/or violent criminals threatening state security. Second, deportees and their family members experience a post-deportation victimization that confounds popular perceptions of these migrants as troublemakers who, at a minimum, have violated prohibitions on unauthorized entry or, at a maximum, have victimized others through violent crime. Some have argued that deportation is a form of "social cleansing," designed to rid society of individuals and groups that are considered undesirable (De Genova 2002; Kanstroom 2000, 2007). For example, the U.S. government claims that its removal policies reduce crime by targeting noncitizen offenders. Through this claim, the government suggests that it is addressing street violence stereotypically associated with undocumented migrants (Chacón 2007; Dingeman and Rumbaut 2010). While such claims appease immigration restrictionists in receiving countries, our research suggests that deportation may, in fact, spread crime by exposing deportees to violence at the hands of gang members, security guards, and even the police. Third, deportees' responses to dislocation are varied. Some are able to develop new and successful lives in their countries of origin, others languish or turn to delinquency, and still others, like Victor and Freddy, defy banishment. While deportation ostensibly keeps people out of the United States, many deportees return clandestinely in spite of formal bans on their re-entry. Such returns push individuals further underground, creating an increasingly vulnerable underclass of migrants ineligible for work authorization and legal documentation and therefore at risk for further victimization.

In this chapter, we address the confounding effects of deportation. Our analysis draws upon interviews we each conducted in El Salvador during the summer of 2008. As part of a larger project examining the experiences of 1.5 generation Salvadorans—that is, Salvadorans who migrated to the United States originally as children—Susan Coutin interviewed 41 deportees, most of whom had migrated prior to the age of 13 and had grown up in the United States. These interviewees were recruited through a nongovernmental organization (NGO), CARECEN Internacional (the Central American Resource Center International), an immigrant rights organization located in San Salvador. CARECEN staff recruited interviewees through their contacts with gang violence prevention organizations (in particular, the San Salvador office of *Homies Unidos*), a deportee working in a San Salvador call center, and a deportee living in Usulután. Additionally, as part of her master's level research, Kathleen Dingeman interviewed 29 deportees who migrated to the United States at different ages and spent different lengths of time there. These interviewees were located in San Salvador and its vicinity through contacts at (1) *Bienvenidos a Casa* (Welcome Home), a program formerly contracted by the Salvadoran government to assist with the reinsertion of deportees; (2) *El Centro de Intercambio y Solidaridad* (The Center for Exchange and Solidarity), an organization that enables international visitors to work on social justice projects in El Salvador; (3) *Alcance Victoria* (Victory Outreach), a Christian alcohol and drug rehabilitation program; and (4) a public defender who worked in the Salvadoran countryside. All participants were men, as our contacts were unable to locate women who were willing to participate in our research. The majority of the individuals interviewed were 1.5 generation migrants, though a few had immigrated to the United States as adolescents or young adults. Many interviewees had become legal permanent residents in the United States prior to deportation. Taken together, these interviews provide a rich source of information about the diverse experiences of Salvadoran men deported after living in the United States for many years. Their experiences detail the many confounding effects of deportation, particularly in an era of heightened social control.

Social Suffering and Deportation

Our analysis of deportation's confounding effects draws on the concept of *social suffering* (Das and Kleinman 2001, see also Sztompka 2000), that is, traumas and forms of adversity that are inflicted on societies, not just on individuals. While deportation may seem to be an individualized process, many have argued that deportation has a *collective* target. For example, Nicholas De Genova (2002) contends that immigration law enforcement is designed less to remove undesirable migrants than to produce *deportability*, the threat of forced removal (see also De Genova and Peutz 2010). Annual numbers of deportations are small relative to the size of the population at risk for removal, yet the ways in which migrants are targeted, such as through highly publicized raids, create a sense of vulnerability that reverberates throughout immigrant communities. Deportability is thus a collective as well as individual form of suffering that helps define certain migrants as illegal aliens and disposable workers.

The concept of social suffering also draws attention to "the more subtle forms of violence perpetrated by institutions of science and the state" (Das and Kleinman 2000: 2). Our focus on deportees' experiences highlights the role of both state and non-state actors in forced exile and post-deportation stigmatization, discrimination, and violence. The United States' historical denial of political asylum to Salvadorans fleeing the 1980–1992 Salvadoran war left many migrants with only temporary legal status and delayed others' eligibility to naturalize, thus leaving them vulnerable to deportation (Coutin 2011). Changes to deportation law in 1996 served to further deportability in the immigrant community by expanding the definition of aggravated felony and removing judicial discretion and any real chance for migrants to appeal removal decisions (Morawetz 2000). In El Salvador, deportees have been subjected to security regimes that not only target gang members and other delinquents, but also uncannily reproduce security doctrines practiced during the civil war (Zilberg 2007, Moodie 2010, see also Allegro 2006). For example, as in the war, citizens have been suspected of being delinquents or subversives, paramilitary death squads have targeted suspected guerrillas or gang members, and military units have supported domestic police activities.

The social suffering of deportation to El Salvador is therefore linked to the historical memory of political violence during the civil war. Attending to such linkages highlights the connections between U.S. immigration and foreign policies, the racialization of crime in the United States, and zero tolerance gang policies adopted in postwar El Salvador.

By focusing on social suffering, we seek to answer Daniel Goldstein's (2010) call for a critical anthropology—and, we would add, sociology—of security. The strategies through which, to paraphrase Das and Kleinman (2001), deportees seek to remake their everyday lives in the wake of a deportation reveal the *indeterminacies* of state and non-state power and action (see also Cabot 2010). Deportation not only ruptures and displaces geographies (Zilberg 2004, 2007, 2011), but also leads deportees to defy removal through unauthorized entry and through acts that aim to recreate the United States beyond the borders of the United States.

Violence, Migration, and Return

The social suffering of individuals deported from the United States to El Salvador is directly tied to the lived experience, collective memory, and reproduction of civil war violence that plagued El Salvador for more than 12 years. Starting in the late 1970s, a coalition of leftist guerrilla armies known as the Farabundo Martí National Liberation Front (FMLN) rose up against the unequal distribution of land, wealth, and power that long characterized Salvadoran society. The Salvadoran government responded with repressive tactics that included sponsoring the assassination of government opponents and supporting privately funded undercover paramilitary groups—or "death squads"—to terrorize individuals and communities suspected of being sympathetic to the guerrillas. In an attempt to quell the spread of what it viewed as "communism in the Americas," the Reagan administration provided direct military and economic support to the Salvadoran government. After a truth commission exposed the wartime atrocities committed by the U.S.-backed Salvadoran government and the guerrillas, a peace agreement was negotiated, formally ending 12 years of brutal civil war.

Between 1980 and 1992, wartime violence penetrated Salvadoran society so deeply that virtually all Salvadorans had been affected either directly or indirectly. Some served as soldiers or guerrilla combatants, others were indirectly targeted as a result of their residence or occupation, and still others witnessed violence and/or lost loved ones (Coutin 2007). Approximately 75,000 people were killed and more than 22,000 were victimized through other human rights abuses committed by the Salvadoran government, death squads, and the *guerrilla* (PNUD 2005). In excess of a half million people from all socioeconomic sectors of Salvadoran society were internally displaced, and another one million migrated abroad to places like Honduras, Mexico, and the United States (Hamilton and Chinchilla 2001).

The civil war and associated economic disruptions gave rise to a migratory flow between El Salvador and the United States that continued in the postwar years. Currently, an estimated 20–35 percent of Salvadoran nationals reside in the United States (PNUD 2005), the vast majority of whom arrived without proper legal documentation. As a supporter of the right-wing government of El Salvador, the U.S. government chose to systematically deny political asylum to Salvadorans fleeing wartime conditions. Advocates working on behalf of the Salvadoran community protested the interjection of foreign policy into asylum practice and eventually succeeded in negotiating a "patchwork strategy of immigration laws and policies" (Mountz et al. 2002: 335–336). These developments transformed Salvadoran migrants from "undeserving economic migrants to "deserving 'protocitizens'" (Coutin 2003: 70), though in practice, most of the new provisions that made Salvadorans a specially protected population also lacked a direct pathway to citizenship and had strict eligibility requirements, and complex procedures, deadlines, and backlogs, which kept many from regularizing their status. The Salvadoran migrant community has consequently remained in a state that Cecilia Menjívar (2006) calls "liminal legality," in which more than 50 percent of Salvadoran immigrants remain undocumented and 75 percent are at risk of deportation (Office of Immigration Statistics 2010).

The politicized implementation of asylum law has worked in conjunction with recent changes in deportation law and increased funding for immigration enforcement to establish conditions under which another forced migratory movement—in the form of deportation—has emerged. Legal status plays an important role in the acculturation and incorporation experiences of ethnic groups (Portes and Zhou 1993; Rumbaut and Ewing 2007). The hostile context of reception in the United States and inner-city ethnic tensions in Los Angeles have thus contributed to the emergence and growth of Salvadoran street gangs such as *Mara Salvatrucha 13* (MS-13) and *Barrio 18* (18th Street). Despite the fact that members of these gangs are largely composed of U.S.-born second-generation minorities (Vigil 2002), the media have sensationalized them in a way that has legitimated the specific targeting of Salvadoran communities by immigration enforcement agencies attempting to appear tough on violent crime (Chacón 2007). The political rhetoric about Salvadoran gangs also has helped to reinforce the perception that Salvadoran deportees are delinquents who intend to wreak havoc in El Salvador, despite the fact that the vast majority, or 77 percent, of the 20,031 Salvadorans deported in 2008 were removed because of immigration violations rather than criminal convictions (Human Rights Watch 2009).

Such everyday forms of violence blur the line between war and peace (Das and Kleinman 2000; Scheper-Hughes and Bourgois 2004) and critically shape the reintegration experiences of Salvadoran deportees. As Philippe Bourgois (2001: 21) writes, "political repression and resistance in wartime reverberate in a dynamic of everyday violence akin to that produced by the fusing of structural and symbolic violence during peacetime." Such everyday violence has characterized postwar El Salvador, a society still struggling with many of the structural economic inequalities that brought on the war (Binford 2002), as well as the collective trauma induced by the war (see Sztompka 2000). Wartime factions have also been reproduced. For example, wartime violence became legitimized through the institutionalization of paramilitary and other security forces into the national civil police force, *La Policía Nacional Civil* (PNC). The ready availability of American-style weapons also interacted with local economic conditions and with the deportation of Salvadoran gang members from the United States to fuel the proliferation of local gangs (Fariña, Miller, and Cavallaro 2010). These gangs, in turn, have come to replace the guerrillas as the scapegoat for the ills of postwar El Salvador (Zilberg 2007). All of these factors have contributed to producing levels of violence in El Salvador comparable to that which occurred during the years leading up to the civil war (Dalton 2002a, 2002b; OSAC 2010).

In a move reminiscent of the civil war, the Salvadoran government and paramilitary groups responded to postwar violence with increased repression of suspected criminals, including deportees. Espousing the zero tolerance policies of the Giuliani administration in New York City in the 1990s, the conservative party ARENA enacted a series of laws known as *Mano Dura* (Hard Hand), *Super Mano Dura* (Super Hard Hand), and *Mano Amiga* (Friendly Hand) (Allegro 2006; Zilberg 2007). Gang membership was made illegal, and individuals with the presumed visual and auditory markers of gang involvement—including tattoos, baggy jeans, and a U.S. accent— were targeted. Deportees from the United States have thus been targeted for random strip searches and imprisonment, as well as subjected to widespread prejudice and discrimination in other spheres of society (Fariña, Miller, and Cavallaro 2010). In the early 1990s, a newly formed paramilitary group known as the *Sombra Negra*, or "Black Shadow," began to disappear suspected gang members who shared these characteristics. Deportees also became the targets of gang members, who sought to initiate and/or threaten them. This context of return thus has not only reproduced the memory and violence of the civil war, but in a very real way, has made reintegration difficult and dangerous for deportees who grew up in the United States (Coutin 2007; Dingeman and Rumbaut 2010; Zilberg 2007).

Confounding Effect I: Home as Exile

Given this history of violence, it is perhaps not surprising that for many deportees, removal is also a violent act; namely, an exile or banishment that is not unlike the sudden uprootings that they and their parents experienced during the civil war. The histories of deportees who grew up abroad provide perhaps the starkest examples of the insufficiency of formal legal citizenship as a measure of social belonging. Immigration scholars have noted that, in practice, the binary between citizenship and alienage is undone by what Linda Bosniak (2006) calls "alien citizenship" and Hiroshi Motomura (2006) refers to as "territorial personhood." In the United States, territorially present noncitizens enjoy numerous legal rights, even when they are officially undocumented. They study, work, own property, pay taxes, form legally recognized relationships, and perform valuable tasks, including the intimate care of children and the elderly. If they are charged with a criminal offense, they also have the right to due process protections, including access to a public defender, although as noted in Cruz's chapter, these protections are not always without challenges. The lives of noncitizens thus may be in many, though not all, respects indistinguishable from those of their citizen family members and neighbors. Clearly then, "territorial persons" or "alien citizens" cannot be regarded as exclusively *alien*, even though deportation policies treat these statuses as dichotomous. Likewise, deportees who lived outside of El Salvador for considerable periods are returned as citizens of that nation, but may be regarded by other Salvadorans as foreign—a reality that further compounds their experiences of deportation-as-exile. Straightforward notions of formal, legal citizenship as determinative of membership are therefore problematic, in multiple ways and in multiple national territories.

Interviewees who immigrated as young children or adolescents frequently developed such strong ties in the United States that they lived as quasi-citizens, regardless of their official legal status. For example, Marcus López, 22, left El Salvador for the United States in 1998, at the age of 12, joining his father, stepmother, and two half-sisters in Washington, DC. Marcus went to school, learned English, took care of his sisters after school, and obtained a work permit through a pending NACARA (Nicaraguan Adjustment and Central American Relief Act) application. Marcus felt comfortable in the United States: "I learned English, I was working, [and] I had my own stuff. I felt independent even in a country that was not my country." Although as a youth Marcus was convicted on a misdemeanor charge of stealing car radios (to supplement his meager income, he explained), he eventually turned his life around. He married his girlfriend, with whom he had a child, and got a job in a medical clinic that provided community services. However, Marcus was then charged with having sex with an underage minor, a charge he claimed was false. When he accepted a plea bargain, Marcus became deportable. His nine years of residence, work history, English skills, U.S. citizen spouse and child, graduation from a U.S. high school, and pending legalization case did not stop the deportation.

Although interviewees like Marcus encountered hardships in the United States, there was also a normalcy to their lives that made formal citizenship seem unnecessary. As another interviewee, Francisco Ramirez, stated, "I had basically felt like any other kid in the United States that was going there. I had went through school there, went through what they went through—girlfriend, going to the movies, parties, school dances, getting involved with school. . . . The only difference was that I wasn't born there." Indeed, interviewees such as Francisco provided rich oral histories of the U.S. neighborhoods in which they were raised. For example, Marcus described tensions in his high school:

> From '99 to 2004, gang stuff was getting really hectic in DC. Just Hispanic gangs. It wasn't even about Hispanic defending their own race against discrimination or racism from Blacks and Whites. It was more between them, within them. But just within, like countries. Because it was just crews. Because in M-S, there were Dominicans, Puerto Ricans, even Chinese guys were involved in that. So it was more about territory. So that's when it got really hectic between them and people getting shot and everything.

Interviewees' locations in neighborhoods that were rife with violence—and police surveillance—are precisely a product of the adverse circumstances within which they immigrated and are not irrelevant to the criminal histories that some developed (see also Portes and Zhou 1993; Rumbaut and Ewing 2007). As a recent immigrant growing up in DC, Marcus was exposed to this violence and continually pressured to join gangs. He stated, "most of my friends got killed by a shoot-out, or got run-over, or shot, or just jumped, or stabbed. . . . They were like, 'You're ashamed to be Salvadoran.' And I was like, 'I'm not ashamed. It's just that you guys are into your own things, and I am into my own things. So, I can't hang out with you, because I don't want to get shot or get stabbed because somebody died I don't even know.'" Marcus's description of racialized and nationalized gang tensions are evidence of the "second-class citizenship"—whether de jure or de facto—experienced by marginalized youth in the United States.

Detention and deportation stripped away the de facto U.S. personae that interviewees developed in the United States, leaving only their alienage (Coutin 2010). Once in detention, Marcus struggled to make officials recognize his identity and relationships:

> [They] locked me [up]. I lost everything. My car just got thrown in the streets . . . The house, all the stuff in the house, my brother had to just throw it away because he had to move into a small room. I had achieved so many things. They just basically got torn up. And like I said, it's just that sometimes the system is too harsh to see that you're really doing good, and they are just based on what you did a long time ago. And they wouldn't even let me see the judge. I requested it so many times. Even though when the detective, officer, from INS took me to the headquarters of INS in Baltimore, I told him, "I'm married to a U.S.-born citizen." He said, "We don't care. That's not the way we work."

As described in this excerpt, Marcus discovered that basic rights to property, family, and a future, all of which he had linked to his identity in the United States, proved irrelevant. As Marcus explained, "As soon as you get to the detention center, you can't get that [a hearing], you can't even see a judge." The confines of the detention center minimize any "personhood" that interviewees acquired through territorial presence. This personhood is later erased through the process of voluntary departure, in which detained migrants are requested to sign a form that authorizes the state to deport them without a formal hearing. Many interviewees reported that if given the opportunity, they would have appealed their removal decisions on the basis of their social membership in the United States. However, they also recognized that appeals could take many years and were unlikely to succeed. Ramiro Castillo had migrated to the United States at the age of 10 and achieved legal permanent residency, but had few positive memories of El Salvador and had no plans to ever voluntarily return to settle. He explained why he nonetheless signed deportation papers:

> [Immigration asked] us if we wanted to fight the case or not. Because based on the experience of others who had been in there in immigration [detention] fighting their cases and wasting their money, I said, "I have nothing to be waiting for." So, I just signed them and came back to El Salvador. For

all the people who have been fighting their cases, they have been there not for one year, but for like three or four. And they had almost the same case as I had. I didn't see no point in wasting my time. . . . My mom wanted to get [an attorney], but I told her no. Why waste the money even if they are going to send you back anyway?

As Ramiro's case indicates, the removal of territorial aliens from the United States—whether conceived of as voluntary or not—can be an implicitly coercive experience that strips away de facto citizenship and transforms it into legal nonexistence. Such stripping away of U.S. identities did not, however, confer recognizable Salvadoranness after deportees were returned to El Salvador, as Marcus and other interviewees related. Marcus and Francisco (who were interviewed together), explained:

SUSAN: Now that you live here [in El Salvador], do you identify more with here than previously?

MARCUS AND FRANCISCO: Actually, even less.

MARCUS: I feel less that I'm from here. Because people don't see you as you're from here.

SUSAN: You've encountered a rejection.

FRANCISCO: You can't go where you want to. I can't enjoy having a good time without people judging me or getting scared. I might be the most harmless person in the world, but just because of the way I look, they might think I'll do something to them.

MARCUS: It's pretty hard. Riding the bus, and seeing this lady standing up, and you're trying to give her your seat. And instead of taking it she walks away, because she thinks you might do something. I've had that happen to me. I'm being courteous. But what they do, they walk away. So it's hard.

FRANCISCO: I do not see myself as being from here.

The gulf between legal and other measures of membership is evident in the above interview excerpt, in which both Marcus and Francisco describe their own feelings of alienation ("I do not see myself as being from here") and other Salvadorans' reactions to their presence. In interviews, deportees used the phrase "back home" to refer to *the United States* rather than to El Salvador. Their foreignness in El Salvador is therefore the counterpart of their quasi-belonging in the United States. Such alienation contributes to the ways in which deportees are themselves victimized through deportation.

Confounding Effect II: The Victimization
of "Criminals" and their Families

Despite popular rhetoric depicting deportation as a means of preventing crime, removal actually subjects deportees to victimization in the forms of stigmatization, discrimination, and even direct violence from the hands of local police, security forces, and gang members. Post-deportation victimization also extends beyond deportees themselves to their family members left behind in the United States. Similar to the *secondary prisonization* (Comfort 2008) experienced by relatives of those serving time in prison, family members of deportees are subjected to a *secondary deportation*, which treats U.S. citizen children like undocumented immigrants, subjecting them to a de facto deportation.[2] Cumulatively, these experiences deeply rupture the lives of deportees and their families.

Interviewees almost unanimously agreed they were perceived as foreigners and gang members upon return to El Salvador. One interviewee, Armando Vargas, explained why he claimed an identity as a tourist rather than a Salvadoran citizen: "People look at you different. Those are some things that you are not used to. . . . To have someone look at you, you can afford. But, everybody look[s] at you different. When you are in the United States, you understand why people look at you different. They know you are not from there. But here, you are the same color skin. And they mistreat you because of the way you walk, the way you talk." Deportees who carry the perceived markers of gang membership experience exaggerated levels of stigmatization in El Salvador. Freddy Mendoza described reactions to the tattoo on his neck, "I wear a lot of collared shirts because I have a tattoo on my neck. I don't like people looking at that, you know what I mean, and making me feel like I am a criminal, or like I am a hoodlum or something like that, because I know that I am not. If people would just take the time, they would find out that I am a great person. I am a good person."

Gang violence often permeated the lives of interviewees, regardless of their efforts to escape it. Luis had never been involved in gangs in the United States, but he reports that in El Salvador, "On the buses, they used to look at me. And they used to ask, 'Where you from fool?' There were a few times, when they put guns to my head and so I would get off the bus then." Another interviewee, Antonio Ruiz, was actively involved in gangs in the United States and was deported for a gang-related criminal offense. After being deported to El Salvador, he immediately returned to the United States, where he found Christianity and turned his life around. He was later deported again for unauthorized presence. In El Salvador, he studied to become a minister and became involved in mentoring men in a drug and alcohol rehabilitation program. Nevertheless, after his second deportation, gang violence seemed to follow Antonio:

> After doing time [in a prison in the U.S.], I came out pretty healthy. And, I started working out again. And, I guess people kinda felt intimidated at the gym that I was going to [in El Salvador]. Word got out around that there was a new guy here in the neighborhood all with tattoos and stuff. [The gang members] decided to come. They didn't jump me, but they just threatened me. They said, if you come around here again, I'm going to kill you. So, I didn't take that as a joke. So, I just decided to move. I went to the beach. I stayed at this hotel for like almost five weeks or close to five weeks. Over there, they have a swimming pool. It was a nice, nice place. And I didn't know. I was going swimming and stuff. But, the local gang members saw me again. And, I decided to go to the pier to avoid them. I was eating some seafood. And they came from behind and were like, "Hey fool, where you from?" And, I was like, "I don't want no prob- lems. I go to church and stuff." They said, "Take your shirt off." And I said no. And that's when they had the knife, a big knife. Lucky, the guy dropped the knife. But, yeah, they beat me up pretty bad. . . . I had bruises all over me. They told me if they see me again, they were going to kill me. That's why now I am more careful.

Antonio's story suggests that, in spite of many deportees' intentions to leave former criminal lives in the United States, gang recruitment tactics in El Salvador often force them either to join gangs or to severely limit their social activities and become, as was the case of Antonio, "imprisoned" in their own homes. Feelings of informal imprisonment were compounded by high levels of suspicion from and dehumanizing interactions with police and security forces. Giovanni and Luis (who were interviewed together) commented:

> GIOVANNI: Like for me, it's been pretty hard for me to adjust to that, to the way the system is being run, like the police. . . . Here, if you are walk- ing and not doing nothing and the police officer wants to stop you for no reason, they can. . . . That is one of the things that I always got a problem with. The cops harass you too much, too much harassment.
> KATHLEEN: Has that happened to you?
> GIOVANNI: Yeah all the time. And they won't let you talk.
> LUIS: You can say that happened to me the second week I was here. I went out of the house. I have tattoos too. But, they are not gang-related. I

mean, I didn't graduate from school, but every time I wanted a tattoo, I went and got it done. And here, the first thing, they looked at it and asked me what it means.

KATHLEEN: Did they ask you to take your shirt off?

GIOVANNI: Yeah.

LUIS: Yeah.

GIOVANNI: Those are violations of your rights. If they want you to take your clothes off, you have to. If you don't, they start kicking your ass right there.

High levels of stigmatization and criminalization experienced by deportees such as Luis and Giovanni directly lead to emotional and socioeconomic deprivation. Systematically denied employment in the local labor market, many deported husbands and fathers who were once primary breadwinners suddenly became dependent upon the remittances, and thus the labor, of their family members in the United States. This outcome suggests that, in spite of formal legal citizenship, Salvadoran deportees who grew up and spent many years in the United States are denied full social membership in El Salvador.

In addition to deportees themselves, deportees' family members are indirectly victimized through deportation. They are like the relatives of prisoners in the United States, who "do time" on the outside while their husbands serve lengthy sentences in prison, becoming "quasi inmates" who "dwell in the juxtaposition of two ostensibly separate worlds. . . both captive and free" (Comfort 2008: 17–18). Similarly, while relatives left behind after their family members are deported usually do not undergo exile themselves, they *are* forcibly separated from their loved ones. Families suffer the socioeconomic consequences of the loss of a primary breadwinner, children grow up without the presence of a parent, and families must find creative ways to negotiate life across borders if they are to maintain their relationships. Some children— even U.S. citizens—accompany parents who are deported, and thus undergo a de facto deportation. In these ways, families' lived experiences, and future trajectories, become inextricably linked to the current deportation regime.

Many of the men we interviewed expressed deep sorrow about separation from their family members. Speaking about how he felt when he was first deported, one interviewee stated, "I was destroyed inside. I was destroyed. It was horrible. It's a horrible feeling. It's like you know you will be so far away from your family, you know. Your friends and your whole life is just like ripped in front of you. . . . They pull you out of everything you know in your life." These painful ruptures are compounded by the changes they must make for not only financial, but also marital survival. Routine phone calls and emails sustain some struggling relationships but, over time, other relationships become permanently severed as deportees and their wives start new families. Deportees' U.S. children are therefore at risk of growing up in single-parent, reconfigured, and foster care homes. One deportee described his predicament:

> I have two kids over there, and it's kind of hard because my kids, I did everything I could for them. I never paid child support, because me and the mother of my kids were not together. But I always took them on weekends. And I worked, I always worked. I used to help them, take them for vacations. They went to Los Angeles, Las Vegas. They've been practically everywhere with me. Now that I'm here, I've lost contact with them. Their mother got hooked on drugs. My kids are with foster parents. I stress about that all the time. Wonder how they are doing. That's practically one of my biggest [sources of] suffering right now. . . . The last I knew, my daughter had problems with her foster parents and she got changed to another house. It's tough knowing that. I speak to my mother all the time, and she tells me to be strong. But it's hard.

Deportees who had young children thus were not only concerned with their own feelings of separation and loss, and multiple experiences of victimization through the process of deportation, but, critically, with the life chances of their children. One interviewee, Mateo, who spent more than 20 years in the United States, expressed his concern:

> And, you know, [the labor migrants] are doing what is right. They are working to support their family and [immigration enforcement is] just going there and just locking them up and deporting them. Who is going to take care of the kids now? Or their families? You got kids over there that they don't got no more parents. They're probably out with their friends. Probably their friends are taking care of them, or another family member. But, they are separating families. And that is like something very bad. What that comes to is the kids that are over there, they are probably going to become criminals or something like that, you know.

Immigration judges in the post-1996 era lack discretion in deportation decisions and therefore cannot consider the length of time a migrant spent in the United States or the fact that they have U.S. citizen and permanent resident spouses and children. Removal thus victimizes not only individuals who are formally removed from U.S. territory and experience life in their home country as second-class citizens, but it also victimizes their families. U.S.-citizen spouses and children pay a heavy price due to the lengthy forced and potentially permanent separation from their loved ones. Awareness of these effects further victimizes deportees emotionally and also profoundly influences the ways in which they remake their lives after deportation.

Confounding Effect III: Resilience and Return

Although deportation removes individuals from the United States, subjecting them in many instances to a de facto exile and to victimization, deportees' responses to the ruptures of removal vary. Some deportees are able to build new lives for themselves in their country of origin, others find their ability to enter the formal economy quite limited, and therefore turn to crime or live in impoverished conditions, and still others opt to return to the United States, in defiance of their formal exclusion. Whether successful or unsuccessful, deportees' responses constitute attempts to *remake lives* ruptured by the collective trauma of war, emigration, crime, deportation, and post-deportation victimization (see Das and Kleinman 2001). Migrants' efforts to recuperate from trauma are largely informal, involving primarily their own resources of kin and social connections, rather than state and even civil society institutions. Nonetheless, migrants' post-deportation lives suggest potential reforms that could ease the social suffering associated with deportation—a topic to which we return in our conclusion.

Remaking one's life following deportation requires successfully mobilizing kin networks, social capital, and financial resources. Francisco, Jorge, and Pablo Ramirez were three brothers who, though still suffering, at the time of our interview in 2008 had developed new lives in El Salvador. These three brothers had been brought to the United States by their parents in 1990, at the ages of 12, 11, and 5 respectively. The brothers grew up on Long Island and were exposed to crime and ethnic tensions. Their parents then moved to Georgia to take advantage of job opportunities and to remove the children from what they considered to be a bad neighborhood. In 2001, the brothers became legal permanent residents, but their legal troubles continued. Francisco was convicted of selling drugs, and his brothers were convicted of drug possession and possessing a weapon. The three were stripped of their legal permanent residency and deported to El Salvador in 2006. They found deportation devastating. Francisco recalled, "It was a shock, just knowing that you were here in *El Salvador*. After all this time . . . when we got to the city, especially, all this smoke and all these buses! All these people on the streets, and all these kids asking for money. I had never seen that before. When I actually saw that, I wept."

Francisco, Jorge, and Pablo were nonetheless better off than some deportees. Though most of their family was in the United States, their aunt was able to meet them at the airport, and provide them with housing when they first arrived. Their mother also came to stay with them in El Salvador for the first two to three months following deportation, and their parents visited during the second year they were in the country. Their parents also sent them money for several months, enabling them to start their own business—a combination barber shop and cybercafé. Their fortunes then took a downturn. Their business was unsuccessful and their father suffered a stroke, which made it impossible for their parents to continue to send money. Francisco got a job working for FedEx but earned very little. Jorge recalled, "There were times we didn't eat. You see us now, we are a little chunky, with meat. You see us then, we were skinny." Luckily, one of the brothers learned of a call center that was employing deportees, and all three obtained jobs earning $500 per month. Pooling their resources, they were able to purchase a car and rent a $300-a-month house in a good neighborhood.

In El Salvador, the Ramirez brothers tried to recreate the life they had in the United States. They and their friend Amilcar explained:

JORGE: At the job site, we speak English. They require us to speak English at all times.

AMILCAR: Amongst ourselves, we speak English.

JORGE: We be, "Hey, wa'sup?"

AMILCAR: Rarely any Spanish.

JORGE: Just when there're people at the house that speak Spanish and no English.

PABLO: Even when we watch TV, it's in English.

AMILCAR: The "set" button.

PABLO: I mean, [we] just get used to it.

AMILCAR: The life that we lived, everything was in English.

JORGE: And if we was with family, we were translating.

SUSAN: So do you try as much as possible to have your same lifestyle?

JORGE: Like we told you, you just gotta make it seem like you're over there.

AMILCAR: I feel like I'm in the States, but when I hear people talking, "Oh, yeah, I'm in El Salvador."

PABLO: When we're in our own homes, it's like we're in the States. We celebrate all the holidays like over there.

JORGE: You get into your own little world.

AMILCAR: And that's it, you forget about everybody else. You try living like
you were over there, which is hard, because life there is totally different
from over here.

The remaking of a U.S. lifestyle in El Salvador often requires deportees to
adapt to certain culturally acceptable standards of dress and behavior. For
example, in order to prevent the high degree of stigmatization associated
with a visible tattoo, deportees often employ "covering" strategies (Goffman
1986) such as wearing long-sleeved shirts or removing tattoos. Two interviewees, Ricardo and Ramiro, who were friends in the United States prior
to their deportations, reported the strategies they utilized when seeking
employment in transnational companies, such as hotels and call centers, that
are managed by Salvadoran employees:

RICARDO: Most of the time, I dress nice. When I go for an interview, I go
with my suit and tie and everything. I go clean!
RAMIRO: You got to hide them!
KATHLEEN: They don't ask you to take off your shirt?
RICARDO: Some parts, yeah.
RAMIRO: Some parts they do.
RICARDO: I cut my hair different, so they can't tell that I have been deported.
KATHLEEN: Your accent?
RAMIRO: You got to have that normal Spanish.
RICARDO: I am lucky, I don't have the Mexican accent no more. So I do
pretty good.

Not all deportees are able to marshal the cultural and socioeconomic
resources to obtain jobs and "cover" their status as deportees. For example,
Lorenzo Gómez was living on the streets at the time of our interview. Lorenzo's parents immigrated to the United States when he was a toddler and then
sent for him in 1978, when he was eight years old. Lorenzo attended elementary school in Los Angeles and grew to love the English language: "I was so
fascinated with it that I became a little book worm. I would grab books, go
through them, and read them. . . . And then throughout junior high and high
school, I couldn't live without the newspaper. I had to really learn words,
and how to spell them. My English class was my favorite class." Lorenzo
became a legal permanent resident in 1984 and worked in a variety of positions, including as a telephone operator and alarm installer. He also became
addicted to drugs, and, after multiple convictions for drug possession, was
deported in 2000. He quickly returned to the United States, and lived in Los

Angeles for two years before being detained for driving without a license. He was deported again but returned to the United States in 2004. Once again he was apprehended, but this time, instead of simply being deported, Lorenzo was prosecuted for unlawful reentry and sentenced to four years in prison. At the time of our interview, Lorenzo had just been deported to El Salvador for the third time. His situation was bleak:

> I don't believe that what they're doing to me is fair at all. I'm just here run-ning around. I don't know anybody in this country. No friends. No family, no support. I live in the streets. I'm homeless. If I could keep my clothes clean it's because some guy is helping me out where I can wash my clothes and shower. But other than that, I don't have a place of my own. I'm going through an extreme and exceptional hardship. It's what I told the judge! "Sir. This is what I'm going to go through. Please, help me." They don't want to listen. They think everyone can go back home and live happily ever after. It doesn't work like that! I have my daughters back home. My mom, dad, brothers, sister, and I'm the only one here. So I would like to go back home. I really would. It's one of my dreams, now. Just to make it back home. For Christ's sake, just to be with my family.

Lorenzo desperately missed his two daughters, aged 16 and 13. He wanted to return to the United States, though he feared being apprehended again and sentenced to more prison time:

> I'm scared. Because if I get busted crossing, I'm going back to the BoP [Federal Bureau of Prisons] for reentry again. This time, I'm gonna get double time. Eight years. So I really don't know what to do. I'm so con-fused. I need time. I miss my family so much! I'm really hurt! For some time, I was drinking a lot here in Salvador, because I was so hurt and con-fused. I don't understand why this happened to me! Why? Why? Why?

Lorenzo's long-term plan was to obtain a job at a call center because he had good English skills, and save money either to return to the United States clandestinely or to move to Tijuana and buy a Mexican ID, so that his rela-tives who were still living in Los Angeles could travel there to visit him.

The agency exhibited by migrants in their responses to deportation con-founds formal removal in at least two senses: first, by recreating elements of their lives in the United States, it is as though deportation transfers not only individuals but also U.S. territory itself—the "little world" that allows Amilcar, Pablo, and Jorge to imagine that they are in the United States. Of course, such spatial movement is quite limited, given that these deportees are still formally forbidden to reenter the United States to reunite permanently with family members. The counterhegemonic potential of such recreations is also limited by transculturation of Salvadoran society, already under pressure from the export of U.S. businesses and media. Second, returning to the United States without authorization literally defies removal. It may be that removal fails to actually prevent deportees from living in the United States but does succeed in confining deportees to an excluded class that cannot legalize its territorial presence. As a form of "resistance," unlawful reentry is limited by the severe risks of physical harm posed by traveling without authorization, the degree of social exclusion experienced by those who live in the United States without legal status, and the fact that, if re-apprehended, unlawful reentrants are criminally prosecuted, incarcerated, and deported again. Indeed, since reentry potentially activates and justifies the U.S. border enforcement apparatus, reentry may fuel rather than undermine the deportation regime.

Conclusion and Recommendations

In uncanny ways, deportation from the United States reproduces the violence of the Salvadoran civil war. During the 1980s and early 1990s, Salvadorans fled death squads, human rights abuses, forced recruitment, and societal violence. Children were left behind, family and community ties were disrupted, and émigrés were denied asylum. The very conditions that gave rise to emigration and that prevented migrants' full legal integration into the United States in turn contributed to the deportation of the individuals interviewed for this chapter. Deportation inflicts violence upon deportees and their family members, both directly, through the process of removal and, indirectly, through stigmatization and impact on family members. Parents and children are once again separated and asylum and other forms of legalization are once again largely out of reach. This indirect victimization, or secondary deportation, raises serious concerns about the future well-being—and incorporation—of spouses and children left behind in the United States.

By terming deportation a form of *social suffering*, we seek to reconnect these confounding effects of deportation to the historical conditions in which deportation is situated. While U.S. deportation policies apply to all non-citizens, not only Salvadorans, it is important to situate both migration and deportation in the labor and geopolitical histories that have shaped migrants' lives, homelands, and connections to the United States. Deportation results not only from particular individuals' "bad choices," but also from these broader social histories.

The modern deportation regime in the United States is based largely on the logic of citizenship-as-membership. Those who qualify for and obtain citizenship in the United States are considered full members of society and granted full rights as part of the larger body politic. The evolution of deportation policies over the last few decades has capitalized on this notion through the extension of what Daniel Kanstroom (2007) dubs *extended border control* and *post-entry social control*. The border enforcement apparatus has grown increasingly militarized and has extended into the interior. Perhaps more problematic, however, is the use of deportation as a tool to cleanse society of unwanted others, such as noncitizens convicted of crimes. Using citizenship as a measure of membership, however, is confounded by the fact that many deportees grew up and were socialized in the United States, identify with the United States more than with their countries of origin, and are perceived and treated as second-class citizens, unworthy of full participation in the nation to which they legally belong after removal. Deportation, then, not only removes "unwanted" others, but also, in a sense, transforms de facto U.S. citizens into de facto stateless persons.

The experiences of victimization and the various ways in which deportees navigate and remake their lives after deportation suggest several reforms that could minimize the collateral consequences of the modern deportation regime. First, many deportees experience deportation as an exile from the home they established in the United States. The restoration of section 212(c) of the Immigration and Nationality Act, which was eliminated by the reforms of 1996, would allow immigration judges discretion in removal decisions and provide removal relief for noncitizens inadmissible due to certain criminal convictions. This reform would permit judges to allow individuals, on a case-by-case basis, to remain in the United States if their equities warranted it, and would thus recognize that legal citizenship is not the only measure of belonging in the United States. Second, deportees who are returned to countries they barely know are often subjected to stigmatization, discrimination, and unjust criminalization. Some are able to remake their lives in the United States, but many others may be forced into gangs or criminal activities to survive. This problem could be addressed through programs that would help deportees learn skills, find employment, and adjust to their post-deportation lives psychologically and socially. In El Salvador, one such program, *Bienvenidos a Casa*, is charged with providing reintegration support, but the assistance it can provide is limited by funding shortages. By helping deportees successfully reintegrate into society, U.S. State Department economic support of programs such as this would proactively help prevent growing gang membership in Latin America. Finally, in response to their experience of deportation-as-exile, post-deportation victimization, and forced separation from family members left behind, many deportees attempt dangerous, clandestine, and criminalizing returns to the United States in spite of formal bans on reentry (see also Hagan, Eschbach, and Rodriguez 2008). Considering this common response, the United States could entertain the idea of the creation of a special humanitarian visa for deportees whose families experience hardship because of separation across borders. The visa would allow deportees to temporarily visit and help their children who are struggling to incorporate successfully into U.S. society following separation from their parents. Cumulatively, these three reforms would acknowledge territorial personhood, or alien citizenship, as a marker of social membership, while also recognizing that deportees' formal legal citizenship in El Salvador does not guarantee social membership and that they have ties and family formations that are not unproblematically undone by removal.

NOTES

The authors thank Marjorie Zatz, Charis Kubrin, and Ramiro Martinez for the invitation to write this chapter, and we thank the reviewers for their helpful comments. Susan Coutin's research would not have been possible without the collaboration of CARECEN Internacional, and the efforts of Luis Perdomo in particular. Jesus Aguilar supported the research from the outset, and Tony Azucar and Samuel Uribe also helped with arrangements. Homies Unidos also generously provided contacts and allowed interviews to take place at its offices. She is grateful to Luis Romero, Edgar Ramirez, Miguel Arévalo and to the individuals in San Salvador and Usulutan who helped to schedule and arrange interviews, but who will remain anonymous for reasons of confidentiality. Tim Goddard also provided valuable research assistance. Research was supported through funds from the National Science Foundation's Law and Social Sciences Program, Award #SES-0518011. Kathleen Dingeman-Cerda would also like to acknowledge CARECEN Internacional and Homies Unidos, as well as Alcance Victoria and el Centro de Intercambio y Solidaridad. She would like to particularly thank Pastor Salvador Fierro, Dra. Sofia de Delgado, and Cristy Ayala for their assistance in locating interviewees, helping with travel arrangements, and assisting with translation in San Salvador. She also owes much gratitude to Rubén G. Rumbaut and Susan Coutin for their support and mentorship throughout the project. Her research was supported through funds from the Human Rights Fellowship Program at the University of California–Berkeley Human Rights Center.

1. Unless otherwise noted, pseudonyms have been used to identify interviewees.
2. We draw here on Daniel Kanstroom's talk at the Immigration Law Teachers Workshop and on Peter Morales's presentation at the annual meeting of the Law and Society Association, both of which occurred in Chicago in May 2010.

BIBLIOGRAPHY

Allegro, Linda. 2006. "Deportations of 'Illegal Aliens' Under a Neoliberal Security Agenda: Implications for Central America." *AmeriQuests* 3(1): Online. Available: http://ejournals. library.vanderbilt.edu/ameriquests/viewarticle.php?id=50. Accessed: January 23, 2009.

Binford, Leigh. 2002. "'Violence in *El Salvador*: A Rejoinder to Philippe Bourgois's 'The Power of Violence in War and Peace." *Ethnography* 3(2): 201–19.

Bosniak, L. 2006. *The Citizen and the Alien: Dilemmas of Contemporary Membership*. Princeton, NJ: Princeton University Press.

Bourgois, Philippe. 2001. "The Power of Violence in War and Peace: Post-Cold War Lessons from El Salvador." *Ethnography* 1(2):5–34.

Cabot, Heath. 2010. *Translating Law and Lives: Asylum and Legal Aid in Athens. Doctoral Dissertation, Sociocultural Anthropology, University of California, Santa Cruz.*

Chacón, Jennifer. 2007. "Whose Community Shield? Examining the Removal of the 'Criminal Street Gang Member.'" *University of Chicago Legal Forum*, 17–357.

Comfort, Megan M. 2008. *Doing Time Together: Love and Family in the Shadow of Prison*. Chicago: University of Chicago Press.

Coutin, Susan. 2003. *Legalizing Moves: Salvadoran Immigrants' Struggle for U.S. Residency*. Ann Arbor: University of Michigan Press.

Coutin, Susan. 2007. *Nations of Emigrants: Shifting Boundaries of Citizenship in El Salvador and the United States*. Ithaca, NY: Cornell University Press.

Coutin, Susan Bibler. 2010. "Confined Within: National Territories as Zones of Containment." *Political Geography* 29(4): 200–208.

Coutin, Susan Bibler. 2011. "Falling Outside: Excavating the History of Central American Asylum Seekers." *Law & Social Inquiry*.

Dalton, Juan José. 2002a. "Armas y muerta van de la mano en El Salvador." *La Opinión*. April 25. Available at www.laopinion.com. Accessed August 5, 2002.

Dalton, Juan José. 2002b. "Reportaje: La violencia no cede en El Salvador." *La Opinión*. March 11. Available at www.laopinion.com. Accessed August 9, 2002.

Das, Veena and Arthur Kleinman. 2000. *Violence and Subjectivity*. Berkeley: University of California Press.

Das, Veena and Arthur Kleinman. 2001. *Remaking a World: Violence, Social Suffering, and Recovery*. Berkeley: University of California Press.

De Genova, Nicholas P. 2002. "Migrant 'Illegality' and Deportability in Everyday Life." *Annual Review of Anthropology*. 31: 419–47.

De Genova, Nicholas and Nathalie Peutz. 2010. *The Deportation Regime: Sovereignty, Space, and the Freedom of Movement*. Durham, NC: Duke University Press.

Dingeman, M. Kathleen and Rubén G. Rumbaut. 2010. "The Immigration-Crime Nexus and Post-Deportation Experiences: En/Countering Stereotypes in Southern California and El Salvador." *University of La Verne Law Review* 31(2): 363–402.

Fariña, Laura Pedraza, Spring Miller, and James L. Cavallaro. 2010. Eds. *No Place to Hide: Gang, State, and Clandestine Violence in El Salvador*. (Human Rights Program Practice Series) Cambridge, MA: Harvard University Press.

Goffman, Irving. 1986. *Stigma: Notes on the Management of Spoiled Identity*. Beaverton, OR: Touchstone Press.

Goldstein, Daniel M. 2010. "Toward a Critical Anthropology of Security." *Current Anthropology* 51(4): 501–502.

Hagan, Jacqueline, Karl Eschbach, and Nestor Rodriguez. 2008. "U.S. Deportation Policy, Family Separation, and Circular Migration." *International Migration Review* 42: 64–88.

Hamilton, Nora L. and Norma Chinchilla. 2001. *Seeking Community in a Global City: Guatemalans and Salvadorans in Los Angeles.* Philadelphia: Temple University Press.

Human Rights Watch (HRW). 2009. "Forced Apart (By the Numbers): Noncitizens Deported for Mostly Nonviolent Offenses." New York. Available at: http://www.hrw.org/en/reports/2009/04/15/forced-apart-numbers-0. Accessed May 2, 2009.

Kanstroom, Daniel. 2000. "Deportation, Social Control, and Punishment: Some Thoughts about Why Hard Laws Make Bad Cases." *Harvard Law Review* 113(8): 1890–1935.

Kanstroom, Daniel. 2007. *Deportation Nation: Outsiders in American History.* Cambridge, MA: Harvard University Press.

Menjívar, Cecilia. 2000. *Fragmented Ties: Salvadoran Immigrant Networks in America.* Berkeley: University of California Press.

Menjívar, Cecilia. 2006. "Liminal Legality: Salvadoran and Guatemalan Immigrants' Lives in the United States." *American Journal of Sociology* 4: 999–1037.

Moodie, Ellen. 2010. *El Salvador in the Aftermath of Peace: Crime, Uncertainty and the Transition to Democracy.* Philadelphia: University of Pennsylvania Press.

Morawetz, Nancy. 2000. "Understanding the Impact of the 1996 Deportation Laws and the Limited Scope of Proposed Reforms." *Harvard Law Review.* 8: 1936–1962.

Motomura, Hiroshi. 2006. *Americans in Waiting: The Lost Story of Immigration and Citizenship in the United States.* New York: Oxford University Press.

Mountz, Alison, Richard Wright, Ines Miyares, and Adrian J. Bailey. 2002. "Lives in Limbo: Temporary Protected Status and Immigrant Identities." *Global Networks* 4: 335–356.

Office of Immigration Statistics. 2010. *2009 Yearbook of Immigration Statistics.* Washington, DC: Department of Homeland Security.

Overseas Security Advisory Council (OSAC). 2010. "El Salvador 2010 Crime & Safety Report." Washington, DC. Available at: https://www.osac.gov/Reports/report.cfm?contentID=116372. Retrieved March 22, 2010.

Portes, Alejandro and Min Zhou. 1993. "The New Second Generation: Segmented Assimilation and its Variants among Post-1965 Immigrant Youth." *Annals of the American Academy of Political and Social Science* 530: 74–89.

Programa de las Naciones Unidas para el Desarollo El Salvador (PNUD). 2005. "Informe sobre Desarrollo Humano de El Salvador 2005: Una Mirada al Nuevos Nosotros, Impacto de las Migraciones." Report. San Salvador, El Salvador.

Rumbaut, Rubén G. and Walter A. Ewing. 2007. "The Myth of Immigrant Criminality and the Paradox of Assimilation: Incarceration Rates among Native and Foreign-Born Men." *Immigration Policy Center Special Report.* Washington, DC: American Immigration Law Foundation.

Scheper-Hughes, Nancy and Philippe I. Bourgois, eds. 2004. *Violence in War and Peace: An Anthology.* Malden, MA: Blackwell Publishing.

Sztompka, Piotr. 2000. "Cultural Trauma: The Other Face of Social Change." *European Journal of Social History* 3(4): 449–466.

Vigil, James Diego. 2002. *A Rainbow of Gangs: Cultures in the Mega-City.* Austin: University of Texas Press.

Zilberg, Elana. 2004. "Fools Banished from the Kingdom: Remapping Geographies of Gang Violence between the Americas (Los Angeles and San Salvador)." *American Quarterly* 56(3): 759–779.

Zilberg, Elana. 2007. "Gangster in Guerilla Face: A Transnational Mirror of Production Between the U.S. and El Salvador." *Anthropological Theory* 7: 37–57.

Zilberg, Elana. 2011. *Transnational Geographies of Violence: An Inter-American Encounter from the Cold War to the War on Terror.* Durham, NC: Duke University Press.

7

Race, Land, and Forced Migration in Darfur

WENONA RYMOND-RICHMOND AND JOHN HAGAN

Tragically, victimization resulting from a genocidal attack continues for survivors long after the attack is over. This has certainly been the case for survivors of the Darfur genocide. Beyond the traumatic experience of genocide itself, Darfur genocide survivors have witnessed further victimization and human rights violations resulting from forced relocation and displacement. Though less apparent, refugees continue to experience ethnic cleansing, rape and sexual assault, and property loss on the journey to and within the camps. Yet forced displacement has not received the same attention as other human rights violations and "often seems to be accepted as a sad but inevitable consequence of war" (Hollenbach 2008: 2).

Making matters worse, new forms of victimization have emerged for the Darfurian refugees after the genocide, including stigmatization, family disruption, domestic violence, and poverty. The fact that the Sudanese government orchestrated and participated in the genocide and forced displacement of its Black African citizens results in additional complexities and difficulties regarding the likelihood of safely returning to one's homeland. Further

complicating the potential of returning to one's homeland is the repopulation of their villages by settlers who often were perpetrators in attacks by
Arab groups.

Our prior work on the Darfur genocide (2008a, 2008b, 2009) has focused
on defining the attacks as genocide, calculating mortality figures, determining who the perpetrators are, illuminating the racial motivation for the
attack, and critiquing the discipline of criminology for being inattentive to
crimes against humanity, war crimes, and genocides. In this chapter, we shift
our attention from the genocidal incident itself to the aftermath of genocide
to understand the hidden consequences and complexities of surviving a
genocidal attack and being forced to take residence in a refugee camp. Hidden consequences and complexities include the perpetuation of violence,
looting, and ethnic cleansings and new forms of violence and alienation
occurring after the genocidal attack. The data we analyze consist of 1,136 surveys, open-ended questions, and interviews with Darfur refugees.

Immigrants, Refugees, and Internally Displaced Persons

Refugees and immigrants share common disadvantages, including high
levels of poverty and discrimination in their home country. Nonetheless,
significant differences exist. Frequently the distinction is made between
whether the migration to another country occurred by choice, and the
degree to which returning home is feasible (see Kunz 1973; Joly 2002). Refugees typically migrate to another country not by choice but because of social,
cultural, or political pressures, which forced them out of their native country.
Moreover, returning home for a refugee is uncertain and typically involves a
lengthy stay in a refugee camp.

The Geneva Refugee Convention defines a refugee as:

Any person who owing to well-founded fear of being persecuted for reasons of race, religion, nationality, membership of a particular social group
or political opinion, is outside the country of his nationality and is unable,
or owing to such fear, is unwilling to avail himself of the protection of that
country; or who, not having a nationality and being outside the country of
his former habitual residence, is unable, or owing to such fear, is unwilling
to return to it.

Refugees have exceptionally diverse historical and political origins, and
the usefulness of the term is "not as a label for a special, generalizable 'kind'
or 'type' of person or situation," but "as a broad legal or descriptive rubric

that includes within it a world of different socioeconomic statuses, personal histories, and psychological or spiritual situations" (Malkki 1995: 496).

According to recent figures published by the United Nations High Commission for Refugees (UNHCR 2010), more than 43 million people worldwide have been forcibly displaced due to conflict and persecution. Of these 43 million, Darfurians account for approximately 250,000 refugees in camps in Chad, and 2.6 million have been internally displaced. The UNHCR is responsible for protecting and assisting refugees; however, there is no comparable organization within the United Nations for internally displaced persons. With little to no international legal protection, internally displaced individuals often suffer greatly at the hands of their government. Such is the case in Darfur, where the Sudanese government has prevented delivery of medical care and humanitarian aid to IDP camps (see ICC 2007; Kostas 2006; Totten 2006).

Survivors of the Darfur genocide who reside in refugee camps in the neighboring country of Chad are the focus of this chapter. Individuals and families that fled to Chad came under the protection of the Geneva Refugee Convention, which entitles them to legal protection, shelter, food, and water. While shelter in the camps, at least initially, often took the form of a plastic tarp, the situation is believed to be far worse for the Black African survivors residing in IDP camps. One ADS interviewer stated, "I found working in the refugee camps in Chad much harder than working in Kosovo and Bosnia. In Chad, the refugees were in areas that had no resources and, for the first time, I saw people who literally had nothing" (Totten and Markusen 2006: 90).

Background: The Genocide in Darfur

The genocidal conflict began in February 2003 and is still disastrously ongoing as of this writing. More than 400,000 Black African Darfurians have been killed and 2–3 million have been forcibly displaced (Hagan, Rymond-Richmond, and Parker 2005; Hagan and Rymond-Richmond 2008a, 2008b, 2009; Hagan and Palloni 2006). The perpetrators are the Sudanese government and the Janjaweed, who are almost exclusively Arab. The victims are Black Africans. Unlike Southern Sudan, where religious differences are frequently attributed as the cause of conflict, in Darfur, the Arabs and Black Africans practice the Muslim religion. The root cause of the genocidal conflict in Darfur is racial and ethnic hatred. Elsewhere we demonstrate the central role of racism and dehumanization motivating the violence through an analysis of the words and phrases shouted by the perpetrators (Hagan and Rymond-Richmond 2008a, 2008b). Legal precedence for examining the words and phrases shouted by the perpetrators to their victims as evidence for genocidal motivation was established in the *Akayesu* decision in Rwanda (UN 1998) and the *Jelisi* decision in Bosnia (UN 1999). This process of dehumanizing the victims in genocidal conflict is similar in meaning and motivation to hate crimes (Green, McFalls, and Smith 2001; Horowitz 2001; Jenness and Broad 1997). In both cases, dehumanizing language diminishes moral and practical constraints on participants and bystanders, and this is an intrinsically important collective action process (see also Hagan and Rymond-Richmond 2008b).

Below we describe the data we analyze. We then examine the perpetuation of violence en route to refugee camps as well as in the camps. Next, we identify new forms of violence, alienation, and gender relationship changes in the camps. Finally, we discuss the difficulties associated with Darfurian refugees returning home when the violence incurred was state sponsored.

Methods

The data we analyze come from the historically unprecedented U.S. State Department Atrocities Documentation Survey (ADS). In the summer of 2004, the U.S. State Department authorized and funded the collection of this data set. The Coalition for International Justice (CIJ) assumed field responsibility for conducting the survey. The data consist of 1,136 surveys, open-ended questions, and interviews with Darfur refugees living in 20 refugee camps and settlements in the neighboring country of Chad (see Howard 2006). This remarkable survey cost the U.S. government nearly $1 million to complete, yet aside from a brief summary presentation before Congress by Colin Powell, it remained largely unused in the archives of the State Department.

The ADS data extensively described and measured victimization during the attack that caused the survivors to flee, while en route to the refugee camp in Eastern Chad, and once in the refugee camps. We know of only one other systematic study of pre-camp violence in Darfur (Depoortere et al. 2004), and none that include sexual violence. Since the beginning of the conflict about 18 months earlier, refugees reported when, how, and why they had left Darfur and if, when, and how they, their family, or fellow villagers were harmed. The survey mixed the closed-ended format of health surveys with the semistructured format of legal witness statements (Respini-Irwin 2005). The ADS interviews include vivid descriptions of violence, rape, property loss, and torture of self, family, and villagers. The data include the age, gender, and group memberships of the displaced individuals, the separate and combined government and Janjaweed militia attacking groups, the forms of attacks, their particular reported targets, the density of settlement clusters, measures of rebel activity, and reports of hearing the racial epithets, as described below.

The strength of the data is the detailed information regarding the attacks on home villages and during the journey to the refugee camp. ADS data are weaker in documenting experiences within the camp. This is largely a result of the research objectives as well as the fact that many of the interviews were conducted with individuals that had recently arrived in the camps. It was not an objective to target new arrivals for interviews; instead, this frequently occurred because interviewers conducted the ADS interviews during the early stages of the genocide.

The Perpetuation of Violence, Looting, and Ethnic Cleansing

Victimization for Black-African Darfurians does not end with the genocidal attack on their village. The data we analyze considered all deaths and disappearances since the beginning of the attacks in February 2003, as well as deaths and disappearances during the journeys to refugee camps in Chad. The ADS data recorded the deaths and disappearances of extended family members (2,701), villagers (9,300), and nuclear family members (360) defined as husbands, wives, sons, and daughters. Of the 360 deaths of nuclear family members, 213 were killed, 119 are missing, and 28 died in the flight to a refugee camp or close to camp or in the camps. Of the 28 who died in flight, 82.1 percent (n=23) died on the journey to the camps, and the remaining 17.9 percent (n=5) died close to or in the camps (see Hagan, Rymond-Richmond, and Parker 2005).

The survey was not explicitly designed to gather information on deaths in the camps that resulted from the displacement. Nonetheless, a small proportion of interviewees provided information on deaths, attacks, stigma, and other forms of violence and exclusion occurring in and near the refugee camps. Their experiences indicate that victimization continues for genocide survivors long after the initial attack is over.[1]

Journey to the Refugee Camp

Starvation, dehydration, inhospitable weather, and injuries incurred from the genocidal conflict were the primary causes of deaths en route to the refugee camps. Babies, children, pregnant women, and the elderly were least likely to survive the journey. Providing a description of the toll the journey took on children, one refugee reports, "many young kids died because of the cold weather. We would walk for three or four days with no food or water. They would also die from this." A pregnant woman who gave birth on the journey was among those who fled from a village near Karnoi after Janjaweed and Sudanese soldiers brutally attacked her village. She and the baby died. In addition, an old woman "died from cold" and fatigue and "two children died of cold."

For some Black Africans, the journey to the refugee camps took months[2] with multiple attacks characterizing the flight. A Zaghawa male from a village near Umm Berro describes his journey:

> My village was attacked three times by Janjaweed and Sudanese soldiers. The final attack on my village included hundreds of perpetrators arriving in more than 22 cars and 200 horses. During the attack, the perpetrators yelled, "Black colours must be killed." His infant daughter died during the journey from what he describes as a "terrible fever" from "bombing smoke." During the journey to the refugee camp, he personally witnessed the raping of two young girls around the age of 7. When asked why the attacks occurred, he responded, "Because of colour. They want to genocide the black. They want us to never be able to go back again."

Multiple attacks and deaths of fellow villagers also occurred during Musa's[3] flight to Chad after his home was bombed and looted. Musa arrived at Goz Beida camp after five days of travel, during which time he was shot at twice. Musa survived the attack, however 20 of his fellow villagers died of gunshot wounds on their way to the camp. At the time of the interview, Musa and the other survivors from his village were "all living under a tree."

Violence in the Camps

Darfurians report that violence, rapes, abductions, property destruction and loss, and ethnic cleansing persisted in and near the refugee camps. Despite these reports being fewer in number than accounts of violence occurring in their home villages, it is important to document the genocide in as holistic a way as possible, and we therefore include a brief summary of victimization reported in or near the refugee camps. Refugees reported that victimization in the camps often occurred when the need for firewood and water required refugees to travel on the edges and outskirts of the camps. Women were typically the victims because of the gendered division of labor among the Darfurian refugees in which collecting wood and water is the delegated responsibility of women. One refugee reported that the Janjaweed regularly stood guard at a water well used by the Darfurian refugees. The Janjaweed "wouldn't allow males to get water from the well. Only women could go and they were beaten and attempts were made to capture them." In this particular situation, the Chadian army intervened; however, other Dafurian refugee camps and camps around the world report similar forms of gendered victimization (see also Hyndman 2004; Hans 2004). In addition to physical attacks, Darfurians also experienced raids by the Janjaweed, the purpose of which usually was to steal their remaining livestock.

New Forms of Violence, Alienation, and Gender Relationships in the Camps

Pain and suffering does not end once the Darfurian enters a refugee camp. Physical and sexual violence, deaths of family members and fellow villagers, and the loss of property continue to haunt Darfurians long after the genocidal conflict. In fact, new forms of victimization have emerged in the camps for the refugees, including stigmatization, ostracism, and family disruption. Though less obvious, these new forms of victimization resulting from forced displacement illuminate the hidden consequences and complexity of the Darfur genocide. Below we discuss (1) the many ways that raped women continue to be victimized in the refugee camps, and the ways in which rape affects not only individuals, but entire communities; (2) how trauma affects refugees' mental health; (3) domestic violence as a new form of abuse experienced in the camps; and (4) transformations in gender roles following the flight from genocide.

RAPE

Physically, sexual violence results in reproductive trauma, sexually transmitted diseases (including HIV), and pregnancy. Psychological effects include profound feelings of helplessness and despair that persist as post-traumatic stress disorders. In the camps, raped women suffer stigma, ostracism, and reduced likelihood of marriage. In broader terms, intergroup rape is a means of controlling reproduction and is a powerful weapon for destruction of social groups. The Rwandan *Akayesu* case identified rape as "an integral part of the process of destruction" outlawed by the Genocide Convention. Much like in Serbia, Kosovo, and other conflict zones in Africa, the perpetrators rape for the purpose of instilling terror, dehumanizing the victims, and as a means of population extermination (see Bracewell 2000; Diken and Laustsen 2005; Salzman 1998; Wood 2006; Mullins and Rothe 2008; Mullins 2009).

Stigma and cultural taboos in Darfur make it difficult to document and estimate the number of rapes. We defined sexual victimization as including rape, sexual assault, acts of sexual molestation such as insertion of foreign objects into the genital opening or anus, and sexual slavery. Four percent of the full sample and 7 percent of women refugees reported personal victimization (Hagan, Rymond-Richmond, and Palloni 2009). The latter approximates reporting of sexual assaults in Sierra Leon (Amowitz et al. 2002). Nearly a third of the Darfur refugees (29.1%) indicated that other villagers were sexually victimized during attacks. ADS interviewers Jan and Brent Pfundheller provide a powerful non-quantitative illustration of how widespread and stigmatized sexual violence is in the refugee camps. They describe an incident in which they waited in a private area on the edge of the camp for women to tell of the sexual violence suffered personally and by fellow villagers. They expected only a few women to assemble; instead, hundreds gathered (see Totten and Markusen 2006: 94–95).

Because of the patriarchal structure of the society in which lineage is determined by patrilineal parentage, children of Black African rape victims are considered Arabic. Inter-group rape is thus a means of controlling biological and cultural reproduction and is a powerful weapon of destruction. The Genocide Convention includes within its definition of genocide "measures intended to prevent births within the group."

The perpetrators' motivation of raping to instill fear, dehumanize the victims, and to control the biological and cultural reproduction of the women by "changing the race" through impregnating the victims is revealed in the words and phrases shouted during the attack. Fatima was gang raped by 10 men and she quotes them as yelling, "You are black people's wives and you bear black children, but now you have to bear white people's children."[4] Near the village of Seleya, the perpetrators told their victims, "We will kill all men and rape the women. We want to change the color. Every woman will deliver red. Arabs are the husbands of those women." A Masalit refugee heard her Arabic attackers say that they would "Kill as many Masalit as they could and that the rest would never live there again." The attackers also announced, "We will take your women and make them ours. We will change the race."

Abducting women and girls for sexual enslavement was a frequent occurrence. In a village near Karnoi, 50 girls were raped and "have been taken as sexual slaves." Mariam, a female refugee from Tine, was one of 20 women who were abducted by government soldiers and Janjaweed when her village was attacked. She escaped and bravely chronicled the abuse with an ADS interviewer in a refugee camp in Chad:

They attacked my village three times. By the last attack, my house was destroyed. There were eight days of bombing. They brought reinforcements. After the first bombing, the men ran and left their families. They took the cars and left. The Arabs took women—they take the pretty ones. They killed any men they found behind. She saw twenty women taken. She was "taken." The attackers said, "We don't like black men or women in this area.

Although she did not report being raped, the interviewer indicated that she likely was. Raped women are often more comfortable discussing the sexual violations of others than discussing victimization in the first person.

Some abducted women were never seen again, while others arrived in the refugee camps after being held captive for days or weeks after being gang raped by Sudanese soldiers and the Janjaweed. Some of these women escaped, while others were returned to their villages or camps by their attackers. These raped women became the living symbols of genocide, dehumanization, and defeat.

Several of the raped women interviewed became pregnant by their attackers. The long-lasting scars of a cohort of children born from rape in Darfur is still tragically unfolding, and it is likely their fate will be similar to that seen in former Yugoslavia and post-war Bangladesh, in which widespread rapes produced mixed ethnic children. In addition to rape altering the children's ethnic lineage, Mullins (2009: 722) includes the following two effects: (1) the children symbolize the genocide and the subsequent humiliation and derogation of the victims; and (2) it causes the creation of a new group of outcasts that "enhances the social disorganization of villages and cities" (see also Diken and Laustsen 2005; Salzman 1998).

MENTAL HEALTH

A significant portion of refugees develop chronic mental health problems, including depression, anxiety, and post-traumatic stress disorder in the aftermath of genocide and ethnic violence (De Jong et al. 2001; Marshall et al. 2005; Fazel, Wheller, and Danesh 2005). A survey of Darfur refugees in Cairo describes numerous depressive symptoms including "hopelessness, tearfulness, apathy, decreased concentration, decreased or increased sleep, low appetite, weight loss, low mood, decreased energy, and guilt" (Meffert and Marmar 2009: 1841).

While all the Darfurian refugees experienced the trauma of genocide, for some, trauma included bearing witness to extremely brutal killing and tortures. A glimpse into the extreme brutality is provided in the following interviews. In addition to being gang raped, Mariam observed "four preg-nant women attacked by soldiers. The soldiers slit open their bellies and desecrated the fetus if it was male." Several other Darfurians interviewed as part of the ADS data reported targeting pregnant women, male babies or fetuses, and children. Another female refugee witnessed extreme torture of young boys in the village, which included slitting their throats, cutting the foot open from the big toe to the ankle, cutting off hands and sexual organs, removal of the brain, and removal of skin. A female Zaghawa from a small village near Karnoi witnessed the death of seven men who were "dismem-bered alive. They cut off their penises and put them in their mouths. Cut off their tongues and cut them into pieces."

Refugees in the ADS used the following words to describe their mental state: "fatigue," "shock," and "nervous shakes." Interviewers frequently pro-vide a description of the interviewees, which often includes "head down," "eyes averted," and "distressed." Demonstrating devastation, injustice, and hopelessness, a female refugee whose husband and son were murdered asserts, "I feel there is no justice in Sudan and maybe in the world. What can I believe in after losing my husband and son? And who will help me with my baby."

NEW PROBLEMS AND OPPORTUNITIES FOR WOMEN?

Research conducted in refugee camps, communities post-conflict, and com-munities in which refugees have returned home upon exile may be par-ticularly insightful in illuminating additional hidden consequences Darfur refugees may experience in the future. Stress, tension, anger, and new com-munity and family arrangements resulting from the genocide may lead to new types of violence and gender relationships. Such is the case in Southern Sudan, where women's victimization may extend beyond the external enemy to include men within the community who transfer aggression and mascu-linity on the battlefield into the home in the form of domestic violence and sexual assaults (Jok 1999, 2000; see also Khawaja and Barazi 2005).

Despite the horrors of war, there is some evidence that women are empowered during wartime (Cockburn 2004). While it might be difficult for some to accept any positives associated with the tragedy of wartime conflict, the following two examples illuminate human agency and resilience. In the first example, the Women's Commission of Human Rights League of Chad (1998, 127) attributes the 1979 civil war with altering the patriarchal structure of Chadian society when survival created the opportunity for women to par-ticipate in the labor force. In another example, Blacklock and Crosby (2004) describe the transformative experience indigenous women underwent in refugee camps. In the camps, and in the absence of a large male presence, the women organized, learned the language of the NGOs, and asserted their right to be involved in decision making. When they returned to their home many years later, their newly acquired skills threatened the male leadership in the community. In addition, "refugee men began to reassert more patriarchal roles within the family and community that they had occupied prior to exile" (2004, 60).

RETURNING HOME?

The process of a refugee returning to their homeland is met with numerous challenges. However, this process encompasses particular challenges when the violence incurred is state sponsored, as is the genocide in Darfur. The Sudanese government denies all charges of war crimes. Yet, state denial does not end there. The government also denies genocide is occurring, the number of deaths, and even that the crime of rape exists in Sudan (Associated Press 2007).[5] In the words of one Darfurian refugee, "Please let the Sudanese government know what we are telling you because they are saying that they don't know anything and that nothing happened to us." Many Darfurians are certain of government participation in the genocide. According to one refugee, "The government wants to kill us. I know it's the government because otherwise how would they have the Antinovs, the helicopters, and the troops?" Elsewhere we have described the participation of both the Sudanese government militia and the Janjaweed in genocidal attacks on Black African villagers in Darfur. Further, through statistical models, we demonstrated that when the Sudanese militia and the Janjaweed join forces to collectively attack Black African villagers, the effect is a greater number of killings than when either group attacks alone.

Despite state denial, the victims now become eyewitnesses with rich, detailed descriptions of perpetrators, including names when known, to ADS interviewers, journalists, and others invested in documenting the "crime of crimes." Indeed, the refugee interviews are a genocidal trove of evidence. They include a large amount of eyewitness evidence including the names of dead and raped victims, descriptions of weapons, locations of mass graves, and accounts of the government direction, supervision, and participation in attacks on Black African groups.

Evidence of the Sudanese government's participation in the genocide is mounting. At the time of this writing, the Chief Prosecutor for the International Criminal Court (ICC) is charging two individuals in the Sudanese government with genocide, including the president of Sudan, Omar al Bashir. It leaves open the question of how victims can return home when the country's president is charged with genocide. Despite criminal charges and a warrant for his arrest, Bashir was reelected as president in April 2010.

Another government official, Ahmad Muhammad Harun, is also charged by the ICC for participating in the violence against Black African villagers and continues to serve in a government position. Charges against Harun include 20 counts of crimes against humanity and 22 counts of war crimes, including murder, rape, and torture. As an example of exceptional cruelty, Harun was appointed as the Minister of State for Humanitarian Affairs (2006–2009). A man charged with participating in and orchestrating the genocidal attacks that killed hundreds of thousands and forcibly displaced 2–3 million Black African Darfurians was subsequently appointed a government position to oversee humanitarian aid to those he victimized. In the United States, the term "double marginalization" or "double victimization" describes victims injured both by the act as well as by a criminal justice system that is insensitive to those harmed. In Darfur, victims are double victimized by the act of genocidal violence and by the government responsible for protecting its citizens participating in attempts to exterminate a segment of the population.

The possibility of safely returning home is highly improbable given that the president and other government officials charged with genocide are still in positions of power. Structural violence, in which violence is "frozen into structures and the culture that legitimizes violence" (Galtung 1996: vii), existed prior to the genocide and remains intact. Demonstrating structural violence and macro-level ideological precursors to the violence, one refugee succinctly stated, "They don't like us. The government of Sudan has never given the black people anything, education or anything. The government gave the Janjaweed guns to kill us." Another reported, "The government does not want to give us anything. The white people of Sudan think that because we are black we should not be in Sudan. The government of Sudan supports giving Whites education and other things but if we ask for it they will kill us." A third refugee stated, "Africans from the area told the Sudanese government, we want our rights (development, education). So the Sudanese government decided to kill everyone to get rid of the headache." In the final example, the interviewee went further back in history to illuminate structural violence. In his own words, "since independence [in the 1950s] the government of Sudan hasn't given anything to people of Darfur—the people were asking for education and other things, and the government did not want us to ask for these things so they are killing us." He concisely concludes, "I think this happened to Darfur because we're all black."

Refugees recognize the improbability of safely returning home. One refugee simply states, "I don't think we can ever go home." Others recognize that return can only occur with the assistance of the United Nations. In the words of one interviewee, "The UN is our father and mother now. We can't return back to that hell without the protection from this cruel government." Another refugee expresses similar sentiments: "The only way this problem will stop is from help by United Nations and other countries because our Government is involved in it." The government of Sudan continues to be predominately Arabic, leaving Black Africans underrepresented in political positions of power. Unfortunately, there is no reason to believe that racial discrimination, the root cause of the Darfur genocide, has disappeared. Nonetheless, a recent report found that nearly all (98 percent) of the Darfurian refugees interviewed wanted to return to the location where they used to live.

What do the refugees have to return to? Many arrived in the camps with no material possessions. Their village was completely destroyed, homes were burned to the ground, water wells were poisoned, food stores and seed were destroyed or looted, and their livestock was taken. These possessions are necessary for physical and cultural survival. In the words of one male refugee, "I am here and have nothing anymore and my other wives are not here with me. Please return our things and our village. In Darfur we have Petroleum and Gold, here we have nothing." Beyond the massive killing and raping of Black Darfurians, looting and property destruction is yet another way that the Sudanese government and the Janjaweed created conditions intended to destroy the group conditions of life for Black Africans in Darfur. Indeed, the attackers engaged in multiple forms of victimization, each of which single-handedly meets the legal criteria of genocide according to Article II of the Genocide Convention.[6]

Further decreasing the probability of safely returning and pursuing livelihoods in their home villages is the repopulation of their village by their genocidal perpetrators. Repopulation threatens to make the displacement of Black African refugees from Darfur permanent and is yet another means of genocide. As illustrated in the following interview excerpts, there is widespread belief among the refugees that the Sudanese government and the Janjaweed intend to—or have already—repopulated their once Black African villages with Arabs:

- Sudanese military and Janjaweed wants to kill all African tribes in Darfur so they can live on the land. The land has very good grass.
- The government want to kill everyone, they have destroyed our houses, and now they will build Arab houses.
- The Arabs wanted to kill everyone in Darfur. The Arabs want to change all the towns to Arab towns.

- Because they want to take our village and give it to the Janjaweed because our place is nice for cattle.

In a recent report conducted by 24 Hours for Darfur (Loeb 2009), Darfurian refugees were asked what they thought was happening to their land. The most frequent response (65 percent) "was that it was being occupied by other people" (24 Hours for Darfur 2009: 37). When elaborated upon, "other people" meant Janjaweed, Arabs, or foreigners (24 Hours for Darfur 2009). Resettlement of Black African areas by Arabs is further documented in a 2004 Human Rights Watch report and by humanitarian workers in Darfur who indicated that the Sudanese government brought tens of thousands of Arab settlers to Darfur from neighboring countries (Bloomfield 2007).

Conclusion

The purpose of this chapter is to expand our understanding of the hidden consequences, complexities, and layered realities surrounding international migration. Refugees' experience with victimization includes forcible displacement from their native country. For survivors of the genocide in Darfur, state-created vulnerabilities do not end with the genocidal attack and forced displacement. Tragically, rape and sexual assault, ethnic cleansing, and property loss that occurred during the genocidal incident perpetuate during the journey to the refugee camps and while in the refugee camps. Making matters worse, new forms of hidden, state-created vulnerabilities have emerged post-genocide. Some of the new vulnerabilities, such as family disruption, poverty, trauma, and the unlikely return to their homeland, affect all Black African Darfurian refugees. Other vulnerabilities, such as stigmatization and impregnation resulting from rape, underscore the gendered nature of victimization in Darfur.

Within the field of international migration is a debate regarding whether immigrants and refugees are fundamentally distinct categories. One the one hand is the realist perspective, which suggests that the groups are distinguished by whether the migration was by choice or not. For refugees the migration is not by choice but a result of social, cultural, or political pressures, which forced them out of their native country. For immigrants, the migration is by choice and typically for economic opportunities. Additional distinctions are made between the categories based on their likely ability to return to one's homeland and their relationship to the state. On the other hand is the nominalist perspective, which suggests that the binary categories are blurry, socially constructed, used to advance state interests, and mask the similarities between immigrants and refugees. Rather than adjudicate between these positions, the purpose here is to link their shared experience and to highlight the role of the state in creating vulnerabilities affecting immigrants and refugees, their families, and their communities.

The underlying dynamics of racial violence Darfurian refugees experience is not unlike similar forms of conflict and discrimination experienced by immigrants and minorities in other parts of the world. In the Global North, social exclusion takes on many forms, notably homelessness and imprisonment. Albeit in different ways and to varying degrees, large numbers of adults and children are denied the human right to secure shelter in the nations of both the Global North and the Global South. Discrimination, stereotypes linking concentrated immigration with violence (see Sampson and Bean 2006; Martínez 2002), and imprisonment are pervasive mechanisms of social exclusion in the late modern Global North; forced migration and mortality are persistent processes of social exclusion in the contemporary Global South.

Domestic policies of legal exclusion in the Global North—with their legal forms of harassment and discrimination, arrest, due process, conviction, and incarceration—exist a world apart from the policies of exclusion in the Global South, with their criminal forms of death squads, militias, disappearances, and displacements. In addition, the individualized punishments of the North are imposed with some protections. The challenge is to see common themes as well as differences.

Weaknesses in legal and other protective measures in both the United States and Darfur result in extensive racial disparities. In the United States, these disparities follow from discriminatory practices of police harassment and arrests, including the right of police to demand immigration documents from any individual perceived as being undocumented (for example, SB 1070 in Arizona), the massively disproportionate incarceration of young Black men, and misapplications of the death penalty. Increased disenfranchisement results. Meanwhile, the racial oppression in Darfur remains catastrophic and the violence is spreading to other regions in Sudan. The racial consequences of the use of the political, military, and paramilitary command structures of the Sudanese state to organize militia attacks on Black African groups in Darfur continue to mount in scale. This results in hundreds of thousands of killings and rapes, displacement, deportation, property loss, and the confinement of millions of homeless Africans in internal displacement camps and refugee camps. At the time of this writing, violence has erupted in another region of Sudan, South Kordofan. Much like the genocide in Darfur, in South Kordofan Black Africans are being killed and displaced. And once again the predominately Arabic northern Sudanese government and army are believed to be perpetuating the violence. The eerie similarities to the genocide in Darfur include Ahmad Muhammad Harun, recently and controversially elected as governor of Southern Kordofan, who is charged by the International Criminal Court with 20 counts of crimes against humanity and 22 counts of war crimes, including murder, rape, and torture for his role in the Darfur genocide.

One important hope is that the institutions of international criminal law can narrow the distance between the troubled settings of the North and South, yet policies in both parts of the world are based on punishment more often than restoration. They share notable features: the impulses to exclude and repress. The alternative impulses, to include and support, are elusive in both the Global North and the Global South. Discrimination against immigrants and racial minorities and genocidal death and displacement display an awkward symmetry along the mean streets of the global village. Their risks and vulnerabilities are joined by parallel and failed policies of punishment and exclusion.

NOTES

Portions of this chapter were published by John Hagan and Wenona Rymond-Richmond in *Darfur and the Crime of Genocide.* 2008. Cambridge: Cambridge University Press.

1. Sexual violence in refugee camps and internally displaced camps is not uniquely a Sudanese problem, as it has been documented in numerous conflict zones.

2. The journeys to the refugee camps can take years. The ADS survey was conducted in the summer of 2004, and most date spring of 2003 as the beginning of the conflict. As of June 2010, the genocide continues making it conceivable that the journey to a refugee camp may take several years, especially taking into account the likelihood of episodic residence in nearby villages and IDP camps prior to arrival.

3. Individuals interviewed have been given pseudonyms in order to protect their anonymity.

4. Use of "white" here and in some other interviews and surveys is used to refer to Arabic rather than Black African.

5. In an interview, Omar al-Bashir stated, "It is not in the Sudanese culture or people of Darfur to rape. It doesn't exist. We don't have it."

6. According to Article II of the Genocide Convention, genocide means any of the following five acts committed with intent to destroy, in whole or in part, a national, ethnic, racial, or religious group:
Killing members of the group
Causing serious bodily or mental harm to members of the group
Deliberately inflicting on the group conditions of life calculated to bring about its physical destruction in whole or in part
Imposing measures intended to prevent births within the group
Forcibly transferring children of the group to another group

REFERENCES

24 Hours for Darfur. 2009. "Darfurian Voices: Documenting Darfurian Refugees' Views on Issues of Peace, Justice, and Reconciliation." http://www.darfurianvoices.org/ee/images/uploads/DARFURIAN_VOICES_DocuVoices_Report.pdf (accessed January 27, 2011).

Amowitz, Lynn, Chen Reis, Kristina Lyons, Beth Vann, Binta Mansaray, Adyinka Akinsulure-Smith, Louise Taylor, and Vincent Iacopino. 2002. "Prevalence of War-Related Sexual Violence and Other Human Rights Abuses Among Internally Displaced Persons in Sierra Leone." *JAMA* 287: 513–521.

Associated Press. 2007. "U.S. Criticizes Sudan's President for Denying Rape in Darfur." *International Herald Tribune*, March 20.

Blacklock, Cathy, and Alison Crosby. 2004. "The Sounds of Silence: Feminist Research across Time in Guatemala." In *Sites of Violence*, ed. Wenona Giles and Jennifer Hyndman 45-72. Berkeley: University of California Press.

Bloomfield, Steve. 2007. "Arabs Pile into Darfur to Take Land 'Cleansed' by Janjaweed." *The Independent*, July 14.

Bracewell, W. 2000. "Rape in Kosovo: Masculinity and Serbian Nationalism." *Nations and Nationalism*, 6: 563–590.

Cockburn, Cynthia. 2004. "The Continuum of Violence: A Gender Perspective on War and Peace." In *Sites of Violence*, ed. Wenona Giles and Jennifer Hyndman. Berkeley: University of California Press.

De Jong, J. T., Komproe, I. H., Van Ommeren, M., El Masri, M., Araya, M., Khaled, N., et al. 2001. "Lifetime Events and Posttraumatic Stress Disorder in Four Post Conflict Settings." *JAMA* 286: 555–562.

Depoortere, Evelyn, Francesco Checchi, France Broilet, Sibylle Gerstl, Andrea Minetti, Olivia Gayraud, et al. 2004. "Violence and Mortality in West Darfur, Sudan (2003–04): Epidemiological Evidence from Four Surveys." *The Lancet* 364: 1315–1320.

Diken, B. and C. B. Laustsen. 2005. "Becoming Abject: Rape as a Weapon of War." *Body and Society* 11(1): 111–128.

Fazel, Mina, Jeremy Wheeler, and John Danesh. 2005. "Prevalence of Serious Mental Disorder in 7000 Refugees Resettled in Western Countries: A Systematic Review." *The Lancet* 365 (9467): 1309–1314.

Galtung, John. 1996. *Peace by Powerful Means: Peace and Conflict, Development and Civilization*. Thousand Oaks, CA: Sage.

Green, Donald, Laurence McFalls, and Jennifer Smith. 2001. "Hate Crime: An Emergent Research Agenda." *Annual Review of Sociology* 27: 479–504.

Hagan, John and Alberto Palloni. 2006. "Death in Darfur." *Science* 313: 1578–1579.

Hagan, John and Wenona Rymond-Richmond. 2008a. *Darfur and the Criminology of Genocide*. Cambridge: Cambridge University Press.

———. 2008b. "The Collective Dynamics of Race and Genocidal Victimization in Darfur." *American Sociological Review* 73: 6.

Hagan, John, Wenona Rymond-Richmond, and Alberto Palloni. 2009. "Racial Targeting of Sexual Violence in Darfur." *American Journal of Public Health* 99(8): 1386–1392.

Hagan, John, Wenona Rymond-Richmond, and Patricia Parker. 2005. "The Criminology of Genocide: The Death and Rape of Darfur." *Criminology* 43: 525–561.

Hans, Asha. 2004. "Escaping Conflict: Afghan Women in Transit." In *Sites of Violence*, ed. Wenona Giles and Jennifer Hyndman 232-248. Berkeley: University of California Press.

Hollenbach, David. 2008. "Human Rights as an Ethical Framework for Advocacy." In *Refugee Rights: Ethics, Advocacy, and Africa 1-9*. Washington, DC: Georgetown University Press.

Horowitz, Donald. 2001. *The Deadly Ethnic Riot*. Berkeley: University of California Press.

Howard, Jonathan. 2006. "Survey Methodology and the Darfur Genocide." In *Genocide in Darfur: Investigating the Atrocities in Sudan*, ed. Samuel Totten and Eric Markusen 59-74. New York: Routledge.

Human Rights Watch. 2004. "Darfur Destroyed: Ethnic Cleaning by Government and Militia Forces in Western Sudan." Human Rights Watch May 2005, 16, 6(A).

Hyndman, Jennifer. 2004. "Refugee Camps as Conflict Zones: The Politics of Gender." In *Sites of Violence*, ed. Wenona Giles and Jennifer Hyndman 193-212. Berkeley: University of California Press.

International Criminal Court (ICC), Office of the Prosecutor. 2007. Situation in Darfur, The Sudan: Prosecutor's Application under Article 58 (7), February 27.

Jenness, Valerie and Kendal Broad. 1997. *Hate Crimes: New Social Movements and the Politics of Violence*. New York: Aldine de Gruyter.

Jok, Jok Madut. 1999. *Africa* 69: 194–212.

———. 2000. *Journal of African and Asian Studies* 34: 427–442.

Joly, Daniele. 2002. "Odyssean and Rubicon Refugees: Toward a Typology of Refugees in the Land of Exile." *International Migration* 40(6): 3–22.

Khawaja, Marwan and Rana Barazi. 2005. "Prevalence of Wife Beating in Jordanian Refugee Camps: Reports by Men and Women." *Journal of Epidemiology and Community Health* 59(10): 840–841.

Kostas, Stephen. 2006. "Making the Determination of Genocide in Darfur." In *Genocide in Darfur: Investigating the Atrocities in Sudan*, ed. Samuel Totten and Eric Markusen 111-126. New York: Routledge.

Kunz, Egon F. 1973. "The Refugee in Flight: Kinetic Models and Forms of Displacement." *International Migration Review* 7(2): 125–146.

Loeb, Jonathan. 2009. "Darfurian Voices: Documenting Darfurian Refugees' Views on Issues of Peace, Justice, and Reconciliation." 24 Hours for Darfur.

Malkki, Liisa. 1995. "Refugees and Exile: From 'Refugee Studies' to the National Order of Things." *Annual Review of Anthropology* 24: 495–523.

Marshall, G. N., T. L. Schell, M. N. Elliott, S. M. Berthold, and C. A. Chun. 2005. "Mental Health of Cambodian Refugees Two Decades after Resettlement in the United States. *JAMA* 294: 571–579.

Martínez, Ramiro, Jr. 2002. *Latino Homicide: Immigration, Violence, and Community*. New York: Routledge.

Meffert, Susan M. and Charles R. Marmar. 2009. "Darfur Refugees in Cairo: Mental Health and Interpersonal Conflict in the Aftermath of Genocide." *Journal of Interpersonal Violence* 24: 1835–1848.

Mullins, Christopher W. 2009. "We are Going to Rape you and Taste Tutsi Women." *British Journal of Criminology* 49: 719–735.

Mullins, Christopher W. and D. L. Rothe. 2008. *Blood, Power and Bedlam: Violations of International Criminal Law in Post-Colonial Africa*. New York: Peter Lang.

Respini-Irwin, Cyrena. 2005. "Geointelligence Informs Darfur Policy." *Geointelligence* September 1, 2005.

Salzman, Todd A. 1998. "Rape Camps as a Means of Ethnic Cleansing: Religious, Cultural and Ethnic Responses to Rape Victims in the Former Yugoslavia." *Human Rights Quarterly* 20: 348–378.

Sampson, Robert and Lydia Bean. 2006. "Cultural Mechanisms and Killing Fields: A Revised Theory of Community-Level Racial Inequality." In *The Many Colors of Crime*, ed. Ruth Peterson, Lauren Krivo, and John Hagan, 8-361. New York: New York University Press.

Totten, Samuel. 2006. "The U.S. Investigation into the Darfur Crisis and Its Determination of Genocide: A Critical Analysis." In *Genocide in Darfur: Investigating the Atrocities in Sudan*, ed. Samuel Totten and Eric Markusen. New York: Routledge.

Totten, Samuel and Eric Markusen. 2006. *Genocide in Darfur: Investigating the Atrocities in Sudan*. New York: Routledge.

UNHCR. 2010. "2009 Global Trends: Refugees, Asylum-seekers, Returnees, Internally Displaced and Stateless Persons." Country Data Sheets. June 15, 2010. Accessed online 9/17/10. http://www.unhcr.org/4c11fobe9.html.

United Nations Judgment Report. *The Prosecutor v. Jean-Paul Akayesu*, Case No. ICTR-96-4-T, 1998, International Criminal Tribunal for Rwanda, Office of the Prosecutor at 7.8.

United Nations Judgment Report. *The Prosecutor v. Goran Jelisi*, Case No. ICTY-95-10-T, 1999, International Criminal Tribunal for the former Yugoslavia, Office of the Prosecutor at 75.

Women's Commission of the Human Rights League of Chad & The Editors. 1998. Women Denounce their Treatment in Chad. In Meredith Turshen and Clotilde Twagiramariya, *What Women Do in Wartime: Gender and Conflict in Africa*. New York: Zed books Ltd.

Wood, Elisabeth Jean. 2006. "Variation in Sexual Violence during War." *Politics and Society* 34: 307–341.

PART III

Layered Realities

8

Situating the Immigration and Neighborhood Crime Relationship across Multiple Cities

MARÍA B. VÉLEZ AND CHRISTOPHER J. LYONS

Since the early waves of immigration into the United States during the late 1800s, the relationship between immigration and neighborhood crime has garnered considerable interest among social scientists and the general public. Although the preponderance of criminological research on the topic during the last century offers little evidence that immigration leads to more crime, until relatively recently, traditional criminological thinking nonetheless held that the presence of immigrants should increase neighborhood crime. Traditional criminological theory contended that immigrants bring deviant and pro-crime orientations to neighborhoods, disrupt social networks and social cohesion among residents, or place strain upon local service institutions (see Martínez 2006 for a review). These general arguments parallel much public opinion, which also equates higher levels of immigration with increased crime rates (Martínez 2006). Despite such claims and in line with what has been stressed throughout this volume, more recent criminological research finds either that immigration has no impact on local crime levels, or, more commonly, that immigration reduces neighborhood crime (Martínez and

Valenzuela 2006). Importantly, this relationship between immigrant presence and neighborhood crime holds true at the cross section, as well as across multiple time points.

To make sense of this pattern, today researchers typically suggest that rather than destabilize communities, immigrants revitalize neighborhoods because they fortify processes related to crime control. Social scientists note that when immigrants move into communities they can strengthen relationships among residents, invigorate local ethnic economies, and help to expand community institutions such as churches, schools, and immigrant-focused agencies (Lee, Martínez, and Rosenfeld 2001; Martínez 2002; Martínez, Lee, and Nielsen 2004). Thus, in contrast to much public opinion and traditional criminology, current social science research expects immigration to translate into lower than expected rates of local crime.

Although the "protective" impact of immigration on local crime rates is relatively well-established (Stowell et al. 2009; Ousey and Kubrin 2009; Wadsworth 2010), we know less about the conditions that may exacerbate or hamper the ability of immigrants to revitalize and reinvigorate communities and shape neighborhood crime. Our goal in this chapter is to identify some of the complexities and layered realities surrounding the immigration and crime relationship. We advance the literature beyond asking *whether* immigrant concentration affects crime to a more nuanced understanding of the conditions under which immigrants shape neighborhood crime processes. We argue that the ability of recent immigrants to revitalize and reinvigorate communities, and therefore reduce neighborhood crime rates, varies by the context of reception. Specifically, the capacity of immigrants to revitalize neighborhoods should be enhanced in areas with more pronounced histories of immigrant settlement. We explore this general idea by investigating two questions. First, as relatively poor neighborhoods receive the greatest proportions of recent immigrants, we ask whether neighborhood socioeconomic disadvantage conditions the relationship between immigration and crime. Second, we ask whether the moderating effect of neighborhood socioeconomic status is further enhanced in "gateway" cities. According to Singer (2004), gateways are cities with established histories of receiving immigrants and populated by significant numbers of immigrants.

Research shows that relatively economically disadvantaged neighborhoods are more likely to receive recent immigrants and to establish supportive immigrant institutional arrangements (Ley 2008; Logan, Zhang, and Alba 2002). Insofar as economically disadvantaged neighborhoods are places with relatively sustained immigration and immigrant institutional infrastructures, we expect the protective association between immigration and crime to be maximized in these neighborhoods. In contrast, we expect this protective association to be weakened, or perhaps even reversed, in more affluent neighborhoods, which tend to have less immigration and limited, if any, institutional arrangements that support immigrants.

Furthermore, just as some neighborhoods may be more accustomed to immigration than others, some cities also have more pronounced histories of immigrant reception and incorporation. Gateway cities, in particular, are well-established ports of entry for immigrants that offer a variety of advantages including strong immigrant institutional infrastructures as well as large shares of co-ethnics who can provide critical housing and employment information (Painter and Yu 2008; Singer 2004; Waters and Jiménez 2005). We expect that the negative association between immigration and crime will be most pronounced in disadvantaged neighborhoods located in gateway cities accustomed to immigration with strong immigrant institutional infrastructures. In contrast, we expect the interaction between immigration and disadvantaged neighborhoods to be less substantial in non-gateway cities unaccustomed to immigration and without the accompanying institutional arrangements to accommodate new arrivals.

In this chapter, then, we explore first whether the often-found negative relationship between recent immigration and neighborhood crime is limited to or enhanced in economically disadvantaged neighborhoods, and second, if this moderating effect of neighborhood disadvantage is further enhanced in gateway cities. We do so by drawing on a unique multilevel data set—the National Neighborhood Crime Study (NNCS) (Peterson and Krivo 2010a)—which provides demographic and violent crime data for 6,926 neighborhoods within 69 cities. The NNCS allows us to begin exploring the neighborhood and city-level contexts of reception that may influence the immigration-crime relationship.

Conceptual Arguments

Historically, criminologists who studied neighborhoods understood that disadvantaged places were places of immigrant settlement (Shaw and McKay 1942). Shaw and McKay (1942) argued that greater proportions of foreign born contributed to neighborhood heterogeneity, which in turn contributed to social disorganization, or the decreased ability of neighborhoods to control crime collectively. Language barriers in heterogeneous neighborhoods and cultural clashes (with Anglo populations and between children of immigrants and their parents' old world values) undermined the forms of social control and cohesion necessary for effective organization against crime. After initial interest by Chicago-school scholars, inquiry into the connections between immigration and crime waned until recently (Martínez and Valenzuela 2006).

The wave of immigration in the 1990s renewed interest in and research on immigration and crime. A major finding in this literature is that immigration often has negative effects on violence at the neighborhood and metropolitan levels (Lee et al. 2001; Martínez 2002, 2006; Martínez et al. 2004; Martínez, Rosenfeld, and Mares 2008; Ousey and Kubrin 2009; Wadsworth 2010). Communities with large shares of immigrants tend to have lower levels of violence than similarly situated neighborhoods with few immigrants (Lee et al. 2001; Martínez et al. 2004)· At the city level, Wadsworth (2010), for example, finds that cities with the largest increases in the proportions of recent immigrants were characterized by the greatest reductions in homicide and robbery between 1990 and 2000, net of important controls such as economic disadvantage and the percentage of young males.

These findings suggest that rather than destabilize communities and cities by way of increasing social disorganization, immigrants contribute positively to areas, an argument consistent with the "immigrant revitalization perspective" (Lee et al. 2001; Martínez 2002; Martínez et al. 2004). Given the strong support for the null or protective "effect" of immigration on crime, we believe it is central to move beyond asking *whether* immigrant concentration affects neighborhood crime to a more nuanced understanding of the *conditions* under which immigrants shape neighborhood crime processes. In the following section, we elaborate on two contexts that likely shape how immigration impacts neighborhood violent crime rates—a neighborhood's level of disadvantage and a city's gateway status.

The Context of Neighborhood Disadvantage

Research on the spatial distribution of crime has long established the robust connection between socioeconomic disadvantage and neighborhood crime rates (Bursik and Grasmick 1993; Krivo and Peterson 1996; Sampson and Wilson 1995; Shaw and McKay 1942; Wilson 1996). Disadvantaged neighborhoods are associated with several community characteristics that make crime more prevalent, including weakened ties between neighbors, limited access to jobs and conventional role models, and reluctance to intervene on behalf of the common good. Consequently, disadvantaged neighborhoods struggle to engage in the kind of community social control necessary to reduce crime, such as organizing neighborhood watches, intervening when suspicious activity occurs, or making the police more accountable to residents' needs.

Drawing on the immigrant revitalization perspective mentioned earlier, we expect that immigrants can revitalize neighborhoods—especially relatively disadvantaged neighborhoods— in three key ways. First, recent immigrants typically develop strong ties to family members, fellow residents including longer-settled immigrants, and to non-kin persons like clergy, social service providers, and school officials. Ebaugh and Curry (2000) found that immigrants create "fictive" ties in their new neighborhoods as a strategy to garner social and economic resources. Most critical for the perspective developed here, these familial and fictive relationships help generate social control.

Second, the influx of recent immigrants in large numbers helps to re-invigorate an ethnic enclave economy. An ethnic enclave is often characterized by the presence of immigrants with sufficient social capital to create new opportunities for economic growth and an extensive ethnic division of labor. Typical enclave businesses are restaurants, street vendors, and open-air markets that generally arise as a response to the needs of the growing immigrant population. As such, enclaves are thought to provide social capital for their residents by creating a context for widespread job opportunities and higher wages not available outside the enclave for immigrants and non-immigrants (Portes and Zhou 1993). Thus, while many residents may still be poor, the majority of them are working and should have greater attachment to the labor market.

Third, an influx of immigrants should expand and strengthen community institutions such as churches, schools, and immigrant-focused agencies like legal counseling and job placement, allowing them to serve more effectively as brokers on the community's behalf (Chinchilla, Hamilton, and Loucky 1993; Theodore and Martin 2007). For example, Theodore and Martin (2007) studied the Albany Park neighborhood in Chicago, a long-standing point of entry for immigrants in the city, and found that its organizations had expanded in scope, number, and size to serve the needs of the recently arrived immigrant community. Such revitalized organizations, for instance, helped Albany Park confront potential threats associated with gentrification like affordable housing and advocate for day laborers who experienced economic injustices. Ley (2008) found that the influx of immigrants helped strengthen neighborhood churches in Vancouver, British Columbia to better facilitate social networks and the delivery of personal and social services to local residents. Community institutions facilitate crime control because they organize activities that create networks among residents, provide programming for community youth, help connect communities to mainstream individuals and institutions, and facilitate the recruitment of external resources for the community (Theodore and Martin 2007).

This discussion leads us to expect a contingent relationship between recent immigrants and neighborhood disadvantage. Because concentrated immigration is associated with social capital, ethnic enclaves, and institutional vitality, recent immigration should counter the criminogenic effects of economic disadvantage on neighborhood crime rates. Furthermore, the protective effect of recent immigrants on violent crime should be *enhanced* in disadvantaged neighborhoods given that these areas traditionally have received greater shares of immigrant populations. In these neighborhoods, immigrants are better situated to draw on the already strong social ties, enclave economies, and immigrant-serving institutions to help revitalize neighborhoods.

Recent work on the immigrant revitalization perspective is broadly consistent with the argument that the revitalization capacity of recent immigrants should be particularly apparent in disadvantaged neighborhoods. One study by Vélez (2009) finds that the negative association between immigration and homicide is limited to contexts of disadvantage, whereas an influx of recent immigrants is associated with more crime in affluent Chicago neighborhoods. In a multi-level study of Chicago neighborhoods, Morenoff and Astor (2006) find that first-generation youth are less likely to engage in violence and property offending if they live in extremely disadvantaged neighborhoods. The authors suggest that first-generation youth who live in disadvantaged communities are likely surrounded by larger shares of foreign-born residents who supply social capital to them by, for instance, increasing economic opportunities, enforcing conventional norms, and reinforcing parental authority over children (Morenoff and Astor 2006).

The Context of City Gateway Status

The two studies discussed above focus on Chicago, a traditional immigrant "gateway" city, which Singer (2004) defines as a large metropolitan area that has had higher than average foreign-born populations since 1950. Is the protective function of immigration in disadvantaged neighborhoods limited to gateway cities? Gateway cities offer critical resources that facilitate immigrant integration into society. The literature points to three major factors of gateway destinations that better position immigrants for integration: (1) the presence of co-ethnics, (2) employment opportunities, and (3) institutional arrangements that lead to a receptive social and legal climate (Hernández-León and Zúñiga 2002; Waters and Jiménez 2005). Each of these factors suggests that the protective function of immigration in disadvantaged neighborhoods should be enhanced in gateway versus non-gateway cities.

The presence of co-ethnics is an important feature of established immigrant destinations. Co-ethnics provide social capital to their fellow immigrants, especially new arrivals, which helps them navigate their new environment. Painter and Yu (2008), for example, find that a homeownership deficit persists for 15–20 years between immigrants residing in gateway versus new gateway metro areas. They argue that ethnic enclaves are contexts for new immigrants to access both financial and non-financial resources from longer-settled immigrants, allowing them to have greater success in finding a home and employment. This gateway advantage is transportable to non-gateways. According to Hernández-León and Zúñiga (2002), immigrants who move from established gateways to non-gateways are able to draw upon their "funds of knowledge" gained from living in gateways to then quickly settle and integrate into new communities and establish soccer leagues, run for local office, or start community organizations.

Established immigrant cities are better positioned to facilitate the economic incorporation of immigrants (Bohon and DeJong n.d.; Bohon, Massengale, and Jordan 2009; Logan, Zhang, and Alba 2002; Painter, Yang, and Yu 2004). For instance, new immigrants may be able to access employment-related information like hiring sites from longer-settled immigrants, allowing them to have greater success upon arrival in the United States. But non-gateways have fewer and smaller ethnic communities available for immigrants, and so residents living there may be less successful in terms of employment, despite sometimes stronger economies in new destinations. In a study of occupational quality, Bohon and DeJong (n.d.) find that Mexican immigrant workers have worse jobs, on average, in new Latino destinations than in traditional gateways, net of age and length of time in the United States. Bohon and colleagues (2009) find that, net of other factors, Mexican immigrants are less likely to be self-employed in non-gateways and that they do not use self-employment as a way of overcoming English and educational deficiencies like they do in gateways. The authors suggest that established gateways are better situated to provide pathways for upward mobility for immigrants compared to non-gateways.

Places accustomed to immigration also have institutional arrangements such as legal aid bureaus, health clinics, and bilingual services that influence immigrant integration (Marrow 2009; Portes and Rumbaut 2006; Waters and Jiménez 2005). These institutional arrangements form in response to the historical presence of immigrants and well-established migrant networks. For example, Trillo (2004) finds that immigrants from Ecuador, Peru,

Colombia, and the Dominican Republic are able to take advantage of educational programs in New York that were originally designed to help earlier waves of immigration but are sustained with constant flows of immigration into the gateway city of New York. Non-gateways, however, have fewer of these institutional arrangements and thus are less able to absorb new influxes of immigrants. Indeed, Waters and Jiménez (2005) describe how the influx of immigrants into non-gateways often places a strain on municipal services to residents. This literature also suggests that an important consequence of this strain is a less receptive social and legal climate, which can be less accommodating to the needs of immigrants.

The key resources for integration provided by gateway cities may also shape the ability of immigrant populations to moderate the effect of disadvantage on neighborhood crime rates. Receptive cities should be better able to support disadvantaged immigrant neighborhoods as they seek external resources and thus help disadvantaged neighborhoods combat crime. In contrast, in newer immigrant destinations, immigrants may be less able to broker the necessary social, economic, and/or political resources to "revitalize" disadvantaged areas. Under less supportive and integrative conditions, the influx of immigrants into economically disadvantaged areas may not lead to revitalization and may instead heighten social disorganization. One study thus far has examined this logic with a sample of U.S. counties (Shihadeh and Barranco 2010). The authors divide counties into two categories—traditional and new destination—and find that linguistic isolation (a measure of immigrant concentration) is related to reductions in Latino homicide victimizations in traditional counties, presumed to be long-established, well-organized, traditional immigrant communities where Spanish is a dominant language. In contrast, Shihadeh and Barranco (2010) find that linguistic isolation increases Latino homicide victimization in new destination counties, partly because linguistic isolation is associated more strongly with economic deprivation in these areas. They conclude that only in traditional destinations, presumed to be well-established and socially organized, can immigrants revitalize communities and "protect" against crime.

In sum, this chapter examines the protective function of immigration on crime by assessing its applicability to two geographical contexts: concentrated disadvantage at the neighborhood level, and gateway status at the city level. We expect that immigrants contribute positively to neighborhoods, but the protective function they serve may be limited to areas of immigrant concentration—specifically, disadvantaged neighborhoods in gateway cities that are equipped with institutional structures to incorporate them into society.

Data and Methods

We utilize a unique data set from the National Neighborhood Crime Study (NNCS) that permits us to examine the relationship between tract-level (neighborhood) disadvantage, immigration, and crime across multiple metropolitan areas. The NNCS includes reported violent crime counts from police departments and census socio-demographic information for all tracts within a representative sample of U.S. cities with populations of more than 100,000 for the year 2000. The large sample of cities generalizes to most urban places and includes traditional gateway and non-gateway cities (Peterson and Krivo 2010b).

Dependent Variable

VIOLENT CRIME

To measure violent crime across tracts, we measure the three-year tract count (1999–2001) of violent crimes (sum of the number of murders and non-negligent manslaughters, forcible rapes, robberies, and aggravated assaults for 1999–2001) reported to the police based upon the location at which the crimes occurred. The NNCS has data on violent crime counts for 6,926 census tracts across 69 cities.

Independent Variables: Tract-level

PERCENT RECENT IMMIGRANTS

Using 2000 Census data, we measure immigrant concentration with the percentage of residents in a census tract who are foreign born and arrived to the United States in 1990 or later. We focus on recent immigrants because we are interested in the dynamic that occurs between disadvantaged neighborhoods and new immigrants, such as the expansion of community organizations and ethnic economies.

CONCENTRATED DISADVANTAGE

Concentrated disadvantage is an index (average z-scores) of the poverty rate, extent of joblessness (percentage of persons aged 16–64 who are unemployed or out of the labor force), low-wage jobs (percentage of workers in the six occupations with the lowest national average incomes), and the percentage of households that are single-mother families (α = .91).

RACIAL COMPOSITION

We include two dimensions of racial composition. First, to capture the percentage African American in a community, we measured the percentage of residents in a census tract who are non-Hispanic African American. Second, to capture the percentage Latino in a community, we measured the percentage of residents in a census tract who are Latino.

RESIDENTIAL INSTABILITY

Residential instability is measured with an index (average z-scores) of the percentage of renter-occupied units and the percentage of residents aged five or older who lived in a different dwelling in 1995 (α = .69).

YOUNG MALES

The percentage of the population that is male and between 15 and 24 years of age controls for the crime-prone population.

City-level Variables

We create a dichotomous measure of city gateway status, where 1 indicates traditional gateway destinations, and 0 indicates all other (non-gateway) cities. Following Singer's (2004) classification, we code Boston, Buffalo, Charlotte, Chicago, Cleveland, Dallas-Fort Worth, Detroit, Denver, Houston, Los Angeles, Miami, Milwaukee, Minneapolis/St. Paul, Philadelphia, Phoenix, Pittsburgh, Salt Lake City, Seattle, San Diego, St. Louis, Tampa, and Washington, DC as gateway cities. In our sample, we find that these gateways are characterized by significantly higher levels of violent crime, recent immigrants, concentrated disadvantage, residential mobility, African Americans, and Latinos at the census-tract level. We acknowledge variation in the history and traditions of the gateway cities above. Singer (2004) classifies gateway cities further in terms of historical emergence, duration, and level of immigration to capture heterogeneity in immigration experiences across metropolitan areas. Although future research should explore the implication of differences among gateway cities for neighborhood crime processes, the limited number of gateway cities in our data set precludes analyses with more specific gateway designations.

Generally following Peterson and Krivo (2010b), we control for several other characteristics of cities that are associated with differential levels of criminal violence: the *percentage of recent immigrants* of a city's total population; the *city-level disadvantage* index, measured in a parallel fashion to the neighborhood indicator; *residential mobility*, measured by the percentage of the city population that moved in the last five years; *log population*; *percentage non-Latino black*; *percentage Latino*; and the *percentage of young males* ages 15 to 24.[1]

Analytic Strategy

We estimate multilevel models with tracts (level-one units) nested within city contexts (level-two units). We grand-mean center all continuous variables. Because we are analyzing relatively rare events within small units, we fit a Poisson model with violence counts as the outcome. We specify that these counts have variable exposure by tract population (which is the same as including tract population as an independent variable with its parameter fixed at 1 in a nonhierarchical Poisson model) and, thereby, make the analysis one of violent crime per capita rates. We tested whether the mean and variance of the dependent variable are equal (an assumption of the Poisson model) and found that the variance of the outcome is considerably larger than its mean (i.e., there is significant over-dispersion). Hence, we control for over-dispersion in the level-one variance. In hierarchical linear models, a Poisson model with over-dispersion is analogous to a negative binomial model.

To create the interaction term between percentage recent immigrants and concentrated disadvantage, we mean centered the component variables. In supplementary analyses, variance inflation factors indicated minimal concern for multi-collinearity in the models.

Results

We first explore whether immigration conditions the effect of disadvantage on crime in neighborhoods across multiple cities. Previous research (e.g., Morenoff and Astor 2006; Vélez 2009) found that immigrants can diminish the criminogenic effects of neighborhood disadvantage on violent crime in Chicago, but does this moderating potential hold for other cities as well? Table 8.1 presents multi-level models predicting violent crime counts for census tracts across 69 cities. The results indicate that the moderating effect generalizes beyond a single city: the significant and negative product term in model 1 shows that, on average across the full sample of cities and tracts, the protective effect of recent immigrants on neighborhood violent crime is enhanced as disadvantage increases. The interaction also indicates that the positive effect of concentrated disadvantage on violent crime levels is *attenuated* as percentage recent arrivals increases in neighborhoods.[2]

Figure 8.1 provides a visual depiction of this contingent relationship between levels of immigration and economic disadvantage, holding constant all other variables at their means. (For recent immigration and economic disadvantage, "Average" reflects the mean value, whereas "High" refers to one standard deviation above the mean, and "Low" refers to one standard deviation below the mean.) This relationship is robust to neighborhood-level controls of residential stability, percentage black and Latino, and young males. Moreover, the model controls for variation across cities in terms of city population, disadvantage, residential stability, percentage black and Latino, new immigrants, and young males.

Table 8.1. Multi-level Poisson Regressions (with Variable Exposure) Predicting Violent Crime (robust standard errors in parentheses)

	Model 1	Model 2	Model 3
	All Cities	Gateway Cities	Non Gateway Cities
	b	b	b
	(SE)	(SE)	(SE)
Tract-Level Covariates			
% Recent Immigrants	-.004*	-.004	-.002
	(.002)	(.004)	(.004)
Concentrated	.693***	.505***	.723***
Disadvantage	(.038)	(.034)	(.054)
Concentrated Disadvantage * % Recent Immigrants	-.007***	-.006**	-.002
	(.002)	(.003)	(.004)
Residential Instability	.255***	.271***	.233***
	(.020)	(.034)	(.022)
% African American	.005***	.008***	.002**
	(.001)	(.001)	(.001)
% Latino	.003*	.005**	.004**
	(.001)	(.002)	(.002)
% Young Males	-.017***	-.015***	-.016***
	(.002)	(.002)	(.004)
Intercept	-3.796***	-3.434***	-4.074***
	(.041)	(.041)	(.050)
N (tract-level)	6920	3673	3238

	Model 1	Model 2	Model 3
	All Cities	Gateway Cities	Non Gateway Cities
	b	b	b
	(SE)	(SE)	(SE)
N (city-level)	69	17	52

Note: * *p* < .05 (one-tailed); ** *p* < .01 (one-tailed); *** *p* < .001 (one-tailed)

Models also control for city-level variables of recent immigrants, concentrated disadvantage, residential mobility, logged population, percentage African American, percentage Latino, and percentage young males (estimates not shown).

We next explore whether the contingent relationship between recent immigrants and neighborhood disadvantage holds across a key city-level characteristic—its gateway status. In models 2 and 3 of table 8.1, we divide the sample by gateway status and examine the interaction between tract-level recent immigration and disadvantage. This is analogous to exploring a three-way interaction between immigration, disadvantage, and gateway designation. The results indicate that the moderating effect of immigration on disadvantage is limited to traditional gateway destinations, which in our sample means cities like Boston, Dallas-Fort Worth, Miami, San Diego, and Washington, DC. Specifically, model 2, which restricts the sample to gateway cities, reveals a negative interaction between immigration and disadvantage. However, this interaction is not statistically significant when applied to non-gateway cities (model 3). We note that these results hold

Figure 8.1. The Effect of Recent Immigrants on Local Violent Crime Levels by Neighborhood Disadvantage

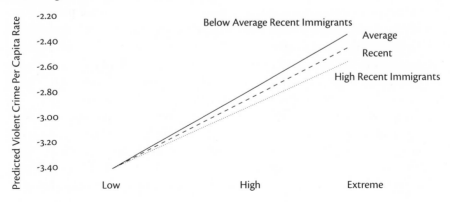

despite the reduced number of cities (and thus reduced statistical power) in model 2.

Together, our results suggest that although immigration helps to reduce the deleterious effects of economic disadvantage on neighborhood crime *on average* (as indicated in model 1), this protective and revitalizing effect is limited to those cities with established resources for immigrant reception and integration. That is, only in established immigrant gateways as defined by Singer (2004) does the influx of immigrants into less affluent areas offset the crime-producing effects of economic disadvantage.

Conclusions

A growing number of criminological studies point to the protective or revitalizing effect of immigrant populations for neighborhood crime rates, yet there is less research that tests the conditionality of this relationship. Drawing on a unique multi-level data set of tracts nested in 69 cities across the country, we set out in this chapter to explore two contexts that might moderate the immigration-crime relationship: neighborhood-concentrated disadvantage and city gateway status. We find that such contexts are important for understanding the relationship between percentage of recent immigrants and crime. Specifically, the negative relationship between recent immigrants and tract-level violent crime is enhanced in disadvantaged neighborhood contexts, where presumably there are stronger institutional arrangements to incorporate immigrants into society. The interaction also indicates that the deleterious effect of disadvantage on violent crime is attenuated as the percentage of recent immigrants increases in a census tract. Although disadvantaged tracts still have more violent crime than affluent tracts, disadvantaged tracts with higher concentrations of recent immigrants have notably fewer violent crimes than their counterparts. Disadvantaged neighborhoods by definition suffer from a variety of deleterious socioeconomic deprivations; however, they also are places where larger numbers of recent immigrants settle and reinvigorate local communities by developing strong "fictive" ties to fellow immigrants (both recent and long term) as well as to non-kin persons like clergy, social service providers, and school officials. Such ties and the trust they generate likely lead to an infusion of social control and reductions in crime.

In addition to exploring the "context of reception" (Portes and Rumbaut 2006) at the local level, we also consider the larger context of gateway status at the city level. We hypothesized that gateway cities—places with historical settlement patterns, continued influxes of immigration, and large shares of co-ethnics—would further condition the moderating effect of immigration on disadvantage. Indeed, our findings suggest that the negative interaction between percentage of recent immigrants and concentrated disadvantage is limited to gateway cities. Insofar as gateway cities provide immigrants with greater resources for integration (Painter and Yu 2008; Waters and Jiménez 2005), these findings suggest that city-level context influences the revitalizing capacity of immigration. Only in cities with traditions of immigrant settlement does the influx of recent immigrants help to revitalize the otherwise crime-producing conditions of neighborhood disadvantage. In non-gateway cities, the influx of immigrants into disadvantaged tracts does not translate into reductions in violent crime; however, neither does the influx of immigrants increase crime.

The argument developed here pertains to issues beyond crime. Given the new geography of immigration, scholars have debated the extent to which receiving communities are better or worse off because of new immigrant residents. Some researchers highlight the economic and social strain that follows waves of immigration into new destinations. Others, however, point to how immigration benefits new destinations by reversing trends of population decline. For instance, Crowley and Lichter (2009) find that among non-metropolitan counties, counties that are new immigrant destinations actually enjoy reductions in crime and increases in employment as a result of influxes of immigration and associated reduction in population loss. Our work provides further evidence that, although established gateways benefit the most from immigration, even non-gateway destinations do not become worse and, in fact, sometimes are better off as a result of immigration.

All macro immigration-crime research confronts methodological challenges in isolating the aggregate "effect" of immigration on crime rates. Might some of the patterns we observe result from the selection of immigrants into certain neighborhoods and cities? Longitudinal panel designs are better positioned to address these concerns. However, we are unaware of any longitudinal, multi-level data set for multiple cities that can address the conditionality of the immigration-crime connection.

A few additional avenues of future work seem particularly promising. First, research should consider whether the protective effect of recent immigrants on neighborhood crime is more consequential for some racial/ethnic groups than others. For instance, census data indicate that majority Latino communities are more likely to have recent immigrants than majority white neighborhoods. Given that, on average, minority neighborhoods are more disadvantaged than white neighborhoods, it could be that the protective effect is greatest in minority disadvantaged neighborhoods (Krivo and Peterson 1996; Wilson 1996).

A second avenue of research should investigate more directly why neighborhood immigration in gateway cities translates into lower crime rates. Is it because gateway cities have receptive institutional arrangements like immigrant elected officials, immigrant-focused service agencies, and bilingual education programs that set the stage for immigrant incorporation and thus less crime? Understanding how recent immigrants shape neighborhood crime outcomes will help criminologists illuminate the intersections of immigration, social capital, and crime-producing conditions.

Third, researchers should explore whether heterogeneity among gateway cities explains variation in the immigration-crime connection. Because of data limitations, we treated all gateway destinations as equal, yet gateway cities differ in terms of the historical onset, duration, and size of the immigration population (Singer 2004). The NNCS provide the unique opportunity to examine tract-level crime across multiple metropolitan areas. Although researchers will be hard-pressed to construct a multi-level data set that encompasses more cities, such a data set might permit exploration of the various sub-designations of gateway cities.

Despite claims to the contrary by media, politicians, and the public, criminological research consistently finds that the immigration-crime correlation is either weak or negative. As part of a larger endeavor to understand the mechanisms linking immigration and crime, we suggest that researchers move beyond asking *whether* immigrants affect crime to a more nuanced understanding of the *conditions* under which immigrants shape neighborhood crime processes. We evaluate two contexts at different levels of geographical aggregation—tract-level disadvantage and city-level gateway status. There are, of course, other conditions that indicate important "contexts of reception" worthy of future study (Portes and Rumbaut 2006). Among other factors that influence immigrant incorporation, future research might explore how the presence and extent of ethnic enclave economies and immigrant institutions at the neighborhood level, or immigrant-related policies (in health care, education, or law enforcement) and political empowerment at the city-level, condition the relationship between immigration and crime. Such analyses would advance our understanding of how variations in the climate of reception influence the experience of immigration and its connection to violent crime.

NOTES

Please direct all correspondence to María B. Vélez (mVélez@unm.edu), Department of Sociology, University of New Mexico, MSC05 3080, 1 University of New Mexico,

Albuquerque, NM 87131-0001.We are very grateful to Ruth Peterson and Laurie Krivo, who provided the data to us before it was made publicly available.

1. While most studies examine the crime-prone populations as the percentage of young males ages 15 to 34 (e.g., Peterson and Krivo 2010b), such a measure is highly collinear with key tract and city-level indicators in our model, especially recent immigrants and residential mobility. We opted instead to use young males aged 15–24, which is significantly less correlated with other covariates yet strongly correlated with tract-level violence.

2. Contrary to our expectations, the models reveal a negative and significant relationship between percentage young males aged 15–24 and violent crime. Given that most research finds percentage young males to have no effect or a positive effect on crime, we explored this pattern further. The effect of percentage young males is strongly positively associated with violent crime counts in reduced-form models. Only net of tract-level concentrated disadvantage does the estimate for young males become negative. We also note that including our measure of young males does not alter the general patterns that we describe. We find substantively identical results if we do not account for young males aged 15–24.

REFERENCES

Bohon, Stephanie A. and Gordon F. DeJong. Not published. Mexican Occupational Attainment in Old and New Immigrant Destination. http://paa2007.princeton.edu/download. aspx?submissionId=71549.

Bohon, Stephanie A., Laura Gerard Massengale, and Audrey Jordan. 2009. "Mexican Self-Employment in Old and New Latino Places." In *Global Connections, Local Receptions: Latino Migration to the Southeastern United States*, ed. Fran Ansley and Jon Shefner 197-219. Knoxville: University of Tennessee Press.

Bursick, Robert J., Jr. and Harold G. Grasmick. 1993. *Neighborhoods and Crime.* New York: Lexington.

Chinchilla, Norma, Nora Hamilton, and James Loucky. 1993. Central Americans in Los Angles. In *In the Barrios*, ed. J. Moore and R. Pinderhughes, 51–78. New York: Russell Sage.

Crowley, Martha and Daniel T. Lichter. 2009. Social Disorganization in New Latino Destinations. *Rural Sociology* 74:573–604.

Ebaugh, Helen Rose and Mary Curry. 2000. Fictive Kin as Social Capital in New Immigrant Communities. *Sociological Perspectives* 43: 189–209.

Hernández-León, Rubén and Victor Zúñiga. 2002. *Mexican Immigrant Communities in the South and Social Capital: The Case of Dalton, Georgia.* UC San Diego: Center for Comparative Immigration Studies. Retrieved from: http://www.escholarship.org/uc/item/9r5749mm.

Krivo, Lauren J. and Ruth D. Peterson. 1996. Extremely Disadvantaged Neighborhoods and Urban Crime. *Social Forces* 75: 619–50.

Lee, Matthew T., Ramiro Martínez, Jr., and Richard Rosenfeld. 2001. Does Immigration Increase Homicide Rates? Negative Evidence from Three Border Cities. *Sociological Quarterly* 42: 559–580.

Ley, David. 2008. The Immigrant Church as an Urban Service Hub. *Urban Studies* 45: 2057–2074.

Logan, John R., Wenquan Zhang, and Richard D. Alba. 2002. Immigrant Enclaves and Ethnic Communities in New York and Los Angeles. *American Sociological Review* 67: 299–322.

Marrow, Helen. B. 2009. Immigrant Bureaucratic Incorporation: The Dual Roles of Professional Missions and Government Policies. *American Sociological Review* 74: 756–776.

Martínez, Ramiro. 2002. *Latino Homicide: Immigration, Violence and Community*. New York: Routledge.

Martínez , Ramiro, Jr. 2006. "Coming to America: The Impact of the New Immigration on Crime." In *Immigration and Crime: Race, Ethnicity, and Violence*, ed. R. Martínez, Jr. and A. Valenzuela, Jr., 1–19. New York: New York University Press.

Martínez, Ramiro, Jr. and Matthew T. Lee. 2000. Comparing the Context of Immigrant Homicides in Miami: Haitians, Jamaicans and Mariels. *International Migration Review* 34: 794–812.

Martínez, Ramiro Jr., Matthew T. Lee, and Amie L. Nielsen. 2004. A Segmented Assimilation, Local Context and Determinants of Drug Violence in Miami and San Diego: Does Ethnicity and Immigration Matter? *International Migration Review* 38: 131–157.

Martínez, Ramiro Jr., Richard Rosenfeld, and Dennis Mares. 2008. Social Disorganization, Drug Market Activity, and Neighborhood Violent Crime. *Urban Affairs Review* 43: 846–874.

Martínez, Ramiro J. and Abel Valenzuela, Jr. (eds.). 2006. *Immigration and Crime: Race, Ethnicity and Violence*. New York: New York University Press.

Morenoff, Jeffrey D. and Avraham Astor. 2006. Immigrant Assimilation and Crime: Generational Differences in Youth Violence in Chicago. In *Immigration and Crime: Race, Ethnicity, and Violence*, ed. R. Martínez, Jr. and A. Valenzuela, Jr., 36–63. New York: New York University Press.

Ousey, Graham C. and Charis E. Kubrin. 2009. Exploring the Connection between Immigration and Violent Crime Rates in U.S. Cities, 1980–2000. *Social Problems* 56:447–473.

Painter, Gary and Zhou Yu. 2008. Leaving Gateway Metropolitan Areas in the United States: Immigrants and the Housing Market. *Urban Studies* 45:1163–1191.

Painter,Gary, Lihong Yang, and Zhou Yu. 2004. Homeownership Determinants for Chinese Americans: Assimilation, Ethnic Concentration and Nativity. *Real Estate Economics* 32: 509–539.

Peterson, Ruth D. and Lauren J. Krivo. 2010a. *The National Neighborhood Crime Study, 2000* [Computer file]. ICPSR27501-v1. Ann Arbor, MI: Inter-university Consortium for Political and Social Research [distributor]. doi:10.3886/ICPSR27501.

Peterson, Ruth D. and Lauren J. Krivo. 2010b. *Divergent Social Worlds: Neighborhood Crime and the Racial Spatial Divide*. New York: Russell Sage Foundation.

Portes, Alejandro and R. G. Rumbaut. 2006. *Immigrant America: A Portrait*. Berkeley: University of California Press.

Portes, Alejandro and Min Zhou. 1993. The New Second Generation. *Annals of the American Academy of Political and Social Science* 530: 74–96.

Sampson, Robert J. and William Julius Wilson. 1995. Toward a Theory of Race, Crime, and Urban Inequality. In *Crime and Inequality*, ed. J. Hagan and R. D. Peterson, 37–54. Stanford, CA: Stanford University Press.

Shaw, Clifford R. and Henry D. McKay. 1942. *Juvenile Delinquency and Urban Areas*. Chicago: University of Chicago Press.

Shihadeh, Edward S. and Ray Barranco. 2010. Latino Immigration and Violence: Regional Differences in the Effect of Linguistic Isolation. *Homicide Studies* 14: 336–355.

Singer, Audrey. 2004. *The Rise of New Immigrant Gateways*. Brookings Institution Living Cities Census Series.

Stowell, Jacob I., Steven F. Messner, Kelly F. McGeever, and Lawrence E. Raffalovich. 2009. Immigration and the Recent Violent Crime Drop in the United States: A Pooled, Cross-Sectional Time-Series Analysis of Metropolitan Areas. *Criminology* 47: 889–928.

Theodore, Nik and Nina Martin. 2007. Migrant Civil Society. *Journal of Urban Affairs* 29: 269–287.

Trillo Alex. 2004. Somewhere between Wall Street and El Barrio: Community College as a Second Chance for Second-Generation Latino Students. In *Becoming New Yorkers: Ethnographies of the New Second Generation*, ed. Phillip Kasinitz, John H. Mollenkopf, and Mary C. Waters, 57–78. New York: Russell Sage Foundation.

Vélez, María B. 2009. Contextualizing the Immigration and Crime Effect: An Analysis of Homicide in Chicago Neighborhoods. *Homicide Studies* 13: 325–335.

Wadsworth, Tim. 2010. Is Immigration Responsible for the Crime Drop? An Assessment of the Influence of Immigration on Changes in Violent Crime between 1990 and 2000. *Social Science Quarterly* 91: 531–553.

Waters, Mary and Tomás R. Jiménez. 2005. Assessing Immigrant Assimilation. *Annual Review of Sociology* 31: 105–125.

Wilson, William Julius. 1996. *When Work Disappears: The World of the New Urban Poor*. New York: Random House.

9

Immigrant Inclusion and Prospects through Schooling in Italy

An Analysis of Emerging Regional Patterns

PAOLA BERTOLINI AND MICHELE LALLA

Education is one of the primary means of integrating immigrant youth into their host country, and it is an important precursor of later economic success. Yet how and in what contexts immigrant youth are best able to draw on education to improve their future prospects is a multi-layered issue requiring micro and macro levels of analysis. For example, in Italy there is evidence that the crime rate is higher among the less educated population: what are the factors affecting dropout rates and potentially increasing crime levels? How do the characteristics of both parents (i.e., their education levels, labor force participation and types of employment, duration of residence in host country) affect their children's school performance? What connections exist between school participation and the economic structure of the territory? Is there any link, or conflict, between school participation and crime in those areas where the criminal organizations are stronger?

While many studies examine the relationship between individual characteristics of the family and the children (gender, duration of residence in host country, but also primary school outcomes), which are the fundamental factors affecting enrollment rates at the micro level, relatively little attention has been given to the economic and social conditions of the territory, both at the micro and macro levels, although some authors have underscored the relevance of labor market dynamics (Bruni 2008) or the general economic conditions of the region (Rodríguez-Pose and Tselios 2010).

This chapter focuses on the territorial economic features influencing the individual choices of immigrants in gaining access to and selecting schools in Italy, at a macro level. The main assumption is that immigrant status influences young people in different ways and to different extents, depending on the characteristics of the territory where they live. In other words, immigrants' weaker status compared to Italians in terms of wealth, employment, and their family's economic status and education level, makes them more dependent on the economic system.

The goal of this analysis is to identify possible patterns in immigrants' school participation, with particular attention to Northern and Southern regions of Italy, the former being among the most developed areas in the European Union (EU) and the latter among the less developed areas. The Southern regions have a well-known and significant presence of organized crime (such as the Mafia in Sicily), even if recently the spread of criminal organizations to the Northern regions has been receiving attention. According to data from the Ministry of Justice (Ministero della Giustizia 2011), a regional pattern of incarceration appears to emerge, characterized by a higher rate of inmates coming from Southern regions (around 40 percent of the total jail population). According to the same statistical source, youth (younger than 29 years old) represent more than one-quarter of the total population in detention (26 percent). This figure increases markedly for immigrant youth. A large percentage of incarcerated immigrants are youth (40.5 percent), and immigrants make up the largest percentage of all youth in jail (57 percent). The causes of this phenomenon are complex, including anti-immigration laws (i.e., detention of undocumented immigrants). On the other hand, the large diffusion of organized crime represents an easy, fast, and well-paid opportunity for employment of young people, especially if they are without legal documents permitting them to work, and most notably in those areas where the differences in income and lifestyles within the population are greater.

Moreover, according to Ministry of Justice data, people with low education levels have the greatest risk of experiencing prison, especially youth. This is particularly relevant in some areas (the largest cities and Southern regions) where we can expect that crime competes with the school system for the enrollment of youth. In turn, for youth, education may play a significant role in curbing crime and the risk of social exclusion linked to detention.

The territorial patterns identified in our study offer a nuanced understanding of the complex set of factors influencing school participation and the success of immigrant youth. The success of immigrant youth in comparison with their Italian-born counterparts is examined at all levels of schooling, from pre-school through high school.

The distinction between first- and second-generation immigrants has been taken into account given the different behavior of the two groups in their performance, interests, and school attendance (European Commission 2008a; Stanat and Christensen 2006), and the expected higher risk of the former to drop out of school (Cortes 2006; Cruz 2009; Gonzalez 2003; Perreira, Harris, and Lee 2006; Riphahn 2003; Worswick 2004). It should be noted that "second-generation" refers to students born in Italy but still considered as foreigners by Italian law, according to the "bloodline law" (*jus sanguinis*). In fact, immigrants born in Italy may acquire citizenship only at 18 years of age and if they have lived continuously in the country. In the analysis, gender is also taken into consideration, in light of different performance, interests, and possibilities for males and females within the educational system and vis-à-vis the labor market.

Particular attention is given to the analysis of high school, as in Italy it is not fully compulsory due to the fact that compulsory education in Italy ends at age 16 and high school lasts for 5 years (from ages 14 to 18). Education beyond compulsory schooling and the type of school attended are both important because they directly affect when and how a person will enter the labor market, thus influencing future career possibilities (Barban 2010). The choice of high school—and mainly of a *liceo* (Italian classical high school) rather than other types such as vocational schools—delays access to the labor market and carries an assumption of university enrollment, increasing future labor market opportunities. Conversely, attendance in technical or vocational school allows early access to the labor market, but it does not carry the guarantee of a high-skilled job (Cappellari 2005). Finally, in the concluding section of this chapter, we discuss implications of our findings.

Theoretical Perspectives and Empirical Findings

Level of education is one of the main factors influencing the social mobility of individuals (Becker 1964; Johnson 1979) and the risk of social exclusion, including social exclusion resulting from delinquency and subsequent implementation of sentences. The fact that 60 percent of inmates in Italy are persons with low education levels, most of them having only attended elementary school (Istat 2001), supports this observation. This becomes even more apparent in the case of immigrants who may face significant difficulties in accessing the labor market and, more generally, in improving their social integration and mobility in the country of arrival (Allasino et al. 2004). Workplace discrimination against foreigners based on non-recognition of their academic or technical qualifications achieved in the country of origin often forces them into less qualified and lower paying positions, reducing opportunities for social mobility (Chiswick and Miller 2008; Chiswick, Lee, and Miller 2005; Weiss, Sauer, and Gotlibovski 2003).

Young immigrants may take advantage of the educational system in their country of arrival from an early age, unlike their parents; therefore, in a broader perspective, school plays a critical role for faster access to the labor market and improvements in career options. However, although demographics show an increasing percentage of foreigners among the youth population in EU countries, the general scenario for the inclusion of immigrants in the education system suggests several areas of concern. In particular, immigrant youth are at an educational disadvantage in comparison to their Italian peers, as evidenced by high dropout rates and low enrollments in higher education (European Commission 2008a). In fact, there is an over-representation of immigrants in vocational schools, which is not a pre-university curricular track, and immigrants are thus unlikely to be admitted to universities, resulting in an under-representation of immigrants attaining academic degrees (European Commission 2008a). Among the many difficulties hindering the integration of young immigrants into the school system, there is the risk of segregation, as students from a non-immigrant background tend to leave schools where there is a high presence of foreign students (Rutter et al. 1979).

The extent of the gap between immigrant and non-immigrant youth varies across Europe, with the deepest gaps seen in those countries with greater economic inequality, low investments in child care, and a poorly developed pre-school educational system (European Commission 2008b). In particular, the EU Southern countries show immigrants to be at a greater disadvantage in relation to years of school attendance, dropout rates, types of school diploma attained (i.e., vocational or pre-university), and school performance skills tested through the PISA[1] test (Stanat and Christensen 2006; OECD 2010).

The Southern areas of the EU, especially in Spain and Italy, are receiving an unprecedented flow of immigrants (coming primarily from the Northern and Central African countries but also from Asia and South America)[2] and appear to be unsuited for offering young immigrants adequate integration through schooling. Student performance in these areas is even worse than in Eastern European countries included in the EU enlargement of 2004 and 2007, whose income levels are the lowest in the EU (European Commission 2008a, 2008b). Although EU school attendance by immigrants indicates some geographic patterns, this has been largely ignored in prior research. As such, efforts to create better and more inclusive policies are hampered.

Several studies have shown that many factors are important in determining immigrant choice (and the success) of schooling. A first group concerns the private sphere of individuals (Rees and Mocan 1997; Rice 1999), such as personal motivations and expectations and awareness of ability, together with knowledge of the language and the level of integration in the host country (Besozzi and Colombo 2006). A second set of factors concerns the relevance of the family's cultural background and its economic conditions (Demarie and Molina 2004; Gang and Zimmermann 1999; Muller and Kerbow 1993; Rumberger 1983), especially in poor areas with lower employment opportunities (Strozza et al. 2009). A third group concerns the effects of the school experience per se, especially time spent in the host-country school system and kindergarten attendance (Heckmann and Schnapper 2003; Worswick 2004; Zhou 1997), failure at middle school (Jimerson, Anderson, and Whipple 2002, Rumberger 1995), advice from teachers and peers, and availability of schools in the area (Barban et al. 2008). Although these factors influence all students, possible discrimination against immigrants, especially in the case of somatically visible diversity, could reinforce and interact with other factors increasing difficulties associated with integration in schools and in the host society (Nesdale and Mak 2000; Zindato et al. 2008).

Within these broader economic concerns, the type and level of educational access is critical to a fuller understanding of the opportunities and barriers facing immigrant youth. Accordingly, we focus here on the school attendance of immigrant youth in Italy, highlighting the different territorial patterns at different local levels and the factors influencing their identification. In particular, we investigate whether, and to what extent, relevant structural aspects such as household income level, economic environment, crime, and labor market conditions of the area significantly affect the territorial pattern of immigrants' school participation (Rodríguez-Pose and Tselios 2010).

Italy's particular characteristics make it an especially interesting case study of the schooling of young immigrants. Even if the North of Italy is one of the richest parts of the EU because of its geographic location and economic and social features, Italy belongs to the Southern area, where the' arrival of immigrants from abroad is a new phenomenon of vast importance and proportions, and where the disadvantages of immigrants in accessing school are, in general, greater. If, as we presume, the external context plays a significant role in distinguishing among different patterns of immigrants' schooling, this could be particularly evident in Italy given the deep economic and social divide among the Italian territories.

Overview of Migration and Panic Concerning Crimes of Migrants

The growing number of immigrants has generated the perception that they represent a threat to the Italian population in terms of competition in the labor market or, more generally, in terms of security. These perceptions are not scientifically supported and are mainly linked to the difficulties of the local population in adapting to a new and relevant phenomenon that is fast changing the traditional social context of the country.

Indeed, according to Eurostat data, in 2008 Italy ranked fourth for foreign migration among all 27 EU countries, following only Germany, Spain, and France. At the beginning of its history as a nation in 1861, Italy was mainly a country of emigrants; from 1876 to the early 1980s, Italy had a net emigration of 19 million people, resulting from a total of 26 million emigrants and 9 million returnees. Unlike other European countries such as France or the United Kingdom, both of which had experiences of immigration of foreigners mainly linked to colonialism, immigration in Italy was largely limited to the sporadic fluxes of Italians coming from the territories given to other countries as a consequence of the War. However, after World War II, as a result of the economic boom of Northern regions, Italy saw a significant influx of internal migration of people, arriving mainly from developing areas of the country and especially from Southern regions, which lost more than 2 million people from 1955 to 1970 (Bonifazi et al. 2009). During those years, Italy was both a country of emigration with a negative net balance of population (mainly directed toward other European countries) and of internal migration.

Given the economic differences already existing between the North and South in terms of per capita revenue (25,500€ in the North and 14,300€ in the South in 2008) and the unemployment rate (4 percent in the North and 12 percent in the South in 2008), internal migration is still a significant factor in Italy. Even if the phenomenon is not as evident as it was during the economic boom, in 2010 the Southern regions registered a negative net population balance of -0.18 percent (Istat 2010).

With regard to the foreign flux, only in the mid-1970s did the country reverse its migration trends, from a prevailing emigration to greater immigration into the country. This process was accelerated during the 1990s and especially in the 2000s. As of January 2011, foreign residents account for 4.5 million people (7.5 percent of the total population of approximately 60 million), with a regular and significant increase each year of about 350,000–450,000 persons. There are about 932,675 minors (under 18 years of age) representing 22 percent of the total foreign population, and more than 50 percent of them (573,000) were born in Italy, representing the second generation.

Foreign immigration has restored the age structure of the Italian population, which in recent years had registered an increasing elderly population (20.3 percent of individuals aged 65 years and older), and also the general population balance which was negative in the absence of foreigners. However, given the economic and social differences between the North and South as described above, the foreigners are part of the migration flux from the Southern to the Northern regions. In the South there is stronger diffusion of a shadow economy and criminality, the wages are lower, and jobs are mainly linked to the agricultural sector and private services for the elderly, while in the North there is a wider variety of employment. At present, 60 percent of legal foreigners are in Northern regions and 13 percent in Southern ones, with faster growth in the latter.

Together with the rapid increase in foreigners, Italy is also registering a change in the nationality of immigrants. While earlier influxes were primarily composed of Asian (mainly Philippine) and African (Morocco, Tunisia, Ghana) populations, more recently, the immigrant flow is from Eastern Europe, primarily Romania and Albania followed by Poland. Half of the foreign population comes from Eastern European countries and 25 percent from new EU acceding countries (Romania is the most significant, representing 21 percent of the total foreign population), although other countries are also relevant (Morocco, Moldova, Ukraine, Pakistan, India, and China).

The Roma (or Gypsies) must be included in the nationalities mentioned above owing to the attention they receive in the press, the fears they arouse in public opinion, and thus the increase in prejudice against foreigners in Italy. They are a minority population, estimated at around 150,000 in Italy and living in (often unofficial) encampments, especially in the outskirts of larger cities such as Milan, Rome, and Naples. They have been living apart from the general European population for many centuries, with a different cultural and ethnic background. As a result of their unique customs (e.g., nomadism), they are often subject to segregation, despite the fact it has been estimated that 40 percent of this population are Italian, the descendants of an early Roma population that settled in Italy many centuries ago. After the last EU enlargement in 2007, when Romania became a Member State, an increase in the arrival of Roma from Romania also contributed to a growing hostile attitude in Italy toward this population, widely accused of not wanting to work and preferring illegal activities. Although a minority, the Roma population in Italy represents a main focus for propaganda, stirring up panic about non-Italian populations.

Although the increase in the number of immigrants involved in crime is lower than the increase in the number of immigrants (CNEL 2010), the relevance of foreigners involved in criminal activity increased significantly (Istat 2001), increasing from 15 percent of total population in prison (in 1991) to 37 percent in 2010 (Ministero della Giustizia 2011). In turn, and as discussed in several of the chapters in this volume, this is often used for building or reinforcing panic against immigrants, with an increasing risk of discrimination against them. As we argue in this chapter, the school system could play a significant role for youth—immigrants and non-immigrants alike—promoting mutual knowledge, improving communication, and fostering integration.

Data and Methods

Three groups of students are systematically compared: Italians, foreign-born immigrants (first generation), and Italian-born immigrants (second generation), who can acquire Italian citizenship only at age 18. The main indicator used for comparing these groups is the participation rate in different schools, implying specific age ranges at which students attend them: preschool enrollment (kindergarten) at 3–5 years, mandatory school (elementary at 6–10 years and middle at 11–13 years), and high school at 14–18 years. The participation rate is defined as the ratio between the total number of students (by groups of Italian and foreign, first and second generation, male and female) enrolled in each type of school and the total population in the corresponding (reference) age range (see appendix for details). For the high school analysis, we distinguish among three main types: vocational school, which generally implies a fast entry into the labor market; liceo, which usually implies access to university education; and technical school, which can lead to labor market entry and/or higher education. The participation rate in the liceo is considered an indicator of social mobility for young foreigners because it reflects their prospects for achieving advanced education and entrance into a higher paying professional career path.

The investigation is based on data at the EU NUTS 3 level, equivalent in Italy to the province.[3] Data on the educational system come from the Ministry of Education, while labor and socioeconomic data are from the

Italian National Institute of Statistics (Istat) (Istat 2008; 2009a–d; Ministero dell'Istruzione 2007, 2008a–d, 2009).

We first examine descriptive patterns among the three groups of students in different regions, mainly distinguishing between Northern and Southern regions of the country. We then propose a new classification of different areas based on the economic features of the territory: metropolitan areas, large industrial areas, large agricultural areas, small industrial areas, and small agricultural areas (Bertolini, Lalla, and Toscano 2010). The metropolitan areas were created following the Istat definition in the 2001 census. The large industrial areas include provinces with a well-developed economy and a significant manufacturing sector. The large agricultural areas include provinces with a well-developed economy and a significant agricultural sector. The small industrial areas include provinces with a less developed economy but that are still based on the manufacturing sector. The small agricultural areas include provinces with a less developed economy based on the agricultural sector. More detailed definitions are given in the appendix.

Our multivariate analysis of the variables affecting educational choice examines a set of school and socioeconomic background factors. The variables referring to the educational system are the number of students enrolled in high school per school year, the type of school, the number of schools per type, and the number of students repeating a grade level (herein referred to as "repeaters") in middle school (11–13 years) and high school per type of school. The number of repeaters may denote the difficulty students face in school because an increase in its value implies an increase in the number of failed students. It may also be an indicator of future educational paths because the experience of failure might affect the decision of both foreign and Italian students to leave school or to continue their studies. Finally, the type and number of schools by territory provides important information on the availability of schools, as this could influence the cost of school access, in terms of time or transportation, and as a consequence the students' choices.

The socioeconomic variables describe the economic status and organization of the areas and their dimensions. Resident population, per capita gross domestic product (GDP), employment in industrial districts, and agricultural and industrial value added describe the general features and development of the territorial economy; Italian and foreign total employment, unemployment rate, and the number of Italian and foreign women in the workforce describe the labor market; and the average household income refers to the economic conditions of the families in that community. The number of crimes reported to the police has been included as a proxy for social context and a factor possibly affecting the school participation rate, given the attraction that organized crime could exercise on youth in some Italian regions. The reference period is the year 2007 for school and socio-economic data, except for the crime data, which refer to the year 2005 to ensure reliable values (see appendix for detailed definitions of the variables).

Schooling of Italian and Foreign Students: A Descriptive Analysis

The performance of foreign and Italian high school students shows the relative disadvantage experienced by immigrants: participation rates in both high school and liceo are lower for immigrants in comparison to the Italian students, while their participation rates in vocational schools and rates of repeaters are higher (almost double the corresponding rates for Italians). In fact, the percentage of foreign students enrolled in all high schools (53.9 percent) and the percentage of first generation enrolled in liceo (6.5 percent) are significantly lower than those of Italians (77.9 percent and 26.0 percent, respectively), with a p-value less than 0.001. On the contrary, the percentage of first-generation immigrants enrolled in vocational schools (20.3 percent) is higher than that of Italians (15.5 percent) and the percentage of foreign repeaters (10.2 percent) is higher than that of Italians (5.4 percent), but neither difference is statistically significant. Given the relevance of high school enrollment and type of high school for entry into the labor market and social mobility through professional careers, the disadvantage experienced by immigrants is salient.

Pre-Mandatory School (3–5 years old)

Participation in kindergarten is relevant for at least two reasons: first, for immigrants it is one of the main steps in their socialization in the new country. Second, foreign children have the opportunity to learn the Italian language before they begin their compulsory education, thus potentially increasing their scholastic performance (Worswick 2004; Heckmann and Schnapper 2003).

There is a high level of participation of immigrants in kindergarten throughout Italy, equal to 75 percent and even higher in some regions. Moreover, the participation rate of immigrants is usually, and again across the country, higher than the Italian participation rate. In general, there is not a clear distinction between Northern and Southern regions, although the rate is slightly higher in Southern than in Northern areas. Many elements might explain regional differences in participation rates for Italian and foreign students: relational networks, family background, local institutional policies. Such factors are particularly relevant to family choices about their child's participation in kindergarten (e.g., the supply of kindergarten, cost of the tuition fees, performance of the schools, presence of alternative relational networks). The active role of relational networks, and especially of grandparents taking care of the children, can explain the lower rate of participation of the Italian children compared to the immigrant youth. Usually, for foreigners, grandparents are not in Italy or are still involved in labor force activities. Thus, they are unable to take care of the children.

Mandatory School (6–13 years old)

The data show there is still a high percentage of Italian students (10.8 percent) who do not attend mandatory school in spite of Italian laws on compulsory education. Even if the lowest participation rates are observed in the Southern regions, this phenomenon is also apparent in the Northern part of the country as 15.3 percent of the children in the Northwest and 12.4 percent in Northeast do not attend school. The non-participation rates are surprising for a rich and developed European country such as Italy, especially for the Northern Italian regions, which are part of the EU area with the highest level of wealth.

At the same time, the figures for non-participation may reflect other aspects connected to internal migration, even with regard to the Italian population. Indeed, the low participation rate observed in some regions could be related to internal migration fluxes—populations could have moved away from their place of residence but have maintained their official residence. As a consequence, their children appear not to be enrolled in compulsory school, even though they are attending school in another province. In other words, the number of residents is overestimated, while the number of participants is underestimated, thereby decreasing the rate of participation. Moreover, we observe that Roma populations, even if they are Italian citizens, often have the highest non-participation rates in mandatory school because of: (i) nomadism; (ii) social stigma against them by local residents, which disincentivizes the participation of Roma children at school; and (iii) poor and large families, where children (especially girls) are involved either in the care of the younger family members or in different work activities. Collectively, these factors suggest that non-participation of Italians in mandatory school is mainly associated with internal migration, which still remains high.

Observing in greater depth the participation rate of foreigners (78.9 percent), which is lower than that of Italians (89.2 percent), it is important to underscore some problematic aspects of their inclusion in Italian schools.

For example, first-generation students arriving in Italy are usually enrolled into classes one year below what their age would suggest. Moreover, this enrollment does not require the residence of the student in the town where the school is located. This occurs, for example, when parents work in another town and so their children go to school near their workplace. As a consequence, in some provinces, the number of students participating in a particular type of school may prove to be greater than the corresponding population of the same age.

The ratio of pupils repeating a year to the total enrolled can be seen as an indicator of difficulties or failure at school. Pupils repeating a year often drop out in the future. The percentages of repeaters in the mandatory middle school show that immigrant students (8.5 percent) are facing greater difficulties than Italian students (3.2 percent). These difficulties can be linked not only to individual skills, but also to the modalities and the stability of migration (e.g., presence of both parents in the family, stability in the same town, absence of seasonal return to the countries of origin, etc.).

At the territorial level, the gap in the rates of repeaters (between Italians and foreigners) is higher than 10 percent, especially in some Southern regions. This is further complicated by differential school achievement levels, with Southern students performing worse in PISA indicators (OECD 2010) compared to Northern students, highlighting the poor educational system in this part of the country.

High School (14–18 years old)

In Italy, young people are required by law to attend school until they are 16 years old. Data show that after the age of 16, in Italy as a whole, school attendance of foreign students is 53.9 percent, far less than that of Italians, which is 77.9 percent. This implies different career options in the labor market: foreign students generally do not continue on to higher education.

This gap in high school participation rates has diverse features in different areas and regions of the country, exhibiting unexpected patterns. For foreigners, secondary school participation in the South (50 percent) is lower than in the North (Northeast with 57.1 percent and Northwest with 52.8 percent) and significantly lower than in Central Italy (58.6 percent, $p < 0.036$). For Italians, school participation has a similar profile to that of foreigners, with the exception of a reversal in the South (79.5 percent), which is higher than in the North. School participation is lower in the Northwest (71.9 percent) than in the Northeast (77.2 percent, $p < 0.083$), Central Italy (82.2 percent, $p < 0.000$), and the South ($p < 0.001$).

Alternatively, Italian regions could be clustered in three different groups unrelated to geography. In a first group of regions, the behaviors of Italian and foreign students do not significantly diverge. These regions show the most inclusive pattern and are located mainly in Central and Northern Italy. In general, these regions belong to the "Third Italy" (Bagnasco 1977; Becattini et al. 2001), with an economy mainly based on small and medium-sized enterprises often constituting industrial districts (Brusco 1989). Moreover, these regions share a common political vision which stresses the importance of public action in supporting schools and education, particularly with regard to pre-schools.[4] The second group of regions are mainly Southern ones, and show the widest differences in the participation rate between the two populations of Italian and foreign students. In these regions, Italian youth have a participation rate which is above the national average, whereas the foreign born have a rate below the national average. As a matter of fact, these data show that Southern regions have in common the low priority given to the inclusion of foreigners (i.e., they are making less effective efforts to integrate foreign youth compared to the Northern regions). The last group is mainly composed of those Northern regions in which the participation rate in high school is low both for Italians and foreigners. These regions are among the most economically developed in the country (as the first group), but they share a different political vision, oriented toward more conservative public policies and the limitation of the welfare state and public spending, including public education. Therefore, in the regions of Piedmont, Lombardy, and Veneto, participation rate tends to be lower, especially for foreigners, implying less inclusive policies for immigrant youth.

The different patterns in high school attendance can be explained by several factors, such as the better well-being of Northern foreign families or the greater effectiveness of inclusive policies developed by the schools. In Northern regions, foreign families are mainly employed in more regular and stable activities (e.g., the manufacturing sector) while Southern regions are often an area of arrival for foreigners directed to Northern areas (both in Italy and in Europe). That is, they are an initial arrival point for foreigners who do not plan to settle there but rather continue on to Northern areas.

Differences in school attendance across regions also can be viewed as reflecting differences in local labor market conditions: lower school attendance rates registered in the Northern area (as a whole) are related to the strong tension of the labor market. In other words, in the North, young people prefer to join the labor market as soon as possible rather than delaying entry by increasing their education. This is compounded by strong labor demand for those who do not necessarily have higher education levels.

This phenomenon is both interesting and worrisome for the future of the country since early access to work by young people is not coupled with ambitious career expectations. Moreover, early access to the labor market decreases the fundamental role that school could play both in the growth of individuals and in the economic growth of territories. It can thus be observed as a dangerous trade-off between school and the labor market, which could lead to a negative impact on the whole Northern socioeconomic context owing to a reduction in employees' skills.

Note that the provinces with the lowest school attendance are located in the Northeast of the country. Once again, the driving factor is the labor market. Where the labor market offers few opportunities, as in the case of Southern regions, students delay their entry into the labor market, choosing instead to attend high school. The opposite is observable in the Northern regions, mainly in the Northeast, which are the most dynamic with respect to the labor market. In fact, these provinces require the highest number of immigrants in order to satisfy their local labor demand.

A latent conflict between school and employment seems to emerge for foreign and Italian students: where the labor market is dynamic, such as in the Northern provinces, labor demand discourages attendance in high school, absorbing low skill employment. On the contrary, in Southern regions where the unemployment rate reaches the highest level in the EU, school is seen as an alternative to unemployment.

Gender Differences

A gender analysis of high school attendance shows a clear pattern both among foreign and Italian youth. Females (62.9 percent of foreign females and 78.8 percent of Italian females) show an equivalent or higher school attendance compared to males (50.9 percent of foreign males and 78.6 percent of Italian males). However, among foreign youth, the gap between males and females widens by about 15–20 percent, with a higher participation rate of foreign females. In fact, in all regions, foreign female enrollment is above 50 percent, though differences exist across regions. In particular, lower attendance overall is recorded in Veneto (males 46.1 percent, females 56.0 percent) and in Lombardy (males 47.4 percent, females 56.1 percent); while Liguria (males 67.8 percent, females 81.9 percent), Emilia-Romagna (males 61.0 percent, females 73.3 percent), and Latium (males 55.5 percent, females 70.9 percent) exhibit the highest percentages. Data confirm the same pattern previously analyzed about local inclusive policies at pre-school: *ceteris paribus*, the most inclusive regions also show a better female participation rate.

The higher participation rate of foreign females suggests the absence of gender discrimination in school. However, in light of the higher school attendance of both Italian and foreign females, this interpretation may change. In both cases, indeed, it is evident that the labor market influences gender differences in school attendance and underlines a dualism in the labor market which penalizes females. In Italy, the female employment rate is very low (about 40 percent); females who are discouraged to enter the labor market may perceive school as a way to fight against unemployment and as a tool for social mobility. However, the labor market dynamic cannot explain all variability in territorial patterns; other important aspects are regional policies regarding education, well-being level of the immigrant families, ethnic composition of the foreign groups, and so on. A better investigation necessitates considering all these factors along with differences among ethnic groups.

The Choice of Different Types of High School

Students enrolled in the liceo, and in some cases in technical schools, are expected to continue on to university, while students enrolled in vocational schools are expected to enter the labor market, often after only three years of school (i.e., at the end of mandatory schooling). Therefore, the choice of high school type, and as a consequence, of university attendance, depends on household economic and social conditions.

The percentage of foreigners enrolled in liceo is lower in the Northwest (5.2 percent) than in the Central regions (8.3 percent, $p < 0.022$) or the South (8.1 percent, $p < 0.010$). Conversely, the percentage of foreigners enrolled in vocational school is lower in the South (17.0 percent) than in the Central regions (24.7 percent, $p < 0.001$), Northeast (25.6 percent, $p < 0.001$), and Northwest (22.0 percent, $p < 0.049$). School participation of Italians in liceo is significantly lower in the Northwest (21.9 percent) than in the Central regions (28.9 percent, $p < 0.001$) and the South (27.4 percent, $p < 0.001$). Participation of Italian students in vocational schools does not differ significantly between areas.

As expected, foreign students mainly choose vocational schools, and accordingly their participation rate in the liceo is generally lower than that of Italians. This pattern implies a possible structural form of discrimination in terms of the future careers of foreigners. And given the fact that the vocational schools are chosen for fast entry into the labor market, albeit limited to manual work, they usually do not garner the highest positions and incomes.

Regional territorial patterns show, however, some unexpected results with regard to the participation rate of foreign students. Considering the economic conditions of the Italian regions (with a low level of income in the South), the expected pattern would reflect a higher participation rate in vocational school in that area. Instead, the strongest participation rates are observed in Northern regions, while in Southern regions, there is a higher preference for liceo.

Once again, the territorial pattern can be explained by labor market conditions. On the one hand, in the more industrialized regions in the North, the dynamism of the labor market requires manual skills and encourages foreign students to attend vocational schools. On the other hand, in the poorest Southern regions, foreign students show a higher participation rate in liceo, which may occur for two reasons: (1) the high unemployment rate that does not encourage early access to the labor market, or (2) imitation of the choices of Italian youth regarding the type of school to attend. In fact, in Southern regions the main career possibilities are linked to the professional activities (lawyers, engineers, physicians, pharmacists, etc.) or to public sector employment, both of which require a university degree, and as a result, both Italian and foreign students are motivated to choose the liceo. The opposite is seen in Northern regions.

Comparison between First- and Second-Generation Immigrants

Second-generation youth throughout Europe often encounter difficulties integrating into a new country; for instance, the phenomena of suburban riots in France and social discontent in the UK are mainly linked to such difficulties. Given that in Italy citizenship is regulated by "blood law," such problems may be aggravated due to the fact that foreign youth—even if born in Italy—are not considered Italian citizens.

The percentage of second-generation immigrants enrolled in liceo (0.6 percent) and vocational school (1.1 percent) does not significantly differ across areas, but these figures depend on the small size of the second generation in Italy, given its recent history of foreign immigration. Similar to the overall patterns discussed above, the percentage of first-generation immigrants enrolled in liceo (4.6 percent) is lower in the Northwest than in Central Italy (7.6 percent, $p < 0.016$) or the South (7.5 percent, $p < 0.007$), and the percentage of first-generation immigrants enrolled in vocational school is lower in the South (16.2 percent) than in the Central regions (23.6 percent, $p < 0.001$) or the Northeast (24.1 percent, $p < 0.001$). Thus, educational choices of first- and second-generation immigrants reveal differences with respect to geographical area and type of school. More foreigners enroll in vocational schools than Italians, with a difference of 9.4 percentage points, but in the South the proportions are the same.

Social integration should produce in the second generation behavior that is not so different from that of the Italian students. Our results confirm this expectation: among second-generation immigrants, we observe a stronger preference to attend liceo than among the first generation. Second-generation immigrants are less oriented to vocational schools. It is expected their future career will benefit from this choice. The second generation seems to assume behavior more similar to that of the Italian students, and this trend characterizes all of the country, even if in the South it is less evident, with a reversal in some areas. The imitation process was previously characterized as a main driver for foreign students; however, from this new information, the imitation of the Italian students' preferences is limited by the general economic condition of the context. Similar to the Italian population, immigrant households in Southern regions have low income and poor working conditions that narrow the choices of pupils, especially if immigrant families, as in the case of second generation, have been living in Southern regions for a long time. Because of their poorer economic conditions, Southern regions generally are arrival areas from which immigrants move in the directions that allow them to attain better living conditions. A decision to stay in the South could be explained by a low education level of the family unit (and skills with regard to work), which in turn influences decisions about school.

From the available evidence, second-generation immigrants mirror the behavior of the Italian population. This finding contrasts with data coming from other parts of the EU, where the second generation experiences greater difficulties at school (European Commission 2008a). However, the number of second-generation students in Italy is too small to assess whether this trend is real or an artifact of the unique characteristics of these immigrants.

Total Participation in High School

The previous analysis outlines some territorial patterns for school participation. These findings suggest the importance of looking further into whether school attendance can be explained by variables related to the labor market and territorial economy. This goal is achieved through a regression model for each school participation rate, for foreigners and Italians. The independent variables are defined in the appendix and refer to both the school supply and social and economic context of the provinces. The results are reported below in a descriptive form.

The school enrollment of foreigners overall, i.e., without distinguishing between first- and second-generation or types of schools, significantly increases when the number of foreign women in the workforce increases (positive influence). This result is expected because the growth of female employment implies a growth in family income and, therefore, the availability of resources to invest in education. The provincial unemployment rate shows a significant negative effect, implying a decrease in the school enrollment rate when the provincial unemployment rate increases, because an increase in the latter could decrease the family income, discouraging continuation in school. The employment rate in the local industrial districts is borderline significant and negative, suggesting that a well-developed industrial or agricultural area offers many job opportunities for all and ease in joining the labor market, encouraging young people to leave school for work. The value added in agriculture reveals a negative impact on the school participation rates with a borderline p-value ($p < 0.056$), for which the above explanation also applies.

Secondary school participation of young Italians shows similarities and differences compared to the enrollment rate of young immigrants. It is positively affected by the number of Italian women in the workforce per child. It is not affected by the provincial unemployment rate, which does, however, affect total school attendance of young foreigners. However, the economic crisis could trigger a negative trend, encouraging younger family members to leave school and seek a job. Secondary school participation of young Italians is negatively influenced by the employment rate in the local industrial districts, similar to immigrant students, and also by per capita GDP. The explanation is similar to that given above for the value added in agriculture. Average family income has a positive impact on secondary school participation of young Italians, as expected, because families enjoying good economic conditions tend to persuade their children to continue studying, hoping they will find an interesting, skilled, and remunerative job.

The distinction between the first and second generation, in general, does not yield many differences between the values for the two generations and Italian students, with some important exceptions discussed in the following sections.

Participation in Liceo

We find a difference between first- and second-generation youth enrollment in liceo. The percentage of the first generation enrolled in liceo decreases when the schools-students ratio for liceo increases ($p < 0.054$) and increases when the number of foreign women in the workforce per child increases. The same is true for Italians.

The percentage of second-generation immigrants enrolled in liceo is positively affected by the provincial unemployment rate (as it was for young Italians) and positively affected by per capita GDP.

The percentage of Italian youth enrolled in liceo shows negative dependence decreases when the average repeater rates increase, i.e., failure at school discourages students from continuing their studies and increases school-leaving rates. Finally, the percentage of Italian youth enrolled in liceo also shows a negative dependence on the employment rate in industrial districts, meaning that the job opportunities offered by a thriving industrial sector tempt young people to leave school to start work immediately, or at least to choose another type of school.

Participation in Vocational School

Enrollment in vocational schools again shows similarities and differences between foreigners and Italians. The percentage of first-generation foreigners enrolled in vocational school is positively affected by the number of foreign women working per child and yields a negative relationship with the provincial unemployment rate, meaning that in those provinces where the unemployment rate increases, the percentage of young foreigners, who do not even attend vocational school, increases because they tend to seek work (presumably unskilled, exploitative, fatiguing manual work).

The percentage of second-generation immigrants enrolled in vocational school shows only a positive dependence on average household income.

The percentage of Italian youth enrolled in vocational school depends, furthermore, negatively on per capita GDP and positively on average household income. In a certain sense, the signs of the two variables are to be expected because an increase in per capita GDP implies both a thriving industrial economic structure and an increase in household income. The former encourages young people to find a job and leave school, while the latter induces parents to press their children to continue to study and invest in their human capital, that is, to acquire highly skilled knowledge in the hope of finding a highly specialized, remunerative job.

Considering some comments made in the first sections, an apparent contradictory pattern seems to emerge. When the unemployment rate is high, as in the Southern regions, the overall participation rate is, as expected, lower than that of foreigners (-2.8 percent) in the Northwest and unexpectedly higher than that of Italians (+6.0 percent) in the Northwest. At the same time, the enrollment in liceo is slightly higher for foreigners (+2.9 percent for the first and +0.1 percent for the second generation) and for Italians (+5.5 percent with respect to the Northwest). This evidence might disappear in a multivariate analysis, when many other factors are considered simultaneously and, moreover, the structure of the territory should be introduced in the model in some way, as has been carried out in the next section for example.

School Enrollment by Uniform Economic Areas

The analysis of school participation in each uniform economic area, defined above, underlines its different complex patterns across the territory and in relation to its economic and social characteristics, but the number of cases in each area is low. Only the overall participation rates of foreigners and Italians are illustrated, both for the sake of brevity and simplicity.

In the metropolitan areas, for foreigners and Italians, the average repeater rate and the value added in industry negatively affect school participation rates, and the impacts on foreigners are greater than on Italians. The school-students ratio yields a negative coefficient for Italians only, and the number of foreign women in the workforce per child yields a negative coefficient only for foreigners. The provincial crime rate and average household income have a positive effect on foreigners only.

The large industrial areas show a complex pattern of relationships. For foreigners and Italians, the average repeater rates and provincial unemployment rate negatively impact school participation rates, as expected. The schools-students ratio, the employment rate in industrial districts, and the average household income provide negative effects only for Italians. It is worth noting that the number of women in the workforce per child influences immigrants positively and Italians negatively, meaning that immigrant families tend to persuade their children to continue their studies once the necessary economic resources are available, as they are in a large industrial area. Conversely, young Italians tend to leave school when good jobs are easy to find, as is the case in a large industrial area. Moreover, value added in agriculture has a positive effect for foreigners, with a high estimated value, implying that in a large industrial area, agriculture employs high numbers of foreigners, who tend to enroll their children at school. Finally, we note the positive coefficient of the provincial crime rate for Italians, which might denote the vexing issue of Italian organized crime and/or Italians' willingness to turn to the courts for less important matters or easily transform disputes into lawsuits.

The large agricultural areas also reveal a complex pattern of relationships. On the one hand, the provincial unemployment rate, value added in agriculture, and per capita GDP have negative impacts on the school participation rates of foreigners and Italians. The employment rate in industrial districts and the provincial crime rate produce negative effects for Italians only. On the other hand, the value added in industry shows a positive impact only for foreigners, while the average repeater ratios, the number of Italian women in the workforce per child, and the average household income only have positive effects for Italians. Therefore, in these areas, it appears that Italian families tend to persuade their children to continue studies in spite of failures.

Small industrial areas show only a few significant variables. The only negative impact, common to both foreigners and Italians, is attributable to the employment rate in industrial districts. The school participation rates increase when the value added in agriculture and household income increase, where the explanations reported again apply.

Small agricultural areas show a simpler pattern. Only the school participation rate of foreigners has statistically significant relationships with some explanatory variables. The employment rate in industrial districts and per capita GDP yield positive relationships, while average household income yields a negative relationship. This may occur because in these areas, an increase in income does not encourage parents to hope that their children may improve their status by aiming higher in education.

Conclusions

This chapter shows significant differences between immigrants and Italians in secondary school enrollment. Across the country, the school participation of foreigners is lower than that of Italians of the same age. Moreover, there are different territorial patterns; in general, however, the enrollment rate of young immigrants is higher in the Center-North and lower in the South.

As research in other countries has pointed out, immigrants' lower participation rates could be linked to their families' economic status (Caille and O'Prey 2002; Nauze-Fichet 2005). Immigrant families often have more children and lower household incomes than Italian families, even if this cannot be generalized for all individuals. Furthermore, school structures are often not tailored to young immigrants' specific needs, such as improvement of language skills. With respect to the territorial pattern, lower participation in the Center-South could be due, apart from lower household income, to the fact that this area is immigrants' initial point of arrival and constitutes an area of transit, i.e., where they stay only for the time necessary to find a better destination.

In line with the literature (e.g., Barban et al. 2008), participation rates for the different types of schools revealed differences between young Italians and young immigrants. For example, foreigners have a higher rate of enrollment in vocational school than Italians, but a lower rate of liceo attendance. There are also differences across the country: in the Center-South a preference for liceo emerges, while in the Center-North there is a preference for vocational school. Presumably, the characteristics of the labor market at the territorial level could explain this difference. The labor market in the Center-South is weaker than in the Center-North, suggesting that it fails to attract young people who spend more time in full-time education in the hopes that it will make it easier to find a good job in the future. On the contrary, in the Center-North, the economic and productive structures are more dynamic than in the Center-South, and tend to attract young people, especially foreigners, who show a preference for shorter courses of study and vocational schools because these allow rapid entrance to the labor market.

The education choices of Italian-born (second-generation) foreigners are somewhat different from those of foreign-born immigrants, and to some extent are similar to those of Italians. However, the size of the phenomenon is small and it is changing quickly over time, so this generalization is not sufficiently robust.

The educational choices are affected by many factors. As reported in the literature (e.g., Brinbaum and Kieffer 2005), in Italy as elsewhere, the number of working women per child positively affects immigrants' secondary school attendance, underlining the positive effects of employment of women in increasing the economic resources available to families. The economic structure of the territory influences enrollment rates in secondary school, expressed by diverse variables. First, the employment rate in industrial districts and the provincial unemployment rate often impact school participation negatively, implying that a dynamic labor market tends to tempt young people to leave school or to choose a shorter course of study. Perhaps in Italy, investment in human capital through education is not fully appreciated by firms in areas with a predominance of small and medium-sized enterprises, which prefer short vocational training. Second, average household income and per capita GDP often significantly affect the secondary school attendance of Italians, with a positive influence for the former and negative for the latter. In particular, the negative influence of per capita GDP is explained by its nature as an indicator of the area's average wealth: an increase in its value implies an increase in employment opportunities, which tend to discourage choices involving a long period of full-time education. Third, the value added in agriculture has a significant negative effect, presumably reflecting provinces' low levels of economic development, which are more likely to affect immigrant families.

The territorial analysis shows that in the poorest areas, young immigrants are facing more difficulties of integration at school. Although the evidence from a single country is not generalizable to the whole EU, our analysis for Italy suggests the importance of carefully considering the risks of policies that do not adequately integrate immigrant youth. In poorer EU regions these risks are higher, especially in the Southern countries, which are especially affected by migration flows. This phenomenon calls for monitoring the capacity of the countries in supporting integration of immigrants at school. As noted in the Green Paper on migration (European Commission 2008a), European societies have to acknowledge the irreversible character of immigration countries, with a significant proportion of their young people being immigrants or with migration background. For this reason, not only the future of immigrants, but the future of the EU, calls for improving their institutions, and particularly educational institutions of all kinds, to increase the educational attainment of immigrant children. As underlined at the beginning of this chapter, this is the first important step for reducing both the panic over the immigrants and the risk of the involvement of youth in crime, which can only lead to future social exclusion and discrimination.

Appendix
A.1. Definitions of the Selected Dependent Variables

The percentage of young immigrants (foreigners) enrolled in all high schools (PF) is the ratio between the total number of foreign students enrolled in high school and the foreign population aged between 14 and 19 years, multiplied by 100.

The percentage of *first*-generation young immigrants enrolled in liceo (P1L) is provided by the ratio between the number of first-generation liceo students and the foreign population aged between 14 and 19 years, multiplied by 100. Similarly, the percentage of first-generation young immigrants enrolled in vocational schools (P1V) is provided by the ratio between the number of first-generation students in vocational schools and the foreign population aged 14–19 years, multiplied by 100. The percentages of *second*-generation young immigrants enrolled in liceo (P2L) and vocational school (P2V) were also obtained as described above.

The percentage of young Italians enrolled in all high schools (PI) is the ratio between the number of Italian students enrolled in secondary school and the Italian population aged 14–19, multiplied by 100. The percentage of Italian young people enrolled in liceo/vocational school (PIL/ PIV) is the ratio between the number of Italian students enrolled in liceo/vocational school and the Italian population aged 14–19 years, multiplied by 100.

A.2. Definitions of the Selected Independent Variables

The school-students ratio for total schools (SSRT) refers to the ratio between the number of schools and the total number of Italian students attending them, multiplied by 1000. This index aims to define the geographical spread of school institutions, which could influence both students' participation and their choice of school type. The two school-students ratios for liceo (SSRL) and vocational school (SSRV) are obtained by the same procedure.

The average percentage of repeaters, for foreigners (PRF) and Italians (PRI), was obtained using the geometric mean of the average rate of foreign/ Italian repeaters at junior secondary school (at age 11–13) and the average rate of foreign/ Italian repeaters in the first three years of secondary school.

The number of foreign/ Italian working women per child (F/ I/ WWC) is the ratio between the number of foreign/ Italian working women and the foreign/ Italian children enrolled in kindergarten. As suggested in the literature (CNEL 2005), the indicator expresses the intensity of women's participation in the labor market, net of children, and an increase in it should yield an increase in school participation. It also reduces the collinearity in the regressions because the number of working women strongly correlates with the number of children enrolled in kindergarten. The other independent variables designed to reflect the effects of labor market and socioeconomic characteristics in the different NUTS 3 are listed below.

The provincial unemployment rate (PUR) is obtained from Istat and follows the official definition.

The employment rate in industrial districts (ERID) is the ratio between the number of workers employed in the industrial district and the total number of workers employed in the province, multiplied by 100.

The provincial crime rate (PCR) is a social indicator and is the ratio between the number of reported offenses against the person for which judicial proceedings have begun and the resident population, multiplied by 1,000.

Four variables capture the economic status and organization of the geographical areas. These include the value added in agriculture (VAA), the value added in industry (VAI), and value added from services (VAS), which indicate these factors' net contribution to the wealth of the area. The per capita GDP is an indicator of the province's economic wealth, while the average household income (AHI) is an index of the average wealth available to families. These four variables are divided by 1000.

A.3. Definitions of Homogeneous Economic Clusters of Provinces

The large industrial areas include provinces with a well-developed economy and a significant manufacturing sector, having a value added in industry, $VAI(p)$ for the p-th province, above the national mean value, $VAI(m)$, and greater than a value added in agriculture, $VAA(p)$ for the p-th province. Given that the mean of $VAA(p)$ is denoted by $VAA(m)$, the rule of inclusion is formally expressed by: $[VAI(p)/VAI(m)] > 1$ and $[VAI(p)/VAI(m)] > [VAA(p)/VAA(m)]$.

The large agricultural areas include provinces with a well-developed economy and a significant agricultural sector, having a value added in agriculture above the national mean and greater than the value added in industry. Formally, it will be: $[VAA(p)/VAA(m)] > 1$ and $[VAA(p)/VAA(m)] > [VAI(p)/VAI(m)]$.

The small industrial areas include provinces with a less developed economy, having a value added in industry less than the national mean value, but greater than the value added in agriculture, i.e., $1 > [VAI(p)/VAI(m)] > [VAA(p)/VAA(m)]$.

The small agricultural areas include provinces with a value added in agriculture less than the national mean value, but greater than the value added in industry, i.e., $1 > [VAA(p)/VAA(m)] > [VAI(p)/VAI(m)]$.

NOTES

We would like to thank our students who helped us in different ways and steps of this work, in particular Valentina Toscano, Linda Tosarelli, Francesco Pagliacci, Riccardo Righi, Francesca Piacentini, Tiziana Ventre, Daniele Ferraguti, Elisabetta Niedda. Thanks also to Enrico Giovannetti for his support in discussing different phases of this research.

1. The PISA (Programme for International Student Assessment) test verifies the skills of the 15-year-old students in reading and in mathematical and science abilities. It is based on surveys, conducted every three years in the participating countries.

2. In Italy, the flows of immigrants in 2007 were about 18.4 percent from Africa, 16.3 percent from Asia, 9.8 percent from America. The countries that recorded the largest number of immigrants in 2008 were Spain (726,000), Germany (682,000), the United Kingdom (590,000), and Italy (535,000). More than two-thirds of total immigrants have been recorded in these four Member States. The total number of non-nationals, i.e., people who

are not citizens of their country of residence, living on the territory of the EU Member States on January 1, 2009, was 31.8 million, constituting 6.4 percent of the total EU population. The stock of non-nationals amounted to 30.8 million on January 1, 2008; that is 6.2 percent of the total EU population (Eurostat 2010).

3. Following the definition of EU, the NUTS classification is a hierarchical system for dividing up the economic territory of the EU into a series of comparable levels. The classification is mainly based on political and administrative systems and population. It moves from the country (NUTS 0) as the largest units, while NUTS 2 are typically regions (800,000–3 million population) and NUTS 3 provinces (150,000–800,000 population).

4. In Italy, pre-school is under the charge of local public government.

REFERENCES

Allasino, Enrico, Emilio Reyneri, Alessandra Venturini, and Giovanna Zincone. 2004. La discriminazione dei lavoratori immigrati nel mercato del lavoro in Italia. Geneva: International Labor Office, *International Migration Papers*, n. 67.

Bagnasco, Arnaldo. 1977. *Tre Italie. La problematica territoriale dello sviluppo italiano*. Bologna: il Mulino.

Barban, Nicola. 2010. *I figli degli immigrati e la scelta della scuola superiore in Italia*,www.neodemos.it (accessed March 11, 2011).

Barban, Nicola, Gianpiero Dalla Zuanna, Patrizia Farina, and Salvatore Strozza. 2008. I figli degli stranieri in Italia fra assimilazione e diseguaglianza. Padua: Department of Statistical Sciences, University of Padua, *Working Paper Series*, n. 16.

Becattini, Giacomo, Marco Bellandi, Gabi Dei Ottati, and Fabio Sforzi, eds. 2001. *Il caleidoscopio dello sviluppo locale. Trasformazioni economiche nell'Italia contemporanea*. Turin: Rosenberg & Sellier.

Becker, Gary S. 1964. *Human Capital: A Theoretical and Empirical Analysis with Special Reference to Education*. New York: Columbia University Press.

Bertolini, Paola, Michele Lalla, and Valentina Toscano. 2010. L'inserimento scolastico degli studenti stranieri di prima e seconda generazione in Italia. Modena: Dipartimento di Economia Politica, Università di Modena e Reggio Emilia, *Materiali di discussione*, n. 631.

Besozzi, Elena and Maddalena Colombo, eds. 2006. *Percorsi dei giovani stranieri tra scuola e formazione professionale in Lombardia. Rapporto 2005*. Milano: Osservatorio regionale per l'Integrazione e la Multietnicità, Fondazione ISMU (Iniziative e Studi sulla MUltietnicità), Regione Lombardia, http://www.orimregionelombardia.it/index.php?c=230 (accessed March 12, 2011).

Bonifazi, Corrado, Frank Heins, Salvatore Strozza, and Mattia Vitiello. 2009. The Italian transition from emigration to immigration country. Rome: CNR and Istituto di Ricerche sulla popolazione e le politiche sociali, Roma, working paper No. 24. http://www.irpps.cnr.it/en/pubblicazioni/working-paper-on-line (accessed March 21, 2011).

Brinbaum, Yaël and Annick Kieffer. 2005. *D'une génération à l'autre, les aspirations éducatives des familles immigrées: ambition et persévérance*. Paris: Ministère de l'Éducation nationale, ftp://trf.education.gouv.fr/pub/edutel/dpd/revue72/article3.pdf (accessed March 12, 2011). Also in *Éducation et formations* 72: 53–75.

Bruni, Michele. 2008. *Il boom demografico prossimo venturo. Tendenze demografiche, mercato del lavoro ed immigrazione: scenari e politiche*. Modena: Dipartimento di Economia Politica, Università di Modena e Reggio Emilia, *Materiali di discussione*, n. 607.

Brusco, Sebastiano. 1989. *Piccole imprese e distretti industriali. Una raccolta di saggi.* Turin: Rosenberg & Sellier.

Caille, Jean-Paul and Sophie O'Prey. 2002. Les familles immigrées et l'école française: un rapport singulier qui persiste même après un long séjour en France. In Données sociales: la société française. Paris: Insee, Èdition 2002–2003, novembre, Collection Références.

Cappellari, Lorenzo. 2005. L'importanza di scegliere bene. In *Per un'analisi critica del mercato del lavoro*, ed. Brucchi Luchino, 37–45. Bologna: il Mulino.

Chiswick, Barry R., Yew Liang Lee, and Paul W. Miller. 2005. A longitudinal analysis of immigrant occupational mobility: a test of the immigrant assimilation hypothesis. *International Migration Review* 39(2): 332–355.

Chiswick, Barry R. and Paul W. Miller. 2008. Why is the payoff to schooling smaller for immigrants? *Labour Economics* 15(6): 1317–1340.

CNEL. 2005. *Adolescenti stranieri e il mondo del lavoro: studio transculturale dei valori inerenti il lavoro.* Rome: CNEL.

CNEL. 2010. *VII Rapporto sugli Indici di integrazione degli immigrati in Italia.* Rome: CNEL.

Cortes, Kalena E. 2006. The effects of age at arrival and enclave schools on the academic performance of immigrant children. *Economics of Education Review* 25(2): 121–132.

Cruz, Vanessa. 2009. Educational attainment of first and second generation immigrant youth. Washington, DC: Urban Institute, Summer Academy for Public Policy Analysis and Research, *Research Brief no. 5.*

Demarie, Marco and Stefano Molina. 2004. Le seconde generazioni. Spunti per il dibattito italiano. In *Seconde generazioni. Un'introduzione al futuro dell'immigrazione in Italia*, ed. Maurizio Ambrosini and Stefano Molina, IX–XXIII. Turin: Edizioni della Fondazione Giovanni Agnelli.

European Commission. 2008a. *Green Paper Migration & mobility: challenges and opportunities for EU education systems.* Brussels: Commission of the European Communities, COM (2008) 423 final.

European Commission. 2008b. *Education and Migration. Strategies for integrating migrant children in European schools and society*, http://www.nesse.fr/nesse/activities/reports (accessed March 12, 2011).

Eursotat. 2010. Migration and migrant population statistics, http://epp.eurostat. ec.europa.eu/statistics_explained/index.php/Migration_and_migrant_population_ statistics#Migration_flows (accessed April 05, 2011).

Gang, Ira N. and Klaus F. Zimmermann. 1999. Is child like parent? Educational attainment and ethnic origin. IZA Discussion Papers, n. 57.

Gonzalez, Arturo. 2003. The education and wages of immigrant children: the impact of age at arrival. *Economics of Education Review* 22(2): 203–212.

Heckmann, Friedrich and Dominique Schnapper. 2003. *The Integration of Immigrants in the European Societies. National Differences and Trends of Convergence.* Stuttgart: Lucius & Lucius.

Istat. 2001. *Gli stranieri e il carcere: aspetti della detenzione.* Rome: Istat.

Istat. 2008. *Gli stranieri nel mercato del lavoro.* Rome: Istat.

Istat. 2009a. http://www.istat.it (accessed March 11, 2011).

Istat. 2009b. http://www.demo.istat.it/ (accessed March 11, 2011).

Istat. 2009c. http://giustiziaincifre.istat.it/Nemesis/index.jsp (accessed March 12, 2011).

Istat. 2009d. *Rilevazione sulle forze di lavoro 2009.* Rome: Istat.

Istat. 2010. *Noi Italia. 100 statistiche per capire il paese in cui viviamo*. Roma: Istat.

Jimerson, Shane R., Gabrielle E. Anderson, and Angela D. Whipple. 2002. Winning the battle and losing the war: examining the relation between grade retention and dropping out of high school. *Psychology in the Schools* 39(4): 441–457.

Johnson, William R. 1979. The demand for general and specific education with occupational mobility. *Review of Economic Studies* 46(4): 695–705.

Ministero della Giustizia. 2011. *Statistiche del Dipartimento dell'Amministrazione penitenziaria*. Rome. http://giustizia.it (accessed June 21, 2011).

Ministero dell'Istruzione. 2007. *Alunni con cittadinanza non italiana, Scuole statali e non statali. Anno scolastico 2005/2006*. Rome.

Ministero dell'Istruzione. 2008a. *Alunni con cittadinanza non italiana, Scuole statali e non statali. Anno scolastico 2006/2007*. Rome.

Ministero dell'Istruzione. 2008b. *La scuola in cifre 2007*. Rome.

Ministero dell'Istruzione. 2008c. *Notiziario sulla scuola dell'infanzia, primaria e secondaria di I e II grado*. Rome.

Ministero dell'Istruzione. 2008d. *La scuola statale: sintesi dei dati. Anno scolastico 2007/2008*. Rome.

Ministero dell'Istruzione. 2009. *10 anni di scuola statale: a.s. 1998/1999 – a.s. 2007/2008. Dati, fenomeni e tendenze del sistema di istruzione*. Rome.

Muller, Chandra and David Kerbow. 1993. Parent Involvement in the Home, School, and Community. In *Parents, Their Children and Schools*, ed. Barbara Schneider and James S. Coleman, 13–42. Boulder, CO: Westview Press.

Nauze-Fichet, Emmanuelle. 2005. *Les projets professionnels des jeunes sept ans après leur entrée au collège*. Paris: Ministère de l'éducation nationale, de l'Enseignement supérieur et de la Recherche, *Les Dossiers d'éducation e formation*, n. 72.

Nesdale, Drew and Anita S. Mak. 2000. Immigrant acculturation attitudes and host country identification. *Journal of Community & Applied Social Psychology* 10(6): 483–495.

OECD. 2010. *PISA 2009 results. What students know and can do*. Paris: OECD.

Perreira, Krista M., Kathleen Mullan Harris, and Dohoon Lee. 2006. Making it in America: high school completion by immigrant and native immigrant youth. *Demography* 43(3): 511–536.

Rees, Daniel I. and Naci H. Mocan. 1997. Labor market condition and high school dropout rate: evidence from New York State. *Economics of Education Review* 16(2): 103–109.

Rice, Patricia. 1999. The Impact of local markets on investment in further education. Evidence from England and Wales youth cohort studies. *Journal of Population Economics* 12(2): 287–312.

Riphahn, Regina T. 2003. Cohort effects in the educational attainment of second generation immigrants in Germany: An analysis of census data. *Journal of Population Economics* 16(4): 711–737.

Robinson, William S. 1950. Ecological correlations and thebehavior of individuals. *American Sociological Review* 15: 351–357.

Rodríguez-Pose, Andrés and Vassilis Tselios. 2010. Returns to migration, education, and externalities in the European Union. *Papers in Regional Science* 89(2): 411–434.

Rumberger, Russell W. 1983. Dropping out of high school: the influence of race, sex and family background. *American Educational Research Journal* 20(2): 199–220.

Rumberger, Russell W. 1995. Dropping out of middle school: a multilevel analysis of students and schools. *American Educational Research Journal* 32(3): 583–625.

Rutter, Michael, Barbara Maughan, Peter Mortimore, and Janet Ouston. 1979. *Fifteen Thousand Hours—Secondary Schools and Their Effects on Children*. Cambridge, MA: Harvard University Press.

Schütz, Gabriela, Heinrich W. Ursprung, and Ludger Wößmann. 2008. Education policy and equality of opportunity. *Kyklos* 61(2): 279–308.

Stanat, Petra and Gayle Christensen. 2006. *Where immigrant students succeed: A comparative review of performance and engagement in PISA 2003*. Paris: OECD.

Stata. 2005. *Stata Base Reference Manual*, vol. 1–3. College Station, TX: Stata Press.

Strozza, Salvatore, Anna Paterno, Laura Bernardi, and Giuseppe Gabrielli. 2009. Migrants in the Italian labour market: gender differences and regional disparities. In *Gender and Migration in 21st Century Europe*, ed. Helen Stalford, Samantha Currie, and Samantha Velluti, 131–160. Aldershot: Ashgate.

Weiss, Yoram, Robert M. Sauer, and Menachem Gotlibovski. 2003. Immigration, search and loss of skill. *Journal of Labor Economics* 21(3): 557–591.

Worswick, Christopher. 2004. Adaptation and inequality: children of immigrants in Canadian schools. *Canadian Journal of Economics* 37(1): 57–77.

Zhou, Min. 1997. Growing up American: the challenge confronting immigrant children and children of immigrants. *Annual Review of Sociology* 23: 63–95.

Zindato, Donatella, Lorenzo Cassata, Fabrizio Martire, Salvatore Strozza, and Mattia Vitello. 2008. L'integrazione come processo multi-dimensionale. Condizioni di vita e di lavoro degli immigrati. *Studi Emigrazione* 171: 657–698.

10

Social Stressors, Special Vulnerabilities, and Violence Victimization among Latino Immigrant Day Laborers in Post-Katrina New Orleans

ALICE CEPEDA, NALINI NEGI, KATHRYN NOWOTNY, JAMES ARANGO, CHARLES KAPLAN, AND AVELARDO VALDEZ

Hurricane Katrina is considered one of most costly and devastating storms ever to occur in the United States (Elliott and Pais 2006). The storm left an estimated $156 billion in damages in 49 counties in southern Alabama, Mississippi, and Louisiana. In New Orleans, the storm surge overpowered the levee system, causing breaches that flooded more than 80 percent of the city. Reports indicate that more than 1,800 people lost their lives during the storm as a result of being trapped by the rising waters. Moreover, the magnitude of the residential and commercial structural damage in New Orleans was devastating owing to the extent and duration of the flooding. Since that time, a massive rebuilding effort has focused on repairing or demolishing these structures. In fact, it is estimated that 90 percent of the over 252,000 owner-occupied housing units that sustained damage as a result of the storm have undergone repair since that time. Concomitantly, many of New Orleans' laborers, mostly low-income African Americans, were displaced throughout the United States. Most were unable to return because they lived in some of the neighborhoods with the worst flooding. This created a need for a flexible and mobile construction labor force for gutting, demolition, and removal, rewiring, dry-walling, and other rebuilding efforts. The demand for this type of labor was the basis for the ensuing dynamic demographic shift of New Orleans as Latino immigrants from other U.S. cities as well as directly from Mexico and Central America migrated to the city to satisfy this need.

Latino settlement in destinations without established communities of Latino immigrants has increased in recent years. States such as New Orleans, Georgia, Arkansas, Maryland, Tennessee, and North Carolina, among others, have experienced a rise in Latino immigrants (Sánchez and Machado-Casas 2009; Lichter and Johnson 2009). These new destinations are marked by increased levels of Latino segregation, exceeding those found in traditional settlements (Lichter et al. 2009). The absence of an established community of Latino immigrants and social structures is highly salient, as it can exacerbate stressors associated with adaptation and heighten vulnerability. As discussed in previous chapters, the growing presence of Latino immigrants within non-traditional destination cities has had wide-ranging effects. For instance, in chapter 3 of this volume, Provine and colleagues discuss the legislative responses to this influx as a social control mechanism, while Vélez and Lyons examine the complex relationship between crime and immigration within the context of a city's positive or negative receptiveness to incoming immigrants. In the case of New Orleans, this emergent community of Latino migrants is especially at risk as a result of the absence of social support structures immediately post-Katrina (when many Latinos migrated into the city), significant workers' rights abuses experienced pre- and post-Katrina, and racial tensions between Latinos and displaced African American workers. The presence of open-air drug markets and high crime also create an important context to study this emergent population's adaptation, social stressors, and vulnerabilities to violent victimization (Valdez et al. 2010).

There have been divergent reports and estimates of the return migration to the city by New Orleans residents (Fussell, Sastry, and VanLandingham 2009). In July 2006, the estimated population of New Orleans was 223,000, approximately 55 percent of the pre-Katrina population (U.S. Census Bureau 2006, 2008). The 2008 census estimate put New Orleans' population at 336,644 (U.S. Census Bureau 2008). Although the population is well over 65 percent of its pre-Hurricane Katrina size, the African American population has fallen substantially from 67 percent prior to the storm (Frey, Singer, and Park 2007). Some argue, "The city has become older (the median age rose from 34 to 38.8), less diverse (the white non-Hispanic population increased from 25.8% to 30.9%), and a bit wealthier (median income rose from $31,369 to $39,530)" (Scott 2010). At the same time, there has been a dramatic increase in the Latino population, from 3 percent pre-Katrina to reports of more than 10 percent (Fletcher et al. 2006). Most of the Latinos are single, poor, undocumented immigrant men working in the demolition and construction trades. The incorporation of Latino immigrants into the New Orleans labor force has created animosity between this new population and African Americans, as documented in other studies and reports (Hunter 2008; Londono and Vargas 2007; Valdez et al. 2010). Despite extensive research on Latino immigration to the United States, little is known about the stress associated with the adaptation and settlement process and the vulnerability for violence victimization in new destination cities for Latino immigrants.

Pre- and Post-Migration Stress and Violence Victimization

For many of the Latino migrants in New Orleans, social vulnerability predates their move to the United States. Many experienced war, lack of resources, difficulties planning a relocation, and the real or imagined danger of the route to the new country (Lee 1966; Saldaña 1992). These experiences are often associated with long-lasting emotional consequences including a brief period of post-traumatic numbness (Aroian and Norris 2003). One study found that Central American immigrants experienced higher levels of generalized distress and psychosocial stress associated with the immigration process, as well as significantly higher ratings of stress related to pre-migration trauma, when compared to Mexican immigrants (Salgado de Snyder, Cervantes, and Padilla 1990). This is likely a result of exposure to violence, political turmoil, and war-like conditions in Central America (Cervantes, Salgado de Snyder, and Padilla 1989) during the 1980s, when civil wars erupted in various countries.

The migration experience itself is wrought with significant stressors as well as financial hardships, which continue through the adaptation process in the United States. Latino migrants often face harsh work and poor housing conditions while in the United States. Among Mexican-origin migrant farm workers, a demographically similar population to the Latino migrant men in New Orleans, the stressors of rigid work demands as well as poor housing conditions have been found to be associated with high levels of anxiety, while rigid work demands and low family income/living in poverty were associated with high levels of depressive symptomology (Magaña and Hovey 2003). Experiences of discrimination also have been found to have an impact on Latino migrants' elevated levels of blood pressure and other markers of health (McClure et al. 2010). For these single men, the absence of instrumental support caused by the long distances separating family members may further exacerbate distress (Aranda et al. 2001). Without the availability of social support to ameliorate feelings of loneliness or distress, migrants are often left to battle discrimination, as well as other stressors, alone.

Latino migrants' significant marginalization also affects their risk for being victimized by crime. As previously stated, many Latino migrants settle in racially segregated and poor neighborhoods that have high crime rates. Despite this population's heightened vulnerability and exposure to violence, little is known about the impact of crime on Latino migrant populations. This is particularly glaring given that recent research indicates an increase in African American crime and violence linked to losses in low-skill jobs to Latino undocumented workers (Shihadeh and Barranco 2010). Similarly, recent news reports indicate a rise in crime against Latino immigrants (Hunter 2008; Londono and Vargas 2007), although increases in immigrant populations have not been found to be associated with increases in community violence and crime (Martínez Jr., Lee, and Nielsen 2004; Nielsen, Martínez Jr., and Lee 2005; Sampson, Morenoff, and Raudenbush 2005; Feldmeyer 2009).

A national survey of day laborers (59 percent of whom were Mexican and 28 percent Central American) by Valenzuela and colleagues found that the most common type of victimization suffered is employer violations of day laborer rights and basic labor standards (Valenzuela et al. 2006). This study found that about half of the day laborers (49 percent) reported being denied payment by an employer, while the same amount (48 percent) reported being underpaid by an employer. In addition to wage theft, day laborers reported they were denied food and water breaks (44 percent); worked more hours than agreed to (32 percent); were threatened or insulted by an employer (28 percent); and were abandoned at the worksite by an employer (27 percent). Most disturbing, 18 percent of day laborers reported having been violently victimized by an employer. This has compelled researchers to call for studies that add to our understanding of both the cultural and structural forces that may contribute to violence and victimization among the Latino immigrant population.

Theoretical Framework

Stress has emerged as a core concept for understanding the life experience of immigrants (Yakushko 2008). The transactional theory of stress has been widely used to explain how individuals experience stress as the result of threatening events, their primary and secondary appraisals of these events, and the coping mechanisms that are employed by the individual (Folkman et al. 1986; Lazarus and Folkman 1984). This theory has been used to explain how Latino immigrants undergo acculturation stress in the transition from their country of origin to the United States (Cervantes, Padilla, and Salgado de Snyder 1991). Complementing the transactional theory of stress, the diathesis stress model has been developed to account for levels of social vulnerability and the availability of coping resources that also shape the stress experience (Struwe 1994). This theory focuses on the resilience displayed by individuals in encountering chronic stressors and the predisposing factors that place individuals at heightened risk for negative consequences when encountering stressful circumstances and contexts.

In this chapter, we develop a theoretical framework integrating these stress theories to help explain our field observations and qualitative interviews of undocumented Latino day laborers in post-Katrina New Orleans and their experiences with violence. The context of New Orleans is particularly important given its new settlement destination status and large urban disenfranchised African American population. The lack of any significant prior Latino immigrant population creates special vulnerabilities and social stressor processes that go beyond those faced by immigrants in more traditional settlement destinations. These vulnerabilities are confounded by a highly racialized social context of New Orleans that is characterized by high rates of crime, thriving open-air drug markets, and drug use (Valdez et al. 2010).

Context: New Orleans Pre-Katrina

Pre-Katrina New Orleans has been described as one of the most disadvantaged urban areas in the United States (National Center for Health Statistics 2005). The city had a population of 485,000 with a racial composition that was 67 percent African American, 28 percent white, and 5 percent other race (U.S. Census Bureau 2000). Compared to other U.S. cities, New Orleans had one of the highest rates of poverty, welfare dependency, and unemployment, and lowest public health indicators (Administration on Children and Families 2004; U.S. Census Bureau 2000). The poor in New Orleans were largely African Americans, who lived in highly segregated and dilapidated public housing located in the old urban center (Cepeda et al. 2010). Others were low-income homeowners living in blighted residential areas, including the Lower Ninth Ward, Ninth Ward, Treme, and Gentily. These were neighborhoods that New Orleans' annual 3.7 million visitors seldom saw when visiting the French Quarter, Mardi Gras, the Jazz and Heritage Festival, Garden District or other popular tourist destinations (New Orleans Convention and Visitors Bureau 2006).

Another distinguishing characteristic of New Orleans was its high drug use prevalence rates (Santibanez et al. 2005). Pre-Katrina research indicated that 78 percent of the adult male and 60 percent of the adult female arrestee population in New Orleans tested positive for any of five drugs (cocaine, marijuana, methamphetamines, opiates, PCP) (Zhang 2003). African American neighborhoods, the areas most devastated by Hurricane Katrina, had the highest levels of crime, drug use, and identified major drug distribution centers (National Drug Intelligence Center 2001; Hartman and Squires 2006).

Methods

Data were collected from 77 undocumented Latino day laborers as part of a National Institute on Drug Abuse funded study conducted in New Orleans in 2008. The purpose of the study was to explore substance use patterns and related risk behaviors among a newly settled population of Mexican and Central American immigrants in post-Katrina New Orleans. A rapid assessment (RA) methodology was implemented in order to collect data on drug use, other risk behaviors, violence and related immigrant experiences (Fitch et al. 2004; Rhodes et al. 1999).

The RA methodology relied on collection of both qualitative and quantitative data to develop sampling frames and accurately assess patterns of risk (Needle et al. 2003). Intensive field observations were conducted by the research team over a six-month period in 2008 (May–October). Initially, the research team conducted a field assessment based on direct observations. This was designed to identify key geographical areas (sites) where Latino immigrant day laborers congregated to seek work. Field staff documented patterns of presence of male Latino day laborers by day, time, and place. The next phase consisted of implementing a more targeted field assessment of four specific sites with high concentrations of Latino day laborers. During this phase, field staff visited sites in order to establish a presence and build trust and rapport with potential respondents. Efforts were made to develop relationships with key informants in order to assess drug use among the population of day laborers in each of the four sites.

Interviews were completed during a one-week time frame in November 2008. A field team consisting of some of the authors of this chapter, an interviewer, and three outreach specialists identified, recruited, and interviewed the sample of Latino day laborers at the four sites. The sites included three home improvement stores and one day labor pick-up site. Inclusion criteria were: being a male 18 years of age or older; self-identified Latino (Hispanic) immigrant; self-reported use of illicit drugs during the past year; currently living in the New Orleans area (at least one year); and did not live in New Orleans prior to Hurricane Katrina. The trained outreach specialists conducted informal eligibility screening of potential subjects in the field. Participants were compensated for their time with $50 cash. Four interviewers trained in open-ended interviewing techniques elicited in-depth qualitative interviews in Spanish lasting 1 to 1.5 hours from each of the 77 participants. All interviews were audio-recorded. They were transcribed and analyzed in Spanish using the NVivo8 qualitative data analysis software. This method is consistent with recommendations to conduct analysis in the native language of respondents to maximize accuracy (Lopez et al. 2008). The data were analyzed using line by line coding. A pattern level analysis allowed for the identification of emerging themes.

Results

LOS JORNALEROS: CHARACTERISTICS OF THE STUDY SAMPLE

A brief demographic survey revealed that all interviewed men were foreign born, with the majority from Honduras (47 percent), followed by Mexico (38 percent), Guatemala (7 percent), and other Latin American countries (8 percent). The mean age was 33.1 years. Living in groups with other men tended to represent the most commonly reported housing arrangements (66 percent). Over half reported having a wife and/or children in their country of origin. The majority (90 percent) had less than a high school education. Respondents reported living in post-Katrina New Orleans for an average of 31 months. During the month prior to the interview, the sample reported seeking day labor work five days out of the week, with mean earnings for the month at approximately $845. Overall, the sample reported an increase in their use of drugs and alcohol since arriving in New Orleans. They cited the use of marijuana (95 percent), cocaine (57 percent), and alcohol (92 percent) since arrival. Of particular interest is the disproportionately high rate of crack cocaine use (64 percent) reported by these immigrants since arriving in the city.

Over 75 percent of the sample reported they had experienced some type of non-payment of wages by employers. Similarly, 85 percent identified having had an experience of underpayment of wages by employers. Experiences of abandonment at work sites, unpaid extra hours, and lack of food or breaks during the workday were reported by more than half of the sample.

Importantly, we note that the employer abuses reported by this sample are overall higher than those reported in the national study conducted by Valenzuela and colleagues (2006). For instance, approximately half of the national sample reported wage theft such as denial of payment and underpayment (49 percent and 48 percent, respectively) compared to the overwhelming majority of day laborers working in post-Katrina New Orleans who reported these types of abuses.

SOCIAL VULNERABILITIES

Respondents arriving in post-Katrina New Orleans found a city in need of inexpensive labor, but with a fractured social infrastructure not able to serve the needs of an unprecedented Latino migrant presence. In this environment, the inability to speak English, and their status as undocumented workers, emerged as vulnerabilities that contributed to their experiences of victimization.

"NO ENTIENDO": VULNERABILITY ASSOCIATED WITH LANGUAGE BARRIERS

Past research has shown that language conflict can contribute to frustration, stress, and even depression (Finch, Kolody, and Vega 2000). It can also contribute to the segregation of migrant workers into marginalized and dangerous jobs, which directly affect their health (Vinck et al. 2009; Ding and Hargraves 2009). The language barrier is an obstacle that is foreseen by migrant laborers. Although communication can be managed in a number of different ways, the intimidation of the language barrier is felt early in the migrant experience. One immigrant describes the gravity of not being able to communicate even the simplest of things during his migration journey.

> We went two complete days without eating, without drinking water, going without sleep, dehydrated. I'll tell you that on the last day almost by a blessing from God, they came to get us and we managed to cross [into the U.S.]. We thought we had made it, we're now up North. Now comes the worst part. Because being here without speaking English, going to a store, wanting to buy chicken or wanting to buy rice without knowing how to say it in English ...without knowing how to say to someone "Hey look, I need work. I can do this, this, and that." Without knowing the language, it is very difficult.

Once they arrived, the undocumented workers were required to negotiate daily activities despite the inability to communicate in English. Respondents found communication especially difficult in New Orleans where there was no significant pre-existing Latino community, which might have facilitated this process. Workers congregated in high-traffic areas of construction supply stores, such as Lowes or Home Depot. Here they hoped to be "picked up" for any number of jobs, ranging from moving furniture to construction. Once picked up, the workers were provided with instructions and paid according to a predetermined amount. At this point, the most common problem they encountered was the inability to understand what they were being asked to do. A Colombian worker explained, "We struggle sometimes because of the language, struggle sometimes because of the job. Sometimes the job isn't done right because we don't know what they are telling us in English ... So sometimes we do the job wrong and there are fights and disturbances because of it."

Many of the men reported having disagreements with the people that had hired them. Without the ability to communicate, these disagreements had the potential to escalate into violence. At times, workers reported the police were brought in to mediate, though the "disturbances" were perceived to be significantly one-sided as many Latinos claimed they were unable to provide their version of the incident to the non-Spanish-speaking law enforcement officials. In instances where immigrants were unable to convey their side of the altercation, participants relayed that law enforcement frequently sided with the English speakers and either dismissed, or in some cases, even arrested, them. A 38-year-old Guatemalan day laborer described how a lack of communication affected options for redress:

> There are a lot of people who because they have disputes about the job, have been hit, you understand? And what are you going to do? Call the police? You can't speak English. And Spanish is going to sound bad to the police officer. "No, no I don't understand friend." And if the police goes over there and asks the other person he tells them, "Oh he took a stick, he wanted to hit me" and they tell him that lie, the other guy is standing there dumb. Total loss. This happens a lot.

This sentiment was echoed by a 21-year-old Honduran day laborer: "There's no support. Because when someone fights some guy out there, and the English speaker talks to the police and says, 'That guy hit me and stole my money.'" This young Honduran goes on to explain that the police always believe the English speaker, leaving the immigrant without any recourse.

Some of the immigrants have been in the United States for years and have a better understanding of the services available to them while acquiring a minor, but generally effective, handle on English. Many of these persons serve as intermediaries between newly arrived migrants and potential employers. A 21-year-old Honduran day laborer with limited English ability describes how a disagreement with employers over payment was dismissed by the police:

> She had told us $800 to paint the wall. Small, right? And so, we said ok $800. Then around seven, once we had finished, the lady was giving us $500. She called the police on us because we were telling her that it was $800. She said that if we didn't leave, she was going to call the police on us. When they arrived I told the police in my half broken English that she said she was going to pay us $800. And the police said, "Get out of here!" And so we left.

Lack of English proficiency and the inability to communicate was also associated with victimization. Specifically, the immigrant men reported they felt exploited precisely due to their inability to speak English. One participant stated, "When a Hispanic don't speak English they take advantage of him. But if you say something to them, like 'What? What do you want?' Then they don't get into it with you. But yeah, when one doesn't speak English, that's when people get screwed."

"SIN PAPELES Y SIN FAMILIA": UNDOCUMENTED IMMIGRANT STATUS VULNERABILITY AND SOCIAL ISOLATION

Many of the men interviewed reported feeling persistent stress due to their undocumented status. Furthermore, they expressed feeling lonely and sad because they are away from family. This loneliness, distrust of peers, and ensuing depression were familiar themes:

> Yeah, I'm here by myself. There are no good friends here in the United States. It's all a lie. Not one. Sometimes you're out there just because one is lonely, "Hey, how're you doing?" But to go out drinking? To be a friend? No. First of all, they'll rob you, screw you over, or talk bad about you at the job, even if it's your best friend. That's why I want to be alone. I'm completely alone.

Often times, depression can have negative health consequences on day laborers. Respondents cite isolation and depression as leading contributors to the harmful consumption of alcohol, drugs, and high-risk sex. Others feel that depression can manifest itself as a biological illness. A Guatemalan day laborer describes how a person can become ill due to loneliness while also illustrating how difficult it can be to adjust to life without a wife and the stress that accompanies the undocumented immigrant status:

> Mostly I get sick of fever, of solitude. Just drained and sometimes I get sick from it, from being alone … I feel lonely. I go to work, get home and I have to do everything. Like, let's say I get off of work, I get home tired, and I say to myself, "Where is my wife to do these things for me?" I still have to do it. I have to do laundry, I have to cook, and I have to do everything. And that's the problem. And I imagine to myself, "Should I look for another woman here, or stay with the one over there [wife in Guatemala]?" I don't know. I start to think it is a mistake for one to feel this way. And that's why I get sick. Yeah. The next morning I feel sick.

This sense of isolation and loneliness is often amplified by problems in their respective country of origin. Frequently, the men reported coping with these issues through the use of drugs and alcohol. A 24-year-old day laborer reported being depressed for three months while his mother in Honduras was sick. He describes this period as one where he wanted to be left alone to drink by himself. He also reported being more inclined to commit hostile behavior at the smallest instigation. Another young man talked about how intimate relationships from their country of origin can play a contributing role in the initiation of drug use:

> I have my wife, I've been married ten years, I have 15- and 16-year-old kids. I send them money. I have ten dollars left. I call home, "Hi Mom, how are you and the family? And the brother? Good, good. Hey so what's up?" Then she says, "Well you know what? She's fooling you. I saw your wife out with some guy," or "I saw her go out to this place with him." And what is a person to do? You get depressed and use drugs and alcohol. What can you do? You know, you haven't achieved what you wanted to do here and you carry that in your mind and you start to drink and do drugs. It's messed up.

This descent into drug and alcohol use further marginalizes a segment of society that is already living on the fringes of the formalized economy. While the presence of substance use is widely cited by these men as a reaction to challenging circumstances, many do not mention knowing of any drug therapy or alcohol counseling available to them. More broadly, many do not know of city, parish, state, or federal social programs that could be available to assist them in any capacity. Some acknowledge that although they do not know of any programs, they would not be able to access them anyway because of their undocumented status. For example, a 38-year-old day laborer from Mexico remembered hearing that without a Louisiana state identification card or driver's license he could not get social services.

While undocumented day laborers do not have access to many government resources and their assistance within peer networks is unstable, there is a significant charitable presence provided by the Archdiocese of New Orleans that is frequently cited by the respondents as their source for external help. This presence is so significant that for many, "social service" was synonymous with the charitable assistance they received from area Catholic churches. These churches, and Saint Joseph in particular, provided clothing, shoes, showers, medical checkups, and occasional dental checkups for people that otherwise would not have access to them. Some reported being allowed to stay the night when they had nowhere else to go. One worker described how the church helped him pay a bill: "It's only the churches that help around here. The church gave me half of what I needed to pay my electricity bill. I was sent there from another office. I went and talked to them and they helped me with half the bill. Between me and my three friends, we sent the payment."

While there were other churches, missions, and charitable organizations available to help undocumented day laborers, in an area where social capital is low, there are few networked channels available to disseminate this kind of information. Outside information is gathered first hand and at the risk and expense of the participant. Once this information is gathered, it can be difficult to spread to others for fear that the resources will disappear, creating an information-hoarding effect. A Mexican with 20 years' experience in undocumented labor explains how this occurs:

> Yeah, there's the Covenant House, Saint Joseph's, and a mobile clinic that's around the Covenant House. There are others by the river, but those are over by the Tulane Hospital. These are for those they call "indigent." But a lot of Hispanics don't know about them. But lots of times, I don't tell others because then that one person will tell three others and those tell others. And then it's me that's finished.

Charitable service as a resource meant a great deal to these men who found themselves without a social safety net and expressed distrust of the police for fear of being deported or detained by immigration or other authorities. For instance, many day laborers report what they perceive to be unfair law enforcement practices because of their immigrant status. A 36-year-old Honduran describes a common experience:

> In the four years I have been here, they've treated us badly. With discrimination. They can't resolve your cases. Just because you're a Latino they can't resolve your problem. So they let it go and turn the page. And every time you look, there are police who are more racist. Only because you're a Latino, for having a Latino face, they stop you on the street and ask for your papers. And if you don't have papers, they send you to immigration. Many cases like this have already happened. Many cases. And so I see sometimes that just for being Latino, they get the police on you.

Respondents reported that interactions with the police are often associated with the risk of deportation. This perception causes a great deal of anxiety among day laborers who worry that even the smallest infraction could lead to them to be processed by immigration officials. A Honduran day laborer stated:

> Here people have car insurance. As an immigrant, you can get an international drivers license and you can use it in this area, New Orleans. We do have access to insurance, but if we do not have a license I get a ticket. They can send me to jail for that. They can even deport me for that. In the Baton Rouge area, they recently deported a Mexican. He got into an accident and didn't have a license or anything.

Distrust of the police further contributed to the workers' sense of powerlessness and feelings of vulnerability, compared to legal residents. One gentleman describes the perceived leverage that legal residents wield: "It's hard here. Since they have papers, they have the power. They have strength. We're illegal. We have our hands tied. How we can do something against a legal resident? We have everything to lose. Everything. If I have a car and I hit a legal resident, I lose."

Labor rights abuses in post-Katrina New Orleans have been widely documented (Fletcher et al. 2006; Gorman 2010; Bernstein 2006). Similarly, respondents overwhelmingly reported that employers had refused payment or had paid less than the agreed upon amount. In many cases the day laborers had no alternative but to accept what they could get. Disputes can occur, but day laborers frequently avoid them because of their vulnerable status. Moreover, these differences have a tendency of escalating into a confrontation such as shouting and threats, even physical assaults and intimidation with firearms: "One time we went to a demolition and instead of paying us, the guy pointed a gun to our head and told us to leave or he was going to kill us. So, we left." In these cases, the respondents were frustrated that even if one turned to the police for help, they typically could not help them resolve their issues. A small number of men resorted to contacting a grassroots organization referred to as *el congreso*. The Congress of Day Laborers operates under the auspices of the New Orleans Workers' Center for Racial Justice and offers advocacy and assistance to day laborers in cases of abuse.

Among the few that used the *congreso*'s services, most acknowledged their services had become less effective over time and were hardly viable at the time of the interviews. As a result, the men began contacting case workers at the Hispanic Apostolate Community Services, a community organization under the direction of the Archdiocese of New Orleans. Others reported using the Hispanic Apostolate Community Services for help, but it appeared that some of their cases had not been resolved to their satisfaction, if at all. Much like the immigrants in Cruz's chapter on the relationship between undocumented workers and criminal defense attorneys, the respondents had little confidence in the organization, and this distrust reinforced feelings of powerlessness in the face of legal abuses and their undocumented status.

Some immigrants in the sample have a different perspective on their role as undocumented workers and victimization. A 35-year-old Guatemalan day laborer responds to the passiveness with which some day laborers take abuse and exploitation:

That's ignorance on their part. I've heard many say that too. I've talked to lots of them on the corner, because on the corner we all know each other and talk. For me, when I tried to file my lawsuit, a lawyer told me, "You can't do anything because you are a wetback. You have no papers [legal residency]." So I told him, "Ok." I grabbed my papers and left to find another lawyer. I told him that the previous lawyer didn't want to take my case because I didn't have any papers. And he told me, "I'm going to tell you something. You too are human, an American, a Hispanic, papers or no papers, and you have the same rights as an American." And so I told everyone that.

Social Stressor Processes

Patterns of violent victimization become apparent when certain stressors combine with the respondents' identified vulnerabilities: limited English proficiency and their status as undocumented workers. Among respondents, the stressors take the form of internal frictions among undocumented Latinos, tensions between Latinos and the local African American population, and the hazards inherent in the labor that is available to them as workers with very little human capital.

"Con Su Misma Gente": Brown-on-Brown Stressors

Of the day laborers interviewed, approximately half were from Honduras. The second largest nationality represented was Mexico, with 38 percent. Guatemala was a distant third with only 7 percent, and the remainder reportedly coming from other Central and Latin American countries. Although social interaction occurred at work sites and job corners between these nationalities, participants described some divisiveness among the workers due to country of origin:

> Well look, I get along with everybody at work or at the corner. I get along with Mexicans, Guatemalans, everybody. With Nicaraguans too. But in terms of outside of work, no. You know, we see each other on the corner, we chat. Good for just talking with them. That's it. But when the evening comes, each one has his place.

Although divisions along nationalities are commonplace and not usually violent, a recurring theme in the interviews was the amount of tension prevalent in interactions between Latinos. We found that social networks tended to be ethnically homogeneous, and tensions based on nationality often erupted into acts of physical aggression and violence:

> There was this one kid who ran over another kid because of a disagreement. And that problem came all the way from Houston, from another corner in Houston. But it was here where they saw each other, he saw him, and he ran him over with the car. Two Latinos. He squashed him, ran him over and broke his hip with the car.

In a separate episode, an inebriated Honduran began insulting some nearby Mexicans and damaged their truck. Four Mexicans retaliated by beating him with a baseball bat, causing head and hip injuries. In yet another incident, a fight between a Honduran and a Mexican resulted in a shooting that killed a Honduran woman nearby. One laborer acknowledged that in New Orleans, Latinos are often their own worst enemies: "It's us same Latinos who put ourselves against the Latinos. I don't see that as a good thing.

Sometimes we're not united as Latinos. Sometimes I see that Latinos are disorganized. They don't like other Latinos and it shouldn't be that way. We should be fairer. Because sometimes it's Latinos who throw down Latinos, here among ourselves."

There appears to be a heightened animosity between Mexicans and Central American respondents. The hostility shared by Hondurans and Mexicans was especially palpable and mutual. This mutual dislike emerged in conversations and interviews with both groups. One Mexican, while talking about how a few Honduran day laborers were recently arrested and sent to prison, punctuated the story with profanity. He later expanded on this sentiment by saying, "It's good that they were Hondurans. Yeah, so that they can finish each other off quicker." There are also examples of Hondurans expressing anti-Mexican sentiment: "There was this guy who when he drank, had a strong resentment towards Mexicans. I don't know why. But when he drank he would always start, 'Mexican sons of bitches.'"

Mexicans' hostility toward Hondurans was not identified, although some Mexican participants relayed feelings that Hondurans are uneducated and vulgar. A Mexican day laborer stated: "I don't know why we don't like each other. It's just that they [Hondurans] don't adjust to our way of being, you understand? They're something else. It's something we [Mexicans] don't like. They're always saying '*Fuck*,' they talk too much. And some are educated and they tell you to shut up."

Hondurans indicated specific reasons for their friction with Mexicans. Much of it was relayed to be because of the dangerous journey that many undertook to the United States from Honduras. For many, the most dangerous part of the journey was through Mexico:

> Yeah the journey was really difficult because you get mugged on the way. A big problem for the immigrants there is all the people who are looking to rob them. Even the train conductor starts asking, "Pay me! If you don't I won't take you anymore and I'll throw you to immigration." And that's the problem that all along the way they want you to pay them. Many get mugged, stabbed, get shot at by Mexicans. So many bad things!

The dangers posed to Central Americans traveling to the United States are also widely publicized in Honduran newspapers. Accounts of Hondurans being raped, murdered, and assaulted in Mexico are commonplace and often intended to deter Hondurans from immigrating (Sladkova 2007). Mexico is seen as a dangerous place with people who make the journey infinitely more difficult. As one respondent noted, "The women from my country

[Honduras] know what's coming. Because in Mexico it's a given they're going to be raped."

Once in the United States, there are notable lifestyle differences between Mexicans and Central Americans that have the potential to create resentment. Among the participants in this study, Mexicans tend to have a higher level of social capital than Central Americans because of their relative proximity to the United States. It is often easier for them to be employed in steadier jobs instead of participating in day labor. Perhaps relatedly, a Mexican in the United States was perceived by some respondents to have higher status than immigrants from Central America:

> The majority of us on the corner are Guatemalans, Hondurans or Salvadorians. There are almost no Mexicans there since they have more prestige than we do here. Seeing two, three Mexicans on the corner is rare. For them, it is easier to find a job . . . . You know that is easier for them. For us on the other hand it's very difficult. They get jobs easier at any company. That's the difference. The Mexican has a little bit more prestige than those of us who came from further away.

"Nos Escupen" Black-on-Brown Stressors

The sudden presence of undocumented Latinos in traditionally low-income African American neighborhoods puts many of the immigrant day laborers in close proximity to unemployed, street-oriented young African American males (Valdez et al. 2010). Simultaneously, the rapid influx of undocumented Latino immigrants into New Orleans appeared to have created competition for low-skill jobs. Some of the men reported employers preferring Latino laborers to African American laborers on the same corner. This tension is compounded by the fact that employment and payment of day laborers is highly visible, making many day laborers easy targets for quick cash by criminal elements and referred to as "walking ATMs" (Nossiter 2009).

Overwhelmingly, undocumented Latino day laborers reported experiencing the most violence and victimization from African American males. Often these crimes include assaults and robberies, though many of them report that as a group they are the targets of other kinds of aggression by African American males, such as intimidation and harassment: "He [African American male] kept telling me 'Hispanics aren't good for anything. They don't have any strength, power. They don't have a head for anything. They don't think. They aren't good for anything." At other times, aggression is much more violent:

> The blacks spit on us here. When they see us, they spit on us. They've actually killed lots of Hondurans here. Last week they killed a guy who had only been here a year and a half. They shot him four times. And now it looks like they [family] don't have a way of taking him back to Honduras. Last time, they killed a man who was working and because he wouldn't give them his money, they killed him. And another man was killed for a little bit of money. For a hundred or even fifty dollars, they'll take your life.

Contact between day laborers and African American males was often limited to job sites and typically avoided outside these settings. Some undocumented workers relayed how they would try to avoid certain neighborhoods, blocks, or streets known to be primarily African American: "Blacks assault us a lot. It's even worse if it's in an African American neighborhood. Here you have to know where to go. I know where all the African American neighborhoods are. And that's why I know don't go in there."

Still, for some drug-using respondents, contact was unavoidable as drug dealers were reported to be mostly African Americans in New Orleans. These drug users also reported victimization and relayed that sellers would frequently take a buyers' money but not provide the drugs: "It's happened to me lots of times. The blacks have pulled guns on me, they've taken my money. The last time, I took one on, and then another and I grabbed another, like six black guys. They didn't give me my drugs or anything. They just took my money. That's how it happens."

Anecdotally, many of the men report Latinos being the victims of senseless crimes in which robbery does not seem to be the motivation. The following is an example of what Latino day laborers experience on a continual basis and the dangers posed to them by African Americans involved in crime and violence:

> Yeah, one day we were just sitting outside drinking beer when we heard, "poom, poom." It was two bullets and they hit the car near where we were. It was a black man who was shooting especially for us right there where we were sitting. I suppose it was racism on his part. He must have said, "I'm going to get them out of here" and so he shot at where we were and hit that truck instead.

In some incidents there appears to be an anti-immigrant undertone to the violence. The men often report being treated badly by the locals, with many

African Americans saying that the day laborers are "taking their jobs." Frequently, undocumented laborers did not seek help from law enforcement. Although language barriers and fear of deportation are significant deterrents as already noted, some carry a perception that African American police officers often either favor their own race, or would act out their prejudices in the course of their duties:

> How can you testify against one of them [African Americans] when they have all their people on the inside? One sees that a Honduran is killed. How can I say, "It was that guy [who shot him]?" They want you to be a witness. They tell you they'll give you security. 'We're going to keep you safe but you have to tell us who it was and all that. "But we're going to send you to jail for your safety so that they don't kill you out there." They may kill me because they are black police officers. They're the same race. They prefer people of their own race. So here, what can you do?

The idea that police activity appears to be motivated by race is reinforced by an Afro-Caribbean Honduran who reports having better interactions with the police on account of his race. In addition to calling the police when needed, he has also called courthouses and ambulances with an ease not found among other immigrant men. He acknowledges having an immigrant experience characterized by a greater degree of comfort and self-reliance than other undocumented Latinos in New Orleans: "Latinos think that police stop them because they're Latinos, you understand? Yeah man, the police despise them [Latinos] badly. And I tell them when they stop me that I'm from Honduras. And the police say, "But you're black. You're black." They don't believe me, I am a Latino."

Discussion

This chapter has documented the nuanced realities produced by the interaction of social stressor processes and special vulnerabilities experienced by a unique population of Latino immigrant day laborers in the United States. Our findings indicate that immigrant Latino men living in New Orleans are exposed to chronic stressful circumstances that are a result of immigration processes specific to the context of post-Katrina New Orleans. These stressors are exacerbated by their vulnerable status as day laborers. The results of our study support recent innovations in measurement models that emphasize the salience and chronicity of the stressful circumstances and the intensity of the stress response, including their appraisal (Bloch, Neeleman, and

Aleamoni 2004). Our study suggests that stressful events are experienced so frequently by these men that they have become a central part of their everyday lives. These stressful circumstances are not simply the result of the level of existing social vulnerabilities, such as language capacities and legal status, shared by many other segments of the Latino immigrant population. Rather, the qualitative data reveal that these social vulnerabilities common to many undocumented Latino immigrants are socially mediated in a complex process of stressors that can be classified as brown-on-brown, black-on-brown, and white-on-brown that are specific to their day labor and transitory social position.

The data also indicate that these stressors engender coping mechanisms in response to the special social position of the Latino day laborers (Goffman 1963; Mobasher 2006). One of the ways in which the men in our sample cope with these situations is to isolate themselves in exclusive ethnically Latino homogeneous social networks (i.e., Mexican, Honduran, etc.). However, an unintended consequence of this is to increase violence victimization associated with the brown-on-brown social stressor processes, as described by our respondents.

Our results also suggest a pattern of instrumental versus expressive motivations for violence (Block and Block 1993; Block and Christakos 1995) that are strongly associated with the stressor processes presented. That is, the employer violence (or labor-related stressors) against the Latino immigrant day laborers appears to be motivated by the explicit instrumental ends of obtaining free or cheap manual labor for their reconstruction efforts. On the other hand, the violence that occurs between Latino immigrants themselves suggests that these incidents typically emerge as episodic acts of anger, rage, or frustration, thus depicting more expressive motivations. The black-on-brown social stressor process, however, appears to be distinctly unique in that the violence occurring between the long-time African American residents and the newly arrived Latino immigrants occurs as both a mix of instrumental and expressive motivations for violence. For instance, some of the violence that Latinos are exposed to at the hands of young African American men tends to be motivated by robbery (acquiring immigrant's money). However, there is evidence that other black-on-brown violence is more expressive in the sense that the increased tension between both groups as a result of the limited employment and housing has resulted in spontaneous altercations.

Despite their pronounced vulnerabilities, chronic stress, the high intensity of their response to these circumstances, limited coping resources, and an elevated risk for violence victimization, the men in our sample generally have a high level of resilience that allows them to survive. Especially apparent in the Central American immigrants, pre-migration stressors associated with surviving civil war in their home countries and traumatic experiences in the transition through Mexico during their migration seemed to increase their resilience. In the case of Mexican immigrants, resilience seems to have developed under relatively less severe immigration processes. These immigrants display the important individual resilience resource factor termed "bridging and bonding capital" enabling them to access support services that are targeted to this special population of New Orleans (Castro and Murray 2010). These resilience resources are largely unknown to other Central American immigrants who may still employ family-based models of pooled resources to deal with stressful circumstances in their home communities. More research is needed to understand the resilience resource factors that sustain these men in the absence of family and community support.

Implications

Findings from this study indicate the need for increased access to social services for this highly stressed and vulnerable population. Some immigrants reported knowledge of religious charities that offered financial assistance. However, it is clear that these men have little knowledge of how to access medical care or mental health services. This is especially problematic given the frequency of on-the-job injuries, violence, and psychosocial symptomology reported by these men. Furthermore, the immigrant men in this study reported multiple instances of employment abuses. The Congress of Day Laborers, which operates under the auspices of the New Orleans Workers' Center for Racial Justice and offers advocacy and assistance to day laborers in cases of abuse, was cited by only a small number of immigrant day laborers as a resource. More community outreach and dissemination of information are needed to educate these men about the services that are available within the community. This can be done by frequenting day labor pick-up sites and distributing written information in Spanish.

Additional outreach efforts to encourage reporting of criminal offenses to law enforcement can help reduce violence and other types of crime. Several stressors reported by this population concerned the lack of knowledge about their legal status and their rights in this country. Ensuring that they will not be deported due to their victim status can build trust with law enforcement and increase crime reporting among this population. Lastly, we see a continuation of black-Latino tensions that we see elsewhere in more traditional settlement areas such as Los Angeles (Hernandez 2007).

One popular explanation for these tensions is the competition for scarce resources, employment, and political power (Gay 2006; Shihadeh and Barranco 2010). This conflict may be exacerbated by the disaster-stricken context of post-Katrina New Orleans, where even five years after the storm made landfall there is a dearth of community resources, affordable housing, and employment opportunities.

REFERENCES

Administration on Children and Families. 2004. Temporary assisstance for needy families (TANF): Sixth annual report to Congress.

Aranda, Maria P., Irma Castaneda, Pey-Jiuan Lee, and Eugene Sobel. 2001. Stress, Social Support, and Coping as Predictors of Depressive Symptoms: Gender Differences among Mexican Americans. *Social Work Research* 25 (1): 37–48.

Aroian, Karen J. and Anne E. Norris. 2003. Depression Trajectories in Relatively Recent Immigrants. *Comprehensive Psychiatry* 44 (5 (September/October)): 420–427.

Bernstein, Aaron. 2006. Also in the Wake: Wage Abuse. *BusinessWeek* (3982): 16–16.

Bloch, George J., Lori Neeleman, and Lawrence M. Aleamoni. 2004. The Salient Stressor Impact Questionnaire (SSIQ): A measurement of the intensity and chronicity of stress. *Assessment* 11 (4): 342–360.

Block, C. R., and R. Block. 1993. Street Gang Crime in Chicago. In *National Institute of Justice Research in Brief*. Washington, DC.

Block, C. R. and A. Christakos. 1995. Major Trends in Chicago Homicide: 1965–1994. Chicago: Illinois Criminal Justice Information Authority.

Castro, Felipe Gonzalez and Kate E. Murray. 2010. Cultural Adaptation and Resilience: Controversies, Issues, and Emerging Models. In *Handbook of Adult Resilience*, ed. J. W. Reich, A. J. Zautra, and J. S. Hall, 375–403. New York: Guilford Press.

Cepeda, Alice, Avelardo Valdez, Charles Kaplan, and Larry E. Hill. 2010. Patterns of Substance use among Hurricane Katrina evacuees in Houston, Texas. *Disasters* 34 (2): 426–446.

Cervantes, Richard C., Amado M. Padilla, and Nelly Salgado de Snyder. 1991. The Hispanic Stress Inventory: A Culturally Relevant Approach to Psychosocial Assessment. *Psychological Assessment: A Journal of Consulting and Clinical Psychology* 3 (3): 438–447.

Cervantes, Richard C., V. Nelly Salgado de Snyder, and Amado M. Padilla. 1989. Posttraumatic Stress in Immigrants from Central America and Mexico. *Hospital and Community Psychiatry* 40: 615–619.

Ding, H. and L. Hargraves. 2009. Stress-associated Poor Health among Adult Immigrants with a Language Barrier in the United States. *Journal of Immigrant & Minority Health* 11 (6): 446–452.

Elliott, James R. and Jeremy Pais. 2006. Race, Class and Hurricane Katrina: Social Differences in Human Responses to Disaster. *Social Science Research* 35 (2): 295–321.

Feldmeyer, Ben. 2009. Immigration and Violence: The Offsetting Effects of Immigrant Concentration on Latino Violence. *Social Science Research* 38 (3): 717–731.

Finch, Brian Karl, Bohdan Kolody, and William A. Vega. 2000. Perceived Discrimination and Depression among Mexican-origin Adults in California. *Journal of Health & Social Behavior* 41 (3): 295–313.

Fitch, C., G. V. Stimson, T. Rhodes, and V. Poznyak. 2004. Rapid Assessment: An International Review of Diffusion, Practice and Outcomes in the Substance Use Field. *Social Science & Medicine* 59 (9): 1819–1830.

Fletcher, Laurel E., Phuong Pham, Eric Stover, and Patrick Vinck. 2006. *Rebuilding after Katrina: A Population-Based Study of Labor and Human Rights in New Orleans.* UC Berkeley: Human Rights Center.

Folkman, Susan, Richard S. Lazarus, Christine Dunkel-Schetter, Anita DeLongis, and Rand J. Gruen. 1986. Dynamics of a Stressful Encounter: Cognitive Appraisal, Coping, and Encounter Outcomes. *Journal of Personality and Social Psychology* 50 (5): 992–1003.

Frey, William H., Audrey Singer, and David Park. 2007. Resettling New Orleans: The First Full Picture from the Census. Washington, DC: Brookings Institution.

Fussell, Elizabeth, Narayan Sastry, and Mark VanLandingham. 2009. Race, Socioeconomic Status, and Return Migration to New Orleans after Hurricane Katrina. In *Report 09-667.* Ann Arbor: Population Studies Center, University of Michigan, Institute for Social Research.

Gay, Claudine. 2006. Seeing Difference: The Effect of Economic Disparity on Black Attitudes toward Latinos. *American Journal of Political Science* 50 (4): 982–997.

Goffman, Erving. 1963. *Stigma: Notes on the Management of Spoiled Identity.* Englewood Cliffs, NJ: Prentice-Hall.

Gorman, Leo B. 2010. Latino Migrant Labor Strife and Solidarity in Post-Katrina New Orleans, 2005–2007. *Latin Americanist* 54 (1): 1–33.

Hartman, C. and G. D. Squires. 2006. *There Is No Such Thing as a Natural Disaster: Race, Class, and Hurricane Katrina.* New York: Routledge.

Hernández, Tanya Kateri. 2007. Latino Anti-Black Violence in Los Angeles: Not "Made in the USA." *Harvard Journal of African American Public Policy* 13: 37–40.

Hunter, M. 2008. Several Teens Linked to Metairie Robberies and Break-ins. *The Times Picayune,* April 2.

Lazarus, Richard S. and Susan Folkman. 1984. *Stress, Appraisal, and Coping.* New York: Springer.

Lee, Everett S. 1966. A Theory of Migration. *Demography* 3 (1): 47–57.

Lichter, D. T. and K. M. Johnson. 2009. Immigration Gateways and Hispanic Migration to New Destinations. *International Migration Review* 43 (3): 496–518.

Lichter, D. T., D. B. Parisi, M. C. Taquino, and M. S. Grice. 2009. Residential Segregation in New Hispanic Destinations: Cities, Suburbs, and Rural Communities Compared. *Social Science Research* 39 (2): 216–230.

Londono, E. and T. Vargas. 2007. Robbers Stalk Hispanic Immigrants, Seeing Ideal Prey. *Washington Post,* A01.

Lopez, G. I., M. Figueroa, S. E. Connor, and S. L. Maliski. 2008. Translation Barriers in Conducting Qualitative Research with Spanish Speakers. *Qualitative Health Research* 18 (12): 1729–1737.

Magaña, Cristina G. and Joseph D. Hovey. 2003. Psychosocial Stressors Associated with Mexican Migrant Farmworkers in the Midwest United States. *Journal of Immigrant Health* 5 (2): 75–86.

Martínez Jr., Ramiro, Matthew T. Lee, and Amie L. Nielsen. 2004. Segmented Assimilation, Local Context and Determinants of Drug Violence in Miami and San Diego: Does Ethnicity and Immigration Matter? *International Migration Review* 38 (1): 131–157.

McClure, Heather H., Charles R. Martínez Jr., J. Josh Snodgrass, J. Mark Eddy, Roberto A. Jiménez, Laura E. Isiordia, and Thomas W. McDade. 2010. Discrimination-related Stress, Blood Pressure and Epstein-Barr Virus Antibodies among Latin American Immigrants in Oregon, US. *Journal of Biosocial Science* 42: 433–461.

Mobasher, Mohsen. 2006. Cultural Trauma and Ethnic Identity Formation Among Iranian Immigrants in the United States. *American Behavioral Scientist* 50 (1): 100–117.

National Center for Health Statistics. 2005. Health: United States, 2004. Hyattsville, MD: Department of Health and Human Services.

National Drug Intelligence Center. 2001. Louisiana Drug Threat Assessment. Johnstown: U.S. Department of Justice.

Needle, R. H., R. T. Trotter, M. Singer, C. Bates, J. B. Page, D. Metzger, and L. H. Marcelin. 2003. Rapid Assessment of the HIV/AIDS Crisis in Racial and Ethnic Minority Communities: An Approach for Timely Community Interventions. *American Journal of Public Health* 93 (6): 970–979.

New Orleans Convention and Visitors Bureau. 2006. New Orleans area visitor profile.

Nielsen, Amie L., Ramiro Martínez Jr., and Matthew T. Lee. 2005. Alcohol, Ethnicity, and Violence: The Role of Alcohol Availability for Latino and Black Aggravated Assaults and Robberies. *Sociological Quarterly* 46: 479–502.

Nossiter, Adam. 2009. Day Laborers Are Easy Prey in New Orleans. *New York Times*, February 16.

Rhodes, Tim, Gerry V. Stimson, Chris Fitch, Andrew Ball, and Adrian Renton. 1999. Rapid Assessment, Injecting Drug Use, and Public Health. *Lancet* 354: 65–68.

Saldaña, D. 1992. Coping with Stress: A Refugee's Story. *Women & Therapy* 13: 21–34.

Salgado de Snyder, V. Nelly, Richard C. Cervantes, and Amado M. Padilla. 1990. Gender and Ethnic Differences in Psychosocial Stress and Generalized Distress Among Hispanics. *Sex Roles* 22 (7/8): 441–453.

Sampson, Robert J., Jeffrey D. Morenoff, and Stephen W. Raudenbush. 2005. Social Anatomy of Racial and Ethnic Disparities in Violence. *American Journal of Public Health* 95: 224–232.

Sánchez, P., and M. Machado-Casas. 2009. At the Intersection of Transnationalism, Latina/o Immigrants, and Education. *High School Journal* 92 (4): 3–15.

Santibanez, Scott S., Richard S. Garfein, Andrea Swartzendruber, Peter R. Kerndt, Edward Morse, and Danielle Ompad, et al. 2005. Prevalence and Correlates of Crack-Cocaine Injection among Young Injection Drug Users in the United States, 1997–1999. *Drug and Alcohol Dependence* 77: 227–233.

Scott, Matthew. 2010. *After Katrina, the New Orleans Population Goes Upscale.* AOL 2010 [cited September 24 2010].

Shihadeh, Edward S. and Raymond E. Barranco. 2010. Latino Employment and Black Violence: The Unintended Consequences of U.S. Immigration Policy. *Social Forces* 88 (3): 1393–1420.

Sladkova, Jana. 2007. Expectations and Motivations of Hondurans Migrating to the United States. *Journal of Community and Applied Social Psychology* 17: 187–202.

Struwe, G. 1994. Training Health and Medical Professionals to Care for Refugees: Issues and Methods. In *Amidst Peril and Pain: The Mental Health and Well-being of the World's Refugees*. Washington, DC: American Psychological Association.

United States Census Bureau. 2000. County and City Data Book: 2000, table C-4.

———. 2000. U.S. Bureau of the Census.

————. 2006. R1701. Percent of people below poverty level in the past 12 months (for whom poverty status is determined). In *American Community Survey*.

————. 2008. 3-Year Estimates, New Orleans, Louisiana Data Profile 2006–2008. In *American Community Survey*.

Valdez, Avelardo, Alice Cepeda, Nalini Junko Negi, and Charles Kaplan. 2010. Fumando La Piedra: Emerging Patterns of Crack Use Among Latino Immigrant Day Laborers in New Orleans. *Journal of Immigrant and Minority Health* 12 (5): 737–742.

Valenzuela, Abel, Nik Theodore, Edwin Melendez, and Ana Luz Gonzalez. 2006. *On the Corner: Day Labor in the United States*. Los Angeles: University of California–Los Angeles.

Vinck, Patrick, Phuong N. Pham, Laurel E. Fletcher, and Eric Stover. 2009. Inequalities and Prospects: Ethnicity and Legal Status in the Construction Labor Force after Hurricane Katrina. *Organization and Environment* 22 (4): 470–478.

Yakushko, Oksana. 2008. Xenophobia: Understanding the Roots and Consequences of Negative Attitudes Towards Immigrants. *The Counseling Psychologist* 37 (1): 36–66.

Zhang, Zhiwei. 2003. Drug and Alcohol Use and Related Matters among Arrestees. In *Arrestee Drug Abuse Monitoring Program*. Chicago: National Opinion Research Center.

11

Conclusion

MARJORIE S. ZATZ, CHARIS E. KUBRIN, AND RAMIRO MARTÍNEZ, JR.

On January 28, 2011, Representative John Kavanagh (R) filed House Bills 2561 and 2562 in the Arizona House of Representatives. These bills and their senate counterparts (Senate Bills 1308 and 1309) would deny citizenship to children born in the United States if at least one parent is not a U.S. citizen, U.S. national, or legal permanent U.S. resident. A coalition of lawmakers from 13 other states has joined Arizona in efforts to negate the automatic citizenship granted to children born in the United States under the Fourteenth Amendment of the Constitution. According to Representative Kavanagh, "it's irresponsible and foolish to bestow citizenship based upon one's GPS location at birth" (Billeaud 2011). Representative Albert Hale (D), a member of the Navajo nation with ancestral roots dating long before immigrants came to the "new world" and what is now Arizona, countered that if these bills passed, "he would be considered an 'anchor baby' because Native Americans were not granted citizenship until 1924. 'My grandfather was not a citizen. My mother, born in 1919, was not a citizen,' he said. "So I am a child of a non-citizen and therefore illegal. Am I to be deported? And if I am, where are you going to deport me to?'" (Rau 2011).

The comments made by these Arizona legislators draw our attention to the contradictions, nuances, and layered realities embedded in contemporary debates on immigration and citizenship. The movement of people from one point on the globe to another is as old as recorded history. And the reasons for that movement have been fairly constant over time, with the search for work and food for one's family and for safety from political strife being the most common. Yet, as Representative Hale's statement reminds us, definitions of citizenship and belonging are inherently political and social, and the extent to which immigrants and refugees have been welcomed or feared, and incorporated into or excluded from civic and legal membership in their host countries, has varied tremendously depending upon the context.

As of the summer of 2011, restrictive immigration legislation has been introduced throughout the United States. These include efforts to criminalize immigration along the lines of Arizona's controversial SB 1070 (which, as noted in previous chapters, makes not having documents evidencing legal residence in the United States a crime), birthright citizenship bills such as that proposed in Arizona, and bans on college and university admissions and financial aid for undocumented immigrants. At the same time, the DREAM Act, which would provide a 6-year-long path to citizenship for qualifying youth who entered the country at age 15 or younger, have lived in the United States for at least five consecutive years, have a high school diploma or GED, and who go on to complete a college degree or two years of military service, is on hold. In 2009 and 2010 alone, over 2,900 immigration-related bills were introduced, 410 laws enacted, 30 bills vetoed, and 269 resolutions adopted by state legislatures across the United States (National Conference of State Legislatures 2010). To provide context, five years earlier (in 2005), a comparatively smaller number of 300 immigration-related bills were introduced in U.S. state legislatures. At that time, only 39 immigration laws were enacted and six of those were vetoed (National Conference of State Legislatures 2010).

While this level of legislative activity may appear extreme, the United States is not alone in wishing to punish immigrants. France, for example, has revised its immigration legislation four times in the past seven years, most recently introducing legislation making it easier to expel irregular immigrants and some recently naturalized French citizens. According to a *Washington Post* correspondent, French President Nicolas Sarkozy's campaign, which has been "denounced as demagoguery by his opponents, reflects swelling concern in Western European countries over large numbers of immigrants pouring in to seek work, political freedom and generous social services. Several European governments have taken new steps to limit the flow, and anti-immigrant political parties scored electoral gains this year even in such normally liberal bastions as Sweden and the Netherlands" (Cody 2010).

In contrast to the negative and often polemic immigration rhetoric so frequently evident in the news media—rhetoric that links immigration with crime and disorder—the contributions to this volume demonstrate that the reality is far more complex. *Punishing Immigrants: Policy, Politics, and Injustice* grew out of our concern, as immigration scholars, that a broader social science perspective on immigration and immigration policy has been missing, and that policy is being made based on faulty and incomplete data. Funded by the National Science Foundation's Sociology and Law and Social Sciences Programs, we hosted an interdisciplinary workshop at Arizona State University in September 2009 to systematically explore the current state of social science knowledge on the topic. In that conference, and more fully in this volume, we have sought to move beyond old debates about immigration and crime to address three interrelated sets of questions with important theoretical and policy implications.

First, we ask, have modes of controlling immigrants and immigration changed in recent decades, and particularly since 9/11? If so, what are their underlying assumptions and what do they seek to accomplish? To what extent are enhanced control strategies tied to fears of terrorism and to the global economic crisis? Do they mask new forms of racism and xenophobia? How do they complicate relations within and across communities, and between communities and the police and other state agencies? *Second*, what are the consequences, both anticipated and hidden, of recent immigration policies and practices for individuals and communities? What are the social and economic losses for families and communities as a result of large-scale deportations and forced relocations? If immigration serves a protective function, as recent research suggests, what social benefits are lost as a consequence of punitive new policies? *Third*, and finally, we examine the nuanced, or layered, realities of immigrants' and refugees' lives. Do restrictive immigration policies and practices result in outcomes that are patterned by gender and race? Do language and cultural differences exacerbate racial tensions? Are immigrants fleeing violence in their home countries especially vulnerable to violence in their new communities? How does immigration status shape educational and employment opportunities, and what local and institutional factors might mediate these effects? These are just some of the questions we have raised in this volume. Our hope is that these questions and their answers will inform immigration policy, as well as future research. Accordingly, we urge scholars to continue to apply an interdisciplinary law and social science lens to their research and to be attentive to immigration policies, practices, and outcomes across the globe.

New Modes of Social Control

Looking first at new modes of controlling immigrants, the chapters by Welch, Provine and colleagues, and Sinema help us understand how these new policies and modes of control emerged, and why the time was ripe for such restrictive approaches. Depictions of immigrants as dirty, disease-ridden, and criminal abound in our history (Calavita 1984; Chavez 2008; Ngai 2003), but the recent assumption that nearly every immigrant is a potential source of danger has ratcheted fear to a new level. The authors in this first section draw on extant theorizing about moral panics (Cohen 1972; Goode and Ben-Yehuda 1994), racial threat, and moral entrepreneurs as their starting points. Welch then takes the moral panics argument a step further, proposing that the latest surge in anti-immigration legislation requires us to go beyond moral panics to what Ericson (2007) has called a "risk society." In a context of pervasive fear, he suggests, enhanced control strategies that may not previously have been tolerated come to appear reasonable, including use of civil and administrative devices to circumvent standards and procedures embedded in our criminal laws. Such "counter-laws" constitute an important new mode of social control now visible throughout the United States, Europe, and Australia. And, as Welch establishes based on data from the United States, Great Britain, and Australia, such policies converge with privatized modes of control to fuel the growth and renovation of private prisons and jails as immigration detention centers.

Yet as Provine and her colleagues demonstrate, there is substantial variation in local responses to the immigration crisis, and particularly to the devolution of responsibility for enforcement of immigration law from the federal to the state and local levels. Based on their survey of police departments across the country, they conclude that most police chiefs have not yet formulated clear policy with respect to how their officers should interact with undocumented immigrants. Thus, while some state legislatures and municipal governments want their police officers to more proactively identify and arrest unauthorized immigrants for civil law violations, the police chiefs expressed concern that such actions would damage the trust they have sought to build within the community, making residents less willing to report on crimes they experience or witness.

In some cases, though, the police have little choice about how they will respond. If the district court lifts the injunction against Arizona's law, then in Arizona and 17 other states (as of February 2011) which have introduced legislation modeled after Arizona's SB 1070, the police will be required to enforce immigration law. As Sinema establishes in her chapter, such legislation does not materialize overnight; rather, momentum builds until the political climate normalizes what previously had seemed unreasonable (see similarly Provine 2010). Add to this mix a moral interpreter committed to enacting anti-immigrant legislation and supported by national organizations that share his perspective, and we have the makings of strategic and effective political action. Such was the case in Arizona, where anti-immigrant legislation had been introduced unsuccessfully for several years. Over time, a number of these laws were passed, only to be vetoed by Governor Janet Napolitano. When Napolitano stepped down as governor to become Secretary of Homeland Security, the position fell to Jan Brewer, who favored stringent anti-immigrant legislation. At that point, proponents of SB 1070 were able to push the bill through.

Nevertheless, many police officers have expressed concerns that enforcement of SB 1070 type laws will require unconstitutional racial profiling and pull needed personnel and other resources away from crime fighting. Trepidation about the consequences of this legislation for police-community relations, which are already delicate in many neighborhoods, led a Tucson, Arizona police officer to step forward and file the first SB 1070-related lawsuit against the state (National Immigration Law Center 2010; Rangel 2010).

Consequences for Individuals and Communities

Turning next to the effects of recent immigration and refugee policies for individuals and communities, we observe that these policies and practices have anticipated, unanticipated, and in some cases hidden consequences that radiate in multiple directions. Chapters by Cruz, Dingeman-Cerda and Coutin, and Rymond-Richmond and Hagan help us look beyond immediate policy goals to identify these broader outcomes that may be quite damaging to our social order.

One arena in which these consequences arise involves limitations on employment. Comprehensive U.S. immigration legislation passed in the 1980s sought to balance legalization of immigration status for long-term residents with employer sanctions. This was followed in the 1990s by more restrictive legislation, with the result that many long-term residents were deported. Also, while some states developed sophisticated employment verification systems, reliance on workplace raids to identify, arrest, and deport undocumented workers took precedence over penalties against employers as we moved into the twenty-first century.

In one such raid on a meat processing plant in Postville, Iowa in 2008, nearly 400 employees were arrested and more than 300 faced criminal charges. As Cruz documents, all were offered the same, standard plea bargain for misuse of false documents. Defense counsel did not have adequate expertise in immigration law, however, and failed to recognize the consequences of the removal agreement embedded in the plea bargain. In 2009, the U.S. Supreme Court accepted a case that explicitly examined whether criminal defense counsel must have sufficient expertise to inform their clients of the immigration consequences of a guilty plea. Their decision, handed down on March 31, 2010 in *Padilla v. Kentucky*, clarified that the criminal justice system can no longer ignore "the primacy citizenship status plays in immigrant communities' relationships to the judicial system…Specifically, the Court acknowledged that the immigration consequences of a criminal conviction and an individual's status as a noncitizen are not collateral, but rather an essential part of a defendant's decision to accept a plea agreement" (see Cruz, pages 92-93 of chapter 5).

According to the Pew Hispanic Research Center, approximately 11.2 million unauthorized immigrants live in the United States, and 8 million of these immigrants are in the labor force (Passel and Cohn 2011). Many live in blended families in which some members are citizens or legal residents and others are undocumented. These families are torn apart when, for example, parents are deported following the workplace raids discussed in Cruz's chapter (see also Chaudry et al. 2010). The ripple effects reverberate throughout entire communities and undermine trust in legal authorities.

Dingeman-Cerda and Coutin's chapter (chapter 6) offers another window into the experiences of deported immigrants and their families. Somewhere between 20 percent and 35 percent of Salvadoran nationals now live in the United States, having fled north in the face of civil war between 1980 and 1992. The United States was a party to that warfare, and systematically chose not to award political asylum to these refugees (Mountz et al. 2002; Coutin 2003). Large numbers of Salvadorans have since been deported back to their homeland, often following arrests for minor offenses. Based on interviews conducted in El Salvador in 2008 with 70 men, Dingeman-Cerda and Coutin recount the men's experiences following repatriation to El Salvador. Many came to the United States as small children, obtained permanent legal residency, and raised families in the United States. They no longer fit into Salvadoran society and, rather than being welcomed home, they were treated as outsiders and potential troublemakers. Thus, as Dingeman-Cerda and Coutin demonstrate, deportation had multiple confounding effects on the individuals who were relocated, as well as on their families and their communities both in the United States and in El Salvador.

Like the chapter by Provine and colleagues, Dingeman-Cerda and Coutin draw our attention to the importance of social membership and belonging, as well as the legal definition of citizenship. As Provine and her colleagues suggest, "those who advocate a state-centered framing of membership are undisturbed by the deportation of even long-settled residents if proper procedures are followed. For those who defend a civil-society view, deportation of long-standing residents is disturbing, particularly if the process claims to be just" (see chapter 3, page 57). Similarly, Dingeman-Cerda and Coutin assert that deportation results in a collective social suffering, not just individualized suffering. Thus, "despite popular and legal rhetoric depicting deportation as the unproblematic return of non-citizens *to* their homelands, deportees frequently experience removal as an exile *from* their home" (see chapter 6, page 114). The consequences, as Dingeman-Cerda and Coutin demonstrate, come full circle when the forced relocation of Salvadoran immigrants who have lived in the United States for years rips families apart, often leaving U.S. citizen children without parental and, in some cases, economic support. They state,

> In uncanny ways, deportation from the United States reproduces the violence of the Salvadoran civil war. During the 1980s and early 1990s, Salvadorans fled death squads, human rights abuses, forced recruitment, and societal violence. Children were left behind, family and community ties were disrupted, and émigrés were denied asylum. The very conditions that gave rise to emigration and that prevented migrants' full legal integration into the United State in turn contributed to the deportation of the individuals interviewed for this chapter. Deportation inflicts violence upon deportees and their family members, both directly, through the process of removal and, indirectly, through stigmatization and impact on family members. Parents and children are once again separated... This indirect victimization, or secondary deportation, raises serious concerns about the future well-being—and incorporation—of spouses and children left behind in the U.S. (Dingeman-Cerda and Coutin, chapter 6, page 132).

The ramifications of forced relocations are also central to Rymond-Richmond and Hagan's chapter. Race and gender are integrally interwoven into this conflict. As the authors demonstrate here and elsewhere (Hagan and

Rymond-Richmond 2008), the Sudanese government orchestrated and participated in the genocide and forced displacement of Black Africans in Darfur, giving their land, crops, and farm animals to Arab government supporters. As they reveal so starkly through interviews conducted in the relocation camps, racial slurs were hurled at victims incessantly, and rape was used as a weapon to force families to flee their villages, to brutalize victims, and as a tool for ethnic cleansing (see also Hyndman 2004; Human Rights Watch 2004).

The chapters in this section underscore the importance of studying immigration and immigration policy in all of its forms—the voluntary migration of individuals in search of a better life, asylum-seekers, those who have been forcibly relocated and displaced, and those who are repatriated, leaving families behind. Moreover, we must consider the political, economic, and social conditions in the sending and receiving countries if we are to make sense of the policy options available to a nation and the consequences of those options for all involved.

Layered Realities

The third section of *Punishing Immigrants* helps us peel back layers of complexity to better understand both the nuanced experiences of immigrants and the contexts within which recent immigration policies have emerged. Much of the political rhetoric in the United States, Western Europe, and other parts of the world assumes that immigration increases crime. Substantial empirical research has demonstrated, on the contrary, that immigration has a protective effect, reducing violent crime rates in immigrant neighborhoods by supporting small local businesses, expanding engagement with churches, schools, and other community institutions, and strengthening relationships among neighbors. Yet we still do not fully understand what conditions this effect, and whether it holds across new as well as more traditional destination points. In chapter 8, Vélez and Lyons contribute to research on this topic through analysis of a unique national data set, providing information at both the neighborhood and city levels. They report that the crime-reducing effects of immigration are strongest in disadvantaged tracts of traditional gateway cities, hypothesizing that these communities have the greatest resources for integrating newcomers. In contrast, the influx of immigrants into disadvantaged sectors of non-gateway cities has no effect—positive or negative—on violent crime rates.

Several chapters in this volume have touched on what has come to be known as the "1.5 generation." These are individuals who immigrated as children. They are technically "first" generation because they were not born in the host country, but because they migrated as children, their experiences and integration into the larger society resemble that of second-generation youth.

Within the United States, one of the key differences between 1.5'ers and second-generation youth is that a significant percentage of the 1.5 generation is undocumented, thereby severely restricting their educational and employment opportunities. Chapter 9, by Bertolini and Lalla, takes us to the European context, demonstrating distinct differences in the school participation rates, type of school (i.e., pre-university or vocational) attended, and labor market opportunities for native Italian, first-generation immigrant, and second-generation youth (note that second-generation youth are defined as foreigners by Italian law, unlike in the United States). These patterns, in turn, are shaped by a number of individual, familial, and community characteristics including, among other factors, the social and economic structure of the region in which the family settled and the parents' educational and employment statuses. This study confirms and expands upon earlier research in the United States and European Union, demonstrating the importance of educational opportunities—and of policies supporting such opportunities—for successful integration of immigrant youth into the larger society.

The final chapter in this section, chapter 10, by Cepeda, Negi, Nowotny, Arango, Kaplan, and Valdez, connects several of the themes raised earlier. They interviewed 77 undocumented Latino day laborers in New Orleans in 2008. New Orleans is an especially interesting research site for the purposes of this book because it is not a traditional gateway city and thus has limited resources available for immigrants. Also, the city was still recovering from the aftermath of Hurricane Katrina at the time of data collection and race relations were tense, especially between African Americans and the Central American and Mexican immigrants who came in search of work.

Because of the gendered nature of Central American migration patterns and employment opportunities, Cepeda and her colleagues, like Dingeman-Cerda and Coutin, were only able to interview men. Many of the day laborers had experienced social vulnerability because of civil war in their home country, lack of resources, difficulties en route to their destination, and limited English-language skills. After arriving in New Orleans, Cepeda and her colleagues found that the men experienced violence and theft on the streets, as well as exploitation and abuse by employers, as everyday occurrences. They were targets of assaults, robberies, intimidation, and harassment from African American males who perceived them to be interlopers, and when they sought help from local authorities, they received little or no support.

Cepeda and her colleagues conclude, "the qualitative data reveal that these social vulnerabilities common to many undocumented Latino immigrants are socially mediated in a complex process of stressors that can be classified as brown-on-brown, black-on-brown and white-on-brown that are specific to their day labor and transitory position" (see chapter 10, page 226).

Policy Implications

Immigration and immigration policy are complex, multidimensional issues that are as much global as national in scope. As the chapters in this volume demonstrate, we must consider the contexts in which migration and refugee flows occur; the economic, political, and social conditions present in the destination sites; and the kinds of social capital available to migrants, among other factors, if we are to unravel and resolve the tensions inherent in designing and implementing comprehensive immigration policy. Lawmaking in the context of immigration also must respond to a variety of conflicts and dilemmas arising from what are often contradictory local, national, and international objectives and concerns (Chambliss and Zatz 1993; Calavita 1984; Newton 2008; Ngai 2003).

One of the key themes running through this volume is the relevance of the destination site, and particularly whether it is a traditional gateway for immigrants and the social and economic conditions of the region. Gateway cities tend to have more resources upon which immigrants can draw, including ethnic enclaves which can enhance an immigrant's social and cultural capital and job prospects. In contrast, while new destination sites may offer economic opportunities in hotel and food services, construction, meat processing, and other industries, there are typically fewer culturally appropriate services and other resources available. Also, the sense of racial threat posed by immigrants may be higher in some regions than others, resulting in more restrictive anti-immigrant legislation and local ordinances. At least, this appears to be the pattern in the United States and parts of Europe today (see, for example, Calavita 2005; Varsanyi 2010).

In the United States, the tension between federal and state governments grows more pronounced on an almost daily basis. Whether the issue is immigration, health care, education, or economic regulations, proponents of states' rights want more local control and fewer federal mandates. This tension is apparent in laws such as Arizona's SB 1070, which seeks to engage local law enforcement officers in immigration control, legislation seeking to repeal "birthright citizenship," legislative attempts to limit immigrants' access to education and public health systems, English-only bills, and a host of other recent attacks on federal control of immigration. Fear of terrorism and high unemployment are often the rallying cry, although there is little evidence to suggest that restrictive immigration policies would solve either problem.

As this book goes to press, two competing legislative initiatives bookend immigration debates. One is the Birthright Citizenship Act; the other is the DREAM Act. We began this chapter with a glimpse at efforts to thwart the 14th Amendment in Arizona, but Arizona is not alone in this effort. A coalition of lawmakers is working closely with Kris Kobach, the law professor and now Kansas Secretary of State who helped draft SB 1070, in an effort to nullify the automatic citizenship granted to children born in the United States under the Fourteenth Amendment. Three states have introduced birthright citizenship bills and another 15 are considering similar legislation (National Conference of State Legislatures 2010). In addition, a Birthright Citizenship Act has been introduced into the House (H.R. 140) and Senate (S.J. Res. 2) to amend either the Immigration and Nationality Act (in the case of the House bill) or the Constitution (in the case of the Senate resolution).

The Fourteenth Amendment was adopted in 1868 as an explicit repudiation of the earlier Supreme Court ruling, in *Dred Scott v. Sandford*, asserting that persons of African descent could never become U.S. citizens. Now, members of the birthright movement want to limit the Fourteenth Amendment, claiming that doing so will stop rewarding families who, they believe, come to the United States only so that their children can become "anchor babies." The reality that children born in the United States must wait 21 years before they can petition for their parents to legally join them does not seem to matter. Nor does it matter that some of the women who cross the border to have children are, according to hospitals reporting to the *New York Times*, frequent border crossers with valid visas (Lacey 2011, A1), or that many undocumented immigrants had lived in the United States for years prior to starting a family. Indeed, the Pew Hispanic Research Center reports that 61 percent of unauthorized immigrants who became parents in 2009 arrived in the United States before 2004 (Passel and Cohn 2010).

The other bookend is the DREAM Act, short for Development, Relief and Education of Alien Minors Act. As was discussed earlier in this chapter, this Act would allow qualified immigrants who came to the United States as children, grew up in the United States, and have a high school diploma or equivalent, to follow a path to citizenship through college education or military service. Proponents of the bill argue that by coming out of the shadows, well-educated youth who know no other home and consider themselves to be Americans—members of the 1.5 generation—can more fully contribute to the nation's progress.

U.S. President Barack Obama has promised to bring comprehensive immigration reform forward. A comprehensive measure is sorely needed at this time, but it will compete with the Model Anti-Immigration Legislation being developed by the state legislators who proposed the Birthright Act. And, as we have seen, the United States is far from alone in facing these challenges. For these reasons, we close with a call for interdisciplinary social science research that can help to shape sensible, empirically driven immigration policy. Comparative analysis of models in place elsewhere in the world may provide insights into more and less successful approaches. Immigration policy will likely need to balance demands for employer sanctions with a path to legal status for at least a subset of long-term undocumented residents who have paid taxes and in other ways contributed to their host country. Border enforcement remains a challenge throughout the world, as nations seek both to regulate access and to ensure the flow of goods and commerce. Yet reasonable border control must be distinguishable from hate-mongering based on racial threat, and it must recognize that the movement of people is integrally interwoven with current political and economic global affairs.

REFERENCES

Billeaud, Jacques. 2011. Arizona Lawmakers File Bill Targeting Automatic Citizenship for Kids of Illegal Immigrants." *Los Angeles Times*. Retrieved February 3, 2011 from http://www.latimes.com/news/nationworld/nation/wire/sns-ap-us-illegal-immigration-citizenship,0,5953664.story.

Calavita, Kitty. 1984. *U.S. Immigration Law and the Control of Labor: 1820–1924*. London: Academic Press.

———. 2005. *Immigrants at the Margins: Law, Race, and Exclusion in Southern Europe*. New York: Cambridge University Press.

Chambliss, William J. and Marjorie S. Zatz (eds.). 1993. *Making Law: The State, the Law, and Structural Contradictions*. Bloomington: Indiana University Press.

Chaudry, Ajay, Randy Capps, Juan Manuel Pedroza, Rosa Maria Castañeda, Robert Santos, and Molly M. Scott. 2010. *Facing our Future: Children in the Aftermath of Immigration Enforcement*. February. Washington, DC: The Urban Institute.

Chavez, Leo R. 2008. *The Latino Threat: Constructing Immigrants, Citizens, and the Nation*. Stanford: Stanford University Press.

Cody, Edward. 2010. Sarkozy's Planned Crackdown on Illegal Immigration Is Introduced as Legislation. *Washington Post* (September 28). Retrieved February 4, 2011 from http://www.washingtonpost.com/wp-dyn/content/article/2010/09/28/AR2010092803217.html.

Cohen, Stanley. 1972. *Folk Devils and Moral Panics*. London: MacGibsonn and Lee. New York: Routledge.

Coutin, Susan. 2003. *Legalizing Moves: Salvadoran Immigrants' Struggle for U.S. Residency*. Ann Arbor: University of Michigan Press.

Ericson, Richard V. 2007. *Crime in an Insecure World*. Cambridge: Polity.

Goode, Erich, and Nachman Ben-Yehuda. 1994. *Moral Panics: The Social Construction of Deviance*. Cambridge, MA: Blackwell.

Hagan, John and Wenona Rymond-Richmond. 2008. *Darfur and the Criminology of Genocide*. Cambridge: Cambridge University Press.

Human Rights Watch. 2004. *Darfur Destroyed: Ethnic Cleaning by Government and Militia Forces in Western Sudan*. May, Vol. 16, No. 6(A).

Hyndman, Jennifer. 2004. Refugee Camps as Conflict Zones: The Politics of Gender. In *Sites of Violence: Gender and Conflict Zones*, ed. Wenona Mary Giles and Jennifer Hyndman, 193–212. Berkeley: University of California Press.

Lacey, Marc. 2011. On Immigration, Birthright Fight in U.S. is Looming. *New York Times*, January 5, A1, A15.

Mountz, Alison, Richard Wright, Ines Miyares, and Adrian J. Bailey. 2002. Lives in Limbo: Temporary Protected Status and Immigrant Identities. *Global Networks* 4: 335–356.

National Conference of State Legislatures. 2010. 2010 Immigration-Related Laws and Resolutions in the States (January 1–December 31, 2010). Retrieved February 4, 2011 from http://http://www.ncsl.org/default.aspx?tabid=21857.

National Immigration Law Center. 2010. *Why Police Chiefs Oppose Arizona's SB 1070* (June). Retrieved February 4, 2011 from http://www.nilc.org/immlawpolicy/LocalLaw/police-chiefs-oppose-sb1070-2010-06.pdf .

Newton, Lina. 2008. *Illegal, Alien, or Immigrant: The Politics of Immigration Reform*. New York: New York University Press.

Ngai, Mae M. 2003. *Impossible Subjects: Illegal Aliens and the Making of Modern America*. Princeton: Princeton University Press.

Passel, Jeffrey S. and D'Vera Cohn. 2011. *Unauthorized Immigrant Population: National and State Trends, 2010*. Washington, DC: Pew Hispanic Center.

Provine, Doris Marie. 2010. Arizona's New Anti-Immigrant Law and Federal Immigration Reform. *Voices of Mexico* 88: 98–102.

Rangel, Danny. 2010. "Police Join Fight Against Arizona SB 1070." Change.org (May 1). Retrieved February 4, 2011 from http://news.change.org/stories/police-join-fight-against-arizona-sb-1070.

Rau, Alia Beard. 2011. "Arizona Lawmakers File 4 Birthright Bills" January 27. Retrieved February 3, 2011 from http://www.azcentral.com/news/articles/2011/01/27/20110127ariz ona-birthright-bills-introduced.html.

Varsanyi, Monica W. (ed.). 2010. *Taking Local Control: Immigration Policy Activism in U.S. Cities and States*. Stanford: Stanford University Press.

James Arango is a Graduate Research Assistant at the University of South Florida's Department of Anthropology and in the Department of Child and Family Studies at the Louis de la Parte Florida Mental Health Institute. His research interests include migrant health, disaster migrations, and vulnerabilities associated with displacement in the Americas and Caribbean. He is currently pursuing graduate degrees in Applied Anthropology and Public Health at the University of South Florida.

Paola Bertolini is Associate Professor of Economics and a member of CAPP (Centre for the Analysis of Public Policies), University of Modena and Reggio Emilia, Italy. After receiving her Master in Philosophy (with honors), she held a Specialization (PhD equivalent) in Agricultural Economics at the University of Naples, Italy. Moving from an interest in common European agricultural and rural policy, she developed an expertise in the area of general economic policies of the European Union, with a special focus on labor market and migration and on inclusion policies. She has written numerous papers on these topics, published in international and national journals.

Alice Cepeda is Assistant Professor in the School of Social Work at the University of Southern California. Her research interests include examining the social and health risks associated with substance use and related risk behaviors among urban Latino populations.

Susan Bibler Coutin is Professor in the Departments of Criminology, Law and Society and Anthropology at the University of California, Irvine, where she is also Associate Dean of the Graduate Division. She is the author of *The Culture of Protest: Religious Activism and the U.S. Sanctuary Movement* (Westview Press, 1993), *Legalizing Moves: Salvadoran Immigrants' Struggle for U.S. Residency* (University of Michigan Press, 2000), and *Nations of Emigrants: Shifting Boundaries of Citizenship in El Salvador and the United States* (Cornell University Press, 2007).

Evelyn H. Cruz teaches Immigration Law and Comprehensive Law Practice at Arizona State University. She also directs the College's Immigration Law & Policy Clinic, which represents unaccompanied minors in immigration removal proceedings. In 2007, Evelyn received the President's Medal for Social Embeddedness at Arizona State University. Professor Cruz writes articles about immigration law, clinical education, and therapeutic jurisprudence, and has co-authored several immigration law manuals used by practitioners and pro-se detainees at Immigration Detention Centers throughout the country.

Scott H. Decker is Foundation Professor and Director in the School of Criminology and Criminal Justice at Arizona State University. His most recent books include *European Street Gangs and Troublesome Youth Groups* (Winner of the American Society of Criminology, Division of International Criminology Outstanding Distinguished book award, 2006) and *Drug Smugglers on Drug Smuggling: Lessons from the Inside* (Temple University Press, 2008).

M. Kathleen Dingeman-Cerda is a PhD student in the Department of Sociology at the University of California, Irvine. Her dissertation analyzes the ways in which deportation interrupts and alters the life courses of individuals returned to El Salvador and family members left behind in Los Angeles, California.

John Hagan is John D. MacArthur Professor of Sociology and Law at Northwestern University and Senior Research Fellow at the American Bar Foundation. He received the Stockholm Prize in Crimonology in 2009, the ASC Edwin Sutherland Award, the Michael J. Hindelang Award, and the C. Wright Mills Award for *Mean Streets: Youth Crime and Homelessness* (with Bill McCarthy; Cambridge University Press, 1997), a Guggenheim Fellowship and the Albert J. Reiss Award for *Northern Passage: American Vietnam War Resisters in Canada* (2001), and the Albert J. Reiss Award and the Michael J. Hindelang Outstanding Book Award for *Darfur and the Criminology of Genocide* (with Wenona Rymond-Richmond; Cambridge University Press, 2008).

Charles Kaplan is Research Professor at the University of Southern California School of Social Work. His research and publications have focused on the relationships among drug abuse, HIV, and mental health conditions, and he established the Addiction Research Institute (IVO) at the Erasmus University in Rotterdam.

Charis E. Kubrin is Associate Professor of Criminology, Law, and Society at the University of California, Irvine. She is co-editor of *Crime and Society: Crime*, 3rd edition (Sage Publications, 2007) and co-author of *Researching Theories of Crime and Deviance* (Oxford University Press, 2008) and *Privileged Places: Race, Residence, and the Structure of Opportunity* (Lynne Rienner, 2006). In 2005, Charis received the American Society of Criminology's Ruth Shonle Cavan Young Scholar Award and the Morris Rosenberg Award for Recent Achievement from the District of Columbia Sociological Society.

Michele Lalla is Full Professor of Social Statistics in the University of Modena and Reggio Emilia, Italy. He is member of CAPP (Centre for the Analysis of Public Policies), SIS (the Italian Statistical Society), and SIEDS (the Italian Society of Economics Demography and Statistics). He received a BA in Physics (with honors) at the University of Rome (1976) and a Master's in Teaching Methodology of Physics at the University of Modena (1977). His research concerns the applications of statistical techniques in medical and economic data analysis; his fields of interest are sampling techniques, measurement problems, duration of data analysis, the evaluation of teaching activity, and fuzzy expert systems. He is the author of many papers on these topics, published in international and national journals.

Paul G. Lewis is Associate Professor of Political Science in the School of Politics and Global Studies at Arizona State University. He is the author of *Shaping Suburbia: How Political Institutions Organize Urban Development* (University of Pittsburgh Press, 1996), which was named an Outstanding Academic Book by *Choice*, and is coauthor of *Custodians of Place: Governing the Growth and Development of Cities* (Georgetown University Press, 2009).

Christopher J. Lyons received his PhD in Sociology from the University of Washington in 2006, and is currently an assistant professor at the University of New Mexico. His previous work (published in *Social Psychology Quarterly*, *Social Forces*, and the *American Journal of Sociology*) has focused on the social construction and social organization of hate crime.

Ramiro Martínez, Jr. is Professor in the School of Criminology and Criminal Justice and the Department of Sociology and Anthropology at Northeastern University. He recently received the American Society of Criminology's Division on People of Color and Crime Lifetime Achievement Award.

Nalini Negi is currently Assistant Professor at the School of Social Work in the University of Maryland, Baltimore. Her research interests include substance abuse and mental health issues of Latino immigrants.

Kathryn M. Nowotny is pursuing a PhD from the Department of Sociology at the University of Colorado at Boulder, where she is also a Research Assistant with the Problem Behavior Program at the Institute of Behavioral Science. She received her MA in sociology from the University of Houston and previously served as the Research Coordinator for the Center for Drug and Social Policy Research at the University of Houston. Her research interests include the gendered and raced aspects of crime, violence, and incarceration as well as drug use and related social and health consequences among high-risk groups.

Doris Marie Provine is Professor of Justice and Social Inquiry in the School of Social Transformation at Arizona State University. Her most recent book is *Unequal Under Law: Race and the War on Drugs* (University of Chicago Press, 2007). Her current research focuses on unauthorized immigration, both in the evolving context of U.S. law and in cross-national context.

Wenona Rymond-Richmond is an Assistant Professor of Sociology at the University of Massachusetts, Amherst. She received the Albert J. Reiss Award and the Michael J. Hindelang Outstanding Book Award for *Darfur and the Criminology of Genocide* (with John Hagan; Cambridge University Press, 2008). Her areas of research include urban ethnography, gentrification, law, war resisters, and communities and crime. She is currently writing a book about the redevelopment of a public housing development in Chicago.

Kyrsten Sinema is the Arizona State Senator for District 15, an area that covers most of central Phoenix. Prior to this, Kyrsten served three terms in the Arizona House of Representatives. Kyrsten holds both a law degree and an MSW from ASU, and is currently pursuing her PhD in the School of Social Justice and Social Inquiry at ASU. Kyrsten is a 2009 Aspen-Rodel Scholar; she completed the Harvard Kennedy School of Government's Women in Power Program in May 2010, and the Harvard Kennedy School of Government's Senior Executive Program in 2008. In 2006, Kyrsten was a Center for Policy Alternative Flemming Fellow, and in 2005 was selected as an American Council of Young Political Leaders delegate to Morocco.

Avelardo Valdez is currently a Professor at the School of Social Work at the University of Southern California. His most recent book is titled *Mexican American Girls and Gang Violence: Beyond Risk* (Palgrave Macmillan, 2007). His current research is examining the long term social and health consequences of gang membership.

Monica Varsanyi is Associate Professor in the Political Science Department at the John Jay College of Criminal Justice and is on the Doctoral Faculty in Geography at the Graduate Center, both at the City University of New York. Her research addresses the politics of unauthorized immigration in the United States, specifically the devolution of immigration policing powers from the federal government to state and local governments, the emergence of grassroots immigration policy activism, and the growing tensions among local, state, and federal scales of government vis-à-vis immigration policy and enforcement.

María B. Vélez is an Assistant Professor in the Department of Sociology at the University of New Mexico. Her research interests include the interrelationships among crime, disadvantage, and race/ethnicity; linking neighborhood crime and victimization to city political processes such as the distribution of resources (e.g., police protection, residential bank loans); and further specifying the relationship between immigrant populations and neighborhood crime.

Michael Welch is a Professor in the Criminal Justice program at Rutgers University, New Brunswick, New Jersey. Welch is author of *Crimes of Power & States of Impunity: The U.S. Response to Terror* (Rutgers University Press, 2009), *Scapegoats of September 11th: Hate Crimes and State Crimes in the War on Terror* (Rutgers University Press, 2006), *Ironies of Imprisonment* (Sage, 2005), *Detained: Immigration Laws and the Expanding I.N.S. Jail Complex* (Temple University Press, 2002), *Flag Burning: Moral Panic and the Criminalization of Protest* (de Gruyter, 2000), *Punishment in America* (Sage, 1999), and *Corrections: A Critical Approach* (2nd edition, McGraw-Hill, 2004).

Marjorie S. Zatz is Professor of Justice and Social Inquiry at Arizona State University. Her publications include *Images of Color, Images of Crime* (3rd edition, 2006 with Coramae Richey Mann and Nancy Rodríguez, Oxford University Press), *Producing Legality: Law and Socialism in Cuba* (Routledge, 1994), and *Making Law: The State, the Law, and Structural Contradictions* (with William Chambliss, 1993, Indiana University Press). She is the recipient of the American Society of Criminology's Herbert Block Award, the Senior Scholar Award from its Division on Women and Crime, and the Lifetime Achievement Award from its Division on People of Color and Crime, as well as the Western Society of Criminology's W.E. B. DuBois Award for Research on Race and the Administration of Justice and its Paul Tappan Award for Outstanding Contributions to Criminology.